Nelson's Lost Jewel

THE EXTRAORDINARY STORY OF THE LOST DIAMOND CHELENGK

MARTYN DOWNER

Cover illustration: Replica jewel on naval hat for dress uniform made to Admiral Lord Nelson's original specifications by Lock & Co., London, 2017. (Author's Collection)

First published 2017
This paperback edition published 2021

The History Press
97 St George's Place, Cheltenham,
Gloucestershire, GL50 3QB
www.thehistorypress.co.uk

British Library Cataloguing in Publication Data.
A catalogue record for this book is available from the British Library.

ISBN 978 0 7509 9427 9

Typesetting and origination by The History Press
Printed and bound in Great Britain by TJ Books Limited, Padstow, Cornwall.

Trees for Life

CONTENTS

PREFACE

Since the first publication of *Nelson's Lost Jewel*, two important new documents have come to light which settle some of the questions posed in the book. The first was the discovery of a large Turkish watercolour of the çelenk diamond jewel selected by Sultan Selim III as an award for Admiral Sir Horatio Nelson after the battle of the Nile. The history of this watercolour, which formerly belonged to Nelson's step-son Josiah Nisbet, will be discussed in the text but it explains why the jewel was so often mis-represented in England. The second breakthrough was finding the original source for the oft-quoted eye-witness account that the jewel which Nelson received at Naples in December 1798 was 'a kind of feather, it represents a hand with thirteen fingers'. From an unknown correspondent and previously dated to April 1799, I have now identified the writer as Thomas Richards, a young English merchant who dined with Nelson within hours of the jewel's presentation by the Turkish envoy. Richards' statement is so at odds with the newly discovered Turkish watercolour of the çelenk painted weeks earlier in Constantinople that the inevitable conclusion is – and this was hinted at in the first edition but, without evidence, left unresolved – that there were two jewels. For reasons which will be explored in this second edition, it is now obvious that before the Turkish envoy departed Constantinople for Naples, the çelenk selected by the sultan was exchanged for another diamond jewel, probably made bespoke for Nelson. The confusion this late substitution caused, to artists and biographers, had persisted until today.

PRELUDE

In January 1839, Admiral Sir Frederick Maitland, commander-in-chief of the Royal Navy in the East Indies, sent a squadron of warships to capture the Red Sea port of Aden. The local Arab tribes put up a valiant resistance, but they were no match for British firepower and the town fell within a day. Aden was the first acquisition of the British Empire during the reign of the young Queen Victoria. To celebrate this auspicious event, Maitland sent six captured guns back to London as gifts for his monarch. The magnificent bronze cannons were Turkish, made for the Ottoman Sultan Suleiman I, 'Suleiman the Magnificent', who ruled the region in the sixteenth century. Delighted with her trophies, the queen handed them to the committee then raising a column to Admiral Viscount Nelson's memory in Trafalgar Square: not to flank the monument, as might be thought, but to be melted down and re-cast. This transfiguration in the furnace saw the guns collapse from cold metal to hot fluid, then to solid again. Today, four of the sultan's guns survive as the large bronze bas-reliefs on the pedestal of Nelson's Column depicting the battles of Cape St Vincent, the Nile, Copenhagen and Trafalgar.[1] To imperial minds, it was fitting to use captured guns in a monument designed as a symbol of national supremacy. Maitland epitomised the heroes the monument celebrated. As a young man, he had sailed in Turkish waters with Nelson and, by a quirk of fate, he had accepted

Napoleon's surrender after Waterloo. For cynics, the later discovery that the bas-reliefs had been illicitly adulterated with other metals and plaster at the foundry proved that even heroes had feet of clay. But for romantics, this fusion of Turkish metal with English stone might have recalled a long-ago story about Nelson and a beautiful Ottoman jewel: his fabled diamond Chelengk. This is that story.

1

THE BATTLE

Aboukir Bay, Egypt, 1 August 1798

They rose in line from the west under a blood-red sky. Thirteen men-of-war falling on their prey. Hood in *Zealous* found the enemy first, and he now led the way into the uncharted bay, sounding as he went. Nelson hailed his friend from *Vanguard*, raising his hat in salute.[1] In their hunger for prizes, *Orion*, *Audacious*, *Theseus* and *Goliath* swept past them both.

Weeks of playing blind man's bluff across the wide Mediterranean Sea – Nelson blind and Bonaparte bluffing – had ended just hours before with the discovery of the French fleet at anchor in Aboukir Bay, at the mouth of the River Nile. With it came the bitter knowledge that the enemy had landed in Egypt. Back in June, the two fleets had sailed within 20 miles of each other, but lacking frigates, Nelson had been unable to probe the sails pricking his distant horizon and Bonaparte had slipped past. To Sir William Hamilton, British envoy to the Kingdom of the Two Sicilies at Naples, Nelson had complained that, "The Devil's children have the Devil's luck'.'[2] Hamilton had been feverishly working behind the scenes to push the reluctant King Ferdinand IV of Naples into actively supporting this lone British effort to stem the French tide of conquest across Europe. He was assisted by his beautiful young wife, Emma, who had lavished attention on Nelson on his visit to Naples in 1793.

Low born, she wanted to prove her worth to her esteemed husband and to dispel her titillating reputation back in England as an artist's model, exotic dancer and aristocratic plaything. Together, the Hamiltons had cajoled the King of Naples, terrified of French repercussions, into allowing Nelson to provision and water his ships at Sicily as he hunted down Bonaparte. Without such help, the British fleet could not stay at sea. Rumours of victory or defeat tormented them both. Even as the British warships finally closed on the anchored enemy on 1 August 1798, Sir William was writing to Nelson to express his disappointment that rumours of him 'having defeated the French fleet in the Bay of Alexandriette on the 30th of June and taken Buonaparte prisoner' were ill founded.[3]

Despite the encouragement of the Hamiltons, Nelson was stressed and exhausted; burdened by responsibility and the expectation of a nation on his shoulders. The target of the enemy's vast battle fleet had been unknown, causing panic across the eastern Mediterranean area from Naples to Malta, Constantinople to Cairo. His officers were also strained, suffering from debilitating ennui in the exhausting heat and drinking heavily at his table day after day. In July, in declining health, Peyton in *Defence* had pleaded to leave his command altogether, 'to return to a climate that may give me a possibility of re-establishing it'.[4] There was unpleasantness too. At Syracuse, a lieutenant in *Orion* jumped ship after being accused of importuning a midshipman for sex.[5] These were men on the edge.

It was the first time Nelson had commanded a fleet in action, but he did not hesitate now as *Vanguard* closed with an enemy wrapped in the first shrouds of night. The hundreds of men below him in the gun decks were blind to their fate, their senses sharpened for the smell, taste and feel of battle and focused only on the task ahead. In *Goliath*, gunner's mate John Nicol would see nothing of his foe. He recalled only the ominous light of a 'red and fiery sun' leaking into the gun deck as they approached.[6] All around him, men prepared for battle in the oppressive heat: stripping to the waist, checking guns, opening ports, spreading sand to soak the blood, maybe their own, which would soon flow in warm sticky streams down the deck.

The enemy were well prepared for an attack and yet were still shocked when it came, suddenly and violently from the west. One by one, the British ships snaked through their line – some inside and some without – with brilliant seamanship, anchoring in turn before unleashing murderous fire on their chosen victim at point-blank range. In his haste to join the action, Troubridge turned *Culloden* into the bay too tightly, thrusting the ship hard into a shoal, where it stuck fast, leaving him to curse and roar at his lost prizes. Ball in *Alexander* drove into the heart of the enemy line to challenge the towering French flagship *L'Orient*. Soon a fire was seen licking hungrily in its bowels.

Vanguard was in the thickest action, locked in a deadly slugging match with *Le Spartiate*. The upper deck was strewn with shattered timbers, shredded sails and torn bodies. Few men exposed to such a maelstrom could escape unscathed, and within an hour Nelson himself was wounded: struck on the head by a piece of red-hot iron which spiralled at him through the heavy air. It slashed through his hat, opening his flesh to reveal brilliant white bone for an instant before blood flooded the wound. His captain, Berry, caught him as he fell. Nelson had been hurt in action before but, stunned, he now feared a fatal injury. His first thought was of Fanny, oblivious and far away in England. 'I am killed', he cried out, 'Remember me to my wife!'[7] He was taken below, where the surgeon discovered a 'wound on the forehead over the right eye. The cranium bared for more than an inch, the wound three inches long.'[8] The gash was washed then closed with adhesive strips before the dazed patient was given opium for the searing pain. Nelson was then sat in the bread room below the waterline to recover his dazed senses.

At the heart of the French line, *L'Orient* was now ablaze from stern to bow, her guns silent and ports burning a fiery chequerboard in the smoke and darkness. Fearing a cataclysm, the nearest British ships pulled away and some of the smaller enemy brigs fled too in panic. Berry went below to find Nelson, leading him back to the quarterdeck to witness the death throes of his enemy's flagship. From masthead to keel, every ship convulsed and every still-living soul shuddered when *L'Orient* went up in an eruption of timber, iron, looted treasure and torn, burning flesh. Oblivious to the scene above, John Nicol felt *Goliath* get 'such a shake we thought the after part of her had blown up, until the boys told us what it was'.[9] Fiery debris, torn limbs and wreckage crashed onto the decks of the nearest ships in a deadly rain of burning embers. Two large timbers ripped from the wooden corpse cartwheeled onto the deck of *Swiftsure*. The holocaust flooded the battle with bright light, revealing ships locked in mortal combat right across the wide bay.

Nine miles away in Alexandria, French officers listening intently to the rumble of distant battle saw the dreadful explosion on the dark horizon and were troubled by its meaning. Nearer, at Rosetta, others clambered onto roofs to watch *L'Orient* burn before she blew up 'with tremendous noise'.[10] For several minutes or maybe an hour – shock made memories fluid – the battle stopped, all energy sucked from it by the vortex at its scorching heart. The bay was shrouded by 'pitchy darkness and a most profound silence' which the horrified French observers took as 'a very unfavourable augury'.[11] Then, like punch-drunk fighters pulling off the ropes, with rising anger, the opposing ships started firing again, hurling hot iron against each other with renewed fury. Their flagship vaporised, their line shredded, the French fought blindly, crazily, bravely on. In *Tonnant*, the captain, both legs and an arm shot away, remained on deck, grotesquely and fleshily propped up on a bran tub, his life soaking away. The horror and the exhaustion was so great it was said that entire gun crews, friend and foe alike, fell asleep at their posts during the raging night.[12]

The battle lurched on sporadically and messily into the next day. As milky dawn broke, firefights still flared across the bay, the now tranquil waters slick with a bloody sheen and broken by wreckage, viscera and bloating dead bodies. Nelson was confused, dazed and disorientated. He lay below decks vomiting, his eyes black from bruising, his head agony and bound with a bloodied bandage. Feverish and irritable, he was enduring the first effects of that severe concussion which would jar his moral compass for months to come, forcing bad decisions and strange behaviour. Weeks of nervous tension had left him weakened and injured but triumphant – and vindicated. He had some hours now to gather his senses and scrambled thoughts: time to compose the perfectly nuanced dispatch for London. He was the master of a good press release. After the Battle of Cape St Vincent just eighteen months before, he had seized the headlines from his commanding officer by leaking accounts of his own boarding of the enemy ship *San Josef* to the newspapers. But this was a much bigger story and one entirely of his own making. So as he lay in his cot, he started turning phrases in his aching head.

He knew that his daring, the brilliance of his captains – who, with Shakespearean flourish, he now dubbed his 'Band of Brothers' - the superb seamanship and gunnery skills of his men, together with the mistakes of the French, had given him victory. He had also been incredibly lucky. His ships had been propelled into Aboukir Bay by a kindly north-westerly on the perfect trajectory for attack, giving the enemy no time to summon men back from the shore. The same wind had also made it difficult (but not impossible) for the rear of the French line, which had escaped, to come to the aid of its centre and van. Not that Nelson ever recognised luck; he called it Providence. With the sounds of occasional gunfire still filtering through the gloomy sweat-heavy deck, he shaped the perfect opening for his dispatch, one which flattered his God, his king and himself. Feeling weak, he called his secretary to his side for dictation, but 'overcome by the sight of blood and the appearance of the admiral', he was not up to the task so Nelson took up the pen himself.[13] 'Almighty God', he wrote, 'has blessed his Majesty's Arms in the late Battle by a great victory over the Fleet of the enemy, who I attacked at sunset on the 1st August, off the mouth of the Nile.' It was said that King George III turned his eyes to heaven with thanks when he read these words some three months later.[14] Off Muslim Egypt, a Christian god had vanquished an atheist foe. 'Almighty

God has made me the happy instrument of destruction', Nelson would tell Emma Hamilton: and that is exactly how he saw it.[15] Satisfied, he summoned his officers to a service of thanksgiving on the deck of *Vanguard*, then ordered his flag captain, Edward Berry, to carry the dispatch in *Leander* down the Mediterranean to Earl St Vincent, his commander-in-chief at Gibraltar. As insurance against Berry being captured (which he was), duplicate dispatches were sent to Naples with 21-year-old flag lieutenant Thomas Capel in the brig *Mutine*, with orders to continue overland to England from there. Capel also carried a letter for Sir William Hamilton from Nelson, seeking urgent aid and safe haven for the damaged British ships. Before Capel sailed, Nelson handed him the sword surrendered by the French admiral Blanquet, its blade inscribed *VIVRE LIBRE OU MOURIR*, for him to present to the Lord Mayor of the City of London when he reached England. Finally, correctly sensing Bonaparte's wider ambitions, Nelson gave a third letter to Thomas Duval, another young lieutenant in *Zealous*, to carry to India to warn British interests there of possible attack.

While their commander recovered, his jubilant captains, anticipating their spoils, resolved to form an 'Egyptian Club', an instinctive desire in a period when London taverns were crowded with private drinking and dining clubs. Even as the last guns echoed across the bay, they gathered in *Orion* under a sky wheeling with hungry sea birds and heavy with the stench of death to pledge 80 guineas each for the families of their dead and wounded: 895 casualties in all. They also vowed to pay for a portrait of Nelson, if he survived his wound, and to give him a luxurious gold sword as a memento of their shared victory.[16] The idea was Saumarez's, who envisaged hanging the portrait in an 'Egyptian Hall' in London where the captains could meet.[17] This giving of gifts was a time-honoured tradition for the victors of battle, a relic from the age of chivalry. So was the hurried grabbing of trophies from this watery battlefield. Captured weapons were traded, and great chunks of *L'Orient* fished out of the bay and stowed away for crafting into snuff boxes and furniture. Nelson took away *L'Orient*'s mast head, while Benjamin Hallowell, 'the gallant but at times eccentric captain of the *Swiftsure*',[18] gathered enough timber for his ship's carpenter to make the admiral a coffin so 'you may be buried in one of your own trophies'.[19] Before the completed box left *Swiftsure*, John Lee, a midshipman in the ship, climbed into it for fun until Hallowell threatened to screw it down and send him with it to Nelson.[20]

As his jarred senses settled over the coming days and the fear of his own death lifted, Nelson's strategic grip grew stronger, and with it came the grim reality of his predicament. Hundreds of miles from safety, unfit to sail away, the British fleet was anchored off a hostile coast in a bloody slick of debris and floating corpses which grotesquely defied efforts to sink them with shot. The shoreline for miles around the bay was strewn with masts, rigging, boats and gun carriages which the watching Arabs gathered into huge pyres to burn for the iron.

A more personally pressing matter for Nelson's officers and his men, discussed by the captains when they met after the battle, was their prize money. This was paid by the Admiralty to the crews of a successful action in return for recycling their captured ships and enemy loot. There now began a lengthy argument over the value of the many Nile prizes, conducted at arm's length by Nelson through his agent Alexander Davison. Sticking points would be the destruction of *L'Orient*, for which there could be no payment but which Nelson grumpily thought had £600,000 of treasure stolen from Malta on board when it exploded; and compensation for those enemy ships too damaged to repair, which he had been forced to burn. It was all very irregular, but although the claim for *L'Orient* was dismissed, in the euphoria of victory the Admiralty did pay out £20,000 for the burnt ships.

As Nelson did his sums, the welcome sight of his missing frigates appeared on the horizon to strengthen his depleted and battle-worn squadron. Less agreeable was the appearance of his stepson, Josiah Nisbet, his wife's son from her first marriage. Nelson's patronage had propelled Josiah through the ranks of the navy until he was made commander at just 17. Despite such privilege, Josiah was portrayed as a sullen, obstinate, inattentive and unreliable youth with, in the words of his commanding officer, a love of 'drink and low company'.[21] He was becoming an embarrassment to Nelson. Overlooked was Josiah's kind nature and obvious bravery, also a debt the admiral knew he could never repay. A year before the Battle of the Nile, Josiah had saved his stepfather's life during an ill-fated beach attack at Tenerife which had cost Nelson an arm. With presence of mind, Josiah had staunched the bleeding from the wound, applied a tourniquet and evacuated Nelson back to his ship to meet the cold edge of the surgeon's saw. Now he was in Aboukir Bay, Josiah was yet another awkward problem facing Nelson. (Strangely, Bonaparte was also having to deal with a wayward stepson on this campaign: 17-year-old Eugene Beauharnais, son of his wife Josephine.)

On 17 August, after composing his letters and dispatches with an aching head, making his damaged ships seaworthy, sending his prizes down the Mediterranean (burning the three most damaged with great regret) and leaving Hood in *Zealous* to blockade the hostile coast, Nelson finally sailed from Egypt. Trusting to Capel's success at Naples, he headed for Italy to re-provision, take stock and set up a base for operations. Wounded and exhausted, he wanted to go home, but without orders or a clear picture of his strategic situation – his latest mail from London was dated April – he was acting in an information vacuum and forced to improvise. He decided his priority was to bolster the paper-thin blockade of Egypt and keep Bonaparte holed up in Egypt; then, if possible, recover Malta, where the ruling Knights of St John had been recently expelled by the French.

Above all, believing Hood could only remain on blockade until the end of September before running out of supplies, he needed allies. So as *Vanguard* limped towards Naples, Nelson dispatched Captain Retalick in *Bonne Citoyenne* to Turkey with a letter for Francis Jackson, the British minister in Constantinople. He calculated that now he was stranded in Egypt, Bonaparte would seek an overland escape route back to France through Syria and Turkey. And so, in the letter he urged the Ottoman government, or Sublime Porte, to confront the French before they reached the gates of the city. The Porte was traditionally friendly towards the French, so in his appeal Nelson tried to stir up antipathy against them. He inflated stories of atrocities in Egypt, part of the rambling Ottoman Empire, by leaking reports that 200 Turks had been massacred at Alexandria in retaliation for his victory at the Nile. Warning that Ottoman Syria would be Bonaparte's next target, Nelson urged Jackson to press the Porte to send an army to Egypt. Just 10,000 Turks could liberate that country, he suggested, as the French troops were 'very sickly' and dying of thirst.[22] Or, as he put it more succinctly to Earl St Vincent, 'If the Grand Signior will but *trot* an Army into Syria, Bonaparte's career is over.'[23]

Nelson wrote to Constantinople more in hope than in expectation. He could not know yet that the aftershocks of his astonishing victory had rippled across Europe, shifting the Rubicon of alliances and age-old enmities. The battle had tipped the Turks, already deeply shocked by the invasion of Egypt, into unlikely alliance with their oldest enemy, the Russians. The Sultan of Turkey had also ordered the Ottoman Governor at Rhodes to send 'a very abundant supply of fresh provisions, vegetables and most exquisite fruits' as quickly as possible to Nelson's starving fleet off Egypt.[24] Despite their many historic differences, the new Russian tsar, Paul I, was as unhappy as the Turkish sultan at the spread of French influence in the eastern Mediterranean. Grand Master of the Knights of St John, Paul was also furious at the loss of Malta. Both imperial rulers now dispatched ships to strengthen the blockade of Alexandria and to seize back Malta and the Ionian Islands of Corfu, Zante and Cephalonia. The Portuguese were also sending ships in support. Overnight on 1 August, the whole outlook of the war had changed, making Bonaparte, seen as invincible since his recent victorious campaigns in Italy, suddenly appear vulnerable.

Captain Samuel Hood was an excellent choice for the difficult and stressful task of managing the blockade of the marooned French army in Egypt, as his ship *Zealous* had escaped relatively unscathed in the recent action. He was also a highly experienced officer, having been at sea almost continuously since the age of 14. The son of a purser, he enjoyed the powerful interest of his admiral cousins: Samuel Hood, Viscount Hood, and Alexander Hood, Viscount Bridport. He was also familiar with these warm waters, having patrolled the Aegean protecting British trade back in 1795. *Zealous* would cruise the Egyptian coast with Hallowell's *Swiftsure*, *Goliath*, Captain Foley and four frigates: *Alcmene*, *Seahorse*, *Emerald* and *La Fortune*. Their aim was to pick off prizes, cut out French transports when they could and, above all, to keep Bonaparte locked up in Egypt.

It was stressful work, so Hood was grateful when a ship carrying Selim Agha, 'a Turkish officer of English extraction', unexpectedly arrived with welcome news.[25] He brought letters from the British embassy in Constantinople and a *firman*, an imperial order, issued by the Sultan of Turkey granting the British fleet assistance throughout the Ottoman Empire. The agha also carried intriguing rumours, Hood reported to Nelson, that a 'Hat set with diamonds, indeed they say *covered*, is preparing for you as a present from the Grand Signior'.[26]

A month later, on 19 October, the sails of a small squadron of Turkish gunboats and corvettes broke the northern horizon. Ill-prepared for the voyage from Constantinople, the ships were in a sorry state, having endured a month of rough autumn seas with just one compass between them. Their commander, Halil Bey, had been given strict orders by the sultan to make all possible haste to join the British fleet, any delay being met 'with the severest punishment'.[27] Fearing the dire consequences of failure, the bey had pressed on without provisioning properly at Rhodes, leaving his ships nearly out of water and food. On board one of the two corvettes was Kelim Efendi, a genial old scribe from the Sultan of Turkey's *divan*, his council of ministers, who had a package for Nelson said to contain the sultan's precious gift. Described as a sort of 'head clerk in a secretary of state's department to us', Kelim was accompanied by a colourful retinue of attendants.[28] These were led by 'Peter Ritor', an anglicised Greek who had worked in London as a translator, or 'dragoman' (an

English corruption of the Turkish *tercüman*), to Yusuf Agah Efendi, appointed first Ottoman ambassador to Britain in 1793. Officially he was in Egypt to translate for Kelim, but he was probably tasked as well with gathering intelligence for the Porte. He could also probably recognise Nelson. On 27 September 1797, Peter had accompanied the Ottoman ambassador to the king's levee at St James's Palace at which Nelson, still suffering the effects of the amputation of his arm, had been invested knight in the Order of the Bath.[29]

To keep an eye on Ritor, the British embassy in Constantinople sent their own interpreter with the efendi called Bartholomew Pisani. He was Italian and a highly experienced, second-generation dragoman, his father Antonio having been appointed 'His Majesty's Translator of the Oriental Languages in Constantinople' in 1749. Bartholomew had already served the British interest in Turkey for thirty-five years, latterly as chancellor at the embassy, and he would remain a further twenty-five. Like Ritor, he had multiple functions. According to the British minister in Constantinople, he was sent 'no less to interpret on this mission, than to remain at the admiral's orders in this theatre of war'.[30] It seems Bartholomew brought his son Robert with him on this exciting venture.

Hood was exasperated with all these unexpected, inconvenient guests in their rich flowing robes and tall hats, and he struggled to know what to do with them. 'He, the Kiélim Effendi, interpreters etc were all dissatisfied with each other,' he complained.[31] Furthermore, 'the Turks are so very deceitful there is scarce believing anything they say.'[32] Unaccustomed to the sea, Kelim was also ill, possibly with scurvy or severe sea-sickness. Conditions in the corvettes were so bad that Hood had the Turks shifted to *Zealous*, which had a good surgeon on board and, courtesy of the governor of Rhodes, plentiful fresh supplies. The Turkish corvettes were sent away whilst the gunboats were taken into Aboukir Bay to bombard the French shore batteries, each boat having been allocated five British sailors 'to set a good example'. But the Turks' gunnery was poor and their courage suspect to prejudiced British eyes. 'Whenever a shot came whistling from the fort towards the Turks,' recalled one officer scathingly, 'they fell down flat on the decks as if shot, and many of them ran below.'[33] Others sloped off to smoke their long pipes behind a breakwater. There were also frequent clashes between the Turkish sailors and the British tars, leading to several deaths, and it was only when Captain Hallowell of *Swiftsure* took charge in person that order and discipline was restored. Hood considered the Turks 'as horrid a set of allies as ever I had'.[34]

While Kelim recovered in *Zealous*, Hood waited for confirmation of Nelson's safe arrival at Naples. He planned to send the efendi and his precious gift after the admiral in a more robust vessel: one better able to resist the Mediterranean in winter. He was anxious, he told the embassy in Constantinople:

> to make this delivery of this ever-memorable acknowledgment of his highness the Grand Signior as conspicuous as possible; but finding this at so late a season of the year I hazarded its delay. The *presents* shall go with the first frigate or ship of the line, it will be best not to send them in a smaller vessel at this season of the year.[35]

In the event, Hood was obliged to entertain his exotic guests for a further month before they could continue their journey. Only on 27 November were the Turks finally entered in the books of *Alcmene*, a 32-gun frigate commanded by Captain George Hope, 'for passage to Adm Nelson'. The efendi's attendants and servants were listed as Kalyl, Jimayl, Suleiman, Basyle and Panajot, with the proper name of 'Peter Ritor' revealed as Petrarky Rhetorides. The efendi's full name was phonetically recorded by the ship's clerk as 'Mukamed Emior Kelim', or more properly Muhammad Amir Kelim. Robert Pisani was also added to the muster, having been brought across from another ship, *Lion*, where he had been quartered and briefed away from prying Turkish eyes.[36] Hope sailed the same day with his valuable cargo and a bundle of letters for Nelson, including Hood's congratulations 'on the present he will bring you'.[37] Yet he could have little idea what awaited him at Naples.

2

THE SULTAN

Constantinople, Turkey, August 1798

The Sultan of Turkey was the first to hear. On 22 August, just three days after Nelson weighed anchor in Aboukir Bay, an enigmatic message was received at Constantinople from the Ottoman Governor of Rhodes, Hassan Bey. A French brig had struggled into his port with the astonishing news that, 'on the 31 July an English squadron consisting of fourteen ships of the line, one frigate and one corvette had come to attack the French squadron anchored at *eboukir* (*Bequieres*), that towards the evening of the same day the English squadron had got into action, and that *L'Orient* was already on fire, when the captain of the brig came away.'[1] This patchy report was onfirmed when *Bonne Citoyenne* reached Rhodes on 27 August and Captain Retalick went ashore with Nelson's letter for the British minister at the Sublime Porte. Hassan Bey immediately forwarded it to Constantinople, leaving Retalick to be 'loaded' with presents including 'a very rich and valuable Gold Medal'.[2]

Writing to the foreign secretary in London from his ramshackle residence in Pera overlooking the glittering Golden Horn, British diplomat (John) Spencer Smith could hardly contain his excitement when he read the letter. 'I lose not a moment in forwarding homewards by this route what I eagerly conjecture may be the first official report of the glorious news my late letters have so anxiously alluded to,' he wrote, his pen running fast over the page. 'I have almost at the same hour received corroborating advices on the subject from Cyprus (dated 22 August), from Aleppo, and from the Porte, whither I am now upon my way, going in consequence of a pressing call.'[3]

Just 29, Spencer Smith was acting minister to the Sublime Porte whilst London searched for a new ambassador to this sleepy diplomatic posting, the previous appointee Francis Jackson having resigned before even reaching Turkey. Despite his relative youth and inexperience, Smith was about to be thrust into an international crisis. From an impecunious but well-connected family – as a boy he had been a page to George III – Spencer had followed his older brother (William) Sidney Smith into the Royal Navy during the American war. When peace came in 1783, and both boys were placed on half-pay, Sidney began dabbling in freelance intelligence work, while Spencer used an inheritance to purchase a commission in the army. Sidney's wanderings had taken him to Morocco, where he reported his fears of an invasion of Europe by the Sultan of Turkey; then to Sweden, where he joined the Swedish navy as a mercenary, earning a knighthood from King Gustavus III for his exploits during that country's war with Russia. Sidney's foreign decoration was derided by his fellow officers in the Royal Navy, but his value as a fearless freebooting agent was noticed by the British government. The Smith brothers had powerful friends, and as cousins of Prime Minister William Pitt they enjoyed 'interest', that essential social currency of the eighteenth century. In December 1793, their father, General Edward Smith, who had held a position in the royal household, had greeted Ottoman ambassador Yusuf Agah to the shores of England. Such connections helped Spencer gain entry to the Levant Company – more popularly known by its earlier title 'Turkey Company' – which had enjoyed a monopoly on British trade in the eastern Mediterranean since the sixteenth century.

With war with revolutionary France looming, both Smith brothers travelled to Constantinople. Sidney went to advise the Turkish navy (and to spy for the British) and Spencer, having served an apprenticeship with the Turkey Company in London, to work as a merchant. Within a couple of years, some strings were pulled and Spencer was made secretary to the newly appointed British ambassador to Constantinople, Robert Liston, previously Sidney's diplomatic handler in Stockholm. In recommending his brother for a career in diplomacy, Sidney, with typical verbosity, described Spencer as 'particularly qualified for that career by epistolary readiness and talent and adapted to it. His knowledge of the place and study of the Turkish language may be an additional recommendation.'[4]

Working for the Turkey Company in the Levant – a term for the eastern Mediterranean taken from the French for the 'rising' of the sun – had once been highly lucrative for British merchants and diplomats. Relations with their hosts were friendly – Britain had never been at war with the Ottomans – and its royal charter gave the company sweeping tax-raising and political powers, including promoting its own merchants, like Spencer Smith, to diplomat posts in the region. From its factories at Aleppo, Constantinople, Smyrna and Alexandria, the company traded cloth and goods shipped from England for silks and spices in the Orient. But like the Ottoman Empire around it, the company was in long decline, pressed by competition from French and Dutch rivals, changing consumer habits and stifled by its own restrictive practises. By 1792, trade had dwindled so much that the company faced bankruptcy and the Sublime Porte – so called after a fabulous gateway leading to the imperial palace at Constantinople, the Seraglio - was seen as a commercial and political backwater. The outbreak of war in Western Europe appeared to make Turkey even more unimportant, and with enemy warships prowling the Mediterranean preying on their merchantmen, the company's fortunes declined still further. When Spain then entered the war as an ally of France, the Royal Navy was forced to abandon the Mediterranean altogether, leaving the company's ships entirely unprotected. Now there were no more than a handful of British merchants still trading at Constantinople, and many of these expressed Jacobin sympathies to curry favour with the dominant French interest. Turkey was so politically disregarded by London that when Liston was transferred to Washington in 1796 and Francis Jackson backed out of the dead-end post, Spencer Smith was placed in charge of the mission as 'Minister Plenopotentiary'. (That Nelson still sent his Nile dispatch to Jackson shows how difficult it was communicating such news whilst at sea.) Not until 1799 would Lord Elgin arrive as a new British ambassador. Refined and well-connected, Spencer took quickly to his unexpected new role, enjoying the expat social life of the diplomatic quarter at Pera with its balls and whist parties and marrying the beautiful daughter of the Austrian ambassador, Baron d'Herbert.

British lack of interest in the Levant matched the decaying condition of the once-mighty Ottoman Empire. In its heyday, the empire had threatened Western Europe, with Suleiman the Magnificent even laying siege to Vienna. Weak leadership, wars, incompetence and corruption had since forced a slow retreat, yet Ottoman rule still stretched, at least in name, halfway around the Mediterranean, from the Balkans to Libya and beyond. At the heart of the empire, hidden behind the high walls of the Seraglio, his palace in Constantinople, was the Sultan of Turkey, the supreme leader of the Ottomans who could claim descent from the medieval founder of the imperial dynasty, Osman I. The sultan, a mysterious and fearful figure, projected his secular power by *firman*, mindful always of the authority of the Grand Mufti, the empire's head of religion, who issued powerful legal and religious opinion through *fatwas*.

The sultan's authority was administered by his appointed pashas and their local beys, who controlled the far-flung regions of the empire in his name. Some like Ali Pasha in Albania, Djezzar Pasha at Acre and Ibrahim Bey in Egypt ruled almost like sultans themselves. They paid lip service and a grudging annual tribute to the Porte, but they were unreliable, duplicitous allies and their constant warring further sapped an empire already tagged the 'sick man of Europe'. Sultans since Suleiman had often been very lazy, very weak or very cruel. All faced plots and coups. The desiccated heads of their enemies and failed ministers, the efendi, decorated the walls of the Seraglio. More recently, a string of disastrous wars with Russia had further exhausted the bankrupt empire of resources and highlighted the woeful and outmoded state of its army and navy. Far from facing these problems, successive sultans had taken the empire further into isolation, turning their back on the technological advances in the west.

The twenty-eighth sultan of the Ottomans was rather different to his forebears. Despite a traditionally sheltered upbringing, Selim III was highly educated, cultivated and liberal minded. He studied and wrote poetry, composed music and, as Sidney Smith observed in 1795, 'showed greater partiality for the arts than is thought consistent with the system of a strict Musselman'.[5] Although his father Mustafa III had been sultan when Selim was born in 1761, the young prince had not been heir to the throne. That precarious position had been occupied by his uncle, Abdu ul-Hamid, as the title always fell to the eldest living male in the ruling Osman family, not by direct descent. Free of this burden, the young prince had been able to explore Constantinople, attend meetings of the divan, his father's council of ministers, and observe the manoeuvres of the artillery and rifles corps. Romantically inclined and strongly idealistic, he developed a close-knit circle of childhood friends: several of whom became efendis when he ascended the throne. One young companion, Ishak, later made agha, had been present at the Battle of Chesme in 1770 when the Russians had destroyed the once-famed Ottoman navy. This devastating defeat was a formative event for Selim. As sultan, he would seek to reform and rebuild his navy along the lines of the all-powerful Royal Navy, coming to idolise its famous and daring officers. This whimsical and romantic aspect of the idealistic young prince was re-imagined by Lord Byron, who named the tragic hero of his poem 'The Bride of Abydos' for Selim. Byron visited Constantinople in 1810 after the sultan's death and was struck by Selim's once magnificent gardens, 'in all the wildness of luxuriant neglect, his fountains waterless and his kiosks defaced but still glittering in their decay'.[6]

The prince's relatively carefree life came to abrupt end in 1774 when his father died and his uncle came to the throne. The shy, dreamy boy was now heir to a great empire, and to protect him (and the new sultan) from plots he was hidden away in the innermost sanctum of the Seraglio. Access to the outside world was now strictly controlled, but the prince still managed to conduct a surreptitious correspondence with a handful of, principally French diplomats, intellectuals and physicians. He even exchanged letters with Louis XVI in Paris. France was the traditional ally of the Porte, and there were strong Francophile elements at the Turkish court and within the divan. The sultan was even known throughout Europe by his French sobriquet 'Grand Seignior'. Britain hardly figured at all.

On 7 April 1789, Selim ascended the throne of an empire again at war with Russia, and now with Austria too. Ottoman losses mounted quickly. The conflict cost the empire the cities of Belgrade and Bucharest, as well as control of the Crimea with its valuable access to the Black Sea. With France consumed by revolution, the Turks signed a treaty with Sweden, which was also fighting the Russians in the Baltic. It was this alliance which brought Sidney and Spencer Smith to Constantinople. The war painfully demonstrated the backward and ramshackle state of the Ottoman armed forces, and when it ended in 1792, Selim launched widespread reforms in his military, which was riddled by corruption, incompetence and nepotism. But he moved slowly and cautiously, as was the Ottoman way. He knew the history of the empire was littered by the bloody corpses of sultans who had acted too rashly. The biggest obstacle to change was the powerful Janissary corps, the imperial bodyguard which enjoyed enormous privilege and was highly reactionary and dangerous.

As sultan, Selim was wrapped in an almost mythical exoticism and strangeness to Western eyes. Invisible to the world, hidden away in the Seraglio with his famed harem of beautiful women (many European), the sultan generated fantastic rumours about his riches, his extravagant tastes, his sexual proclivities and his bloodthirsty appetite. Very few Englishmen entered this magical world, and still fewer women. One who did was Mary Elgin, who accompanied her husband to Constantinople when he eventually replaced Francis Jackson as ambassador in 1799. Raised on tales from the *Arabian Nights*, first published in English in 1706, Mary was so determined to accompany her husband to the palace that she disguised herself as a man. The procession to the Seraglio was led by 2,000 janissaries, with the foreigners, as was custom, roughly handled all the way. After a huge meal of roasted meats, rose-flavoured sweetmeats and sherbet served in gold dishes, the visitors were ushered by eunuchs into the audience chamber, a small, dimly lit, heavily scented panelled room decorated with bejewelled treasures. In the gloomy midst of all this magnificence, perched on a bed covered with 'immense large pearls', was the 'monster' himself, Selim III. 'By him was an inkstand of one mass of large Diamonds,' reported an awed Mary, 'on his other side lay his sabre studded all over with *Brilliants*. In his turban he wore the famous Aigrette, his robe was of yellow satin with black sable, and in the window there were two turbans covered with diamonds.'[7] Nothing in the *Arabian Nights* equalled such opulence. Mary could gaze with wonder at the sultan, but etiquette prevented him from looking at her, or any foreigner. Another privileged English guest to the audience chamber recalled Selim as 'a man of about forty-three years of age; his beard is become grisly, his countenance is attractive, the tout ensemble of his physiognomy benign; he never lifted his eyes, nor even gave a side glance'.[8]

The audience with the sultan climaxed with the keenly anticipated exchange of gifts, or *douceurs*, an essential and timeless Turkish tradition designed to secure mutual interest and obligation. *Douceurs* were a tool of diplomacy: a projection of status and wealth and a material adhesive for valuable relationships. At an international level, the presents were often stupendously extravagant. During the 1790s, forced to build long-neglected links with foreign courts, Selim had dispatched ambassadors across Europe laden with lavish gifts. When Yusuf Agah arrived as the first Ottoman ambassador in London, he carried with him from Turkey four beautiful horses, a pair of gold pistols and a gold dagger to present to King George III. In addition, Queen Charlotte and her eldest daughter, the Princess Royal, were each given 'a chest of silks, embroidered with gold; a Plume of Feathers for the head-dress, ornamented with diamonds'.[9]

What presents Lord Elgin should give the sultan on reaching Constantinople had exercised the mandarins at the Foreign Office in London for months. They had been flooded with offers from makers of luxury goods, all eager to supply them. A London representative of the Turkey Company advised that the Turks liked nothing better than English 'clocks, watches, jewellery, arms, crystal ware and porcelain'.[10] They especially loved expensive 'toys': small precious objects glittery with gems and glossy with enamelling, often with hidden clockwork mechanisms to surprise the viewer. So Lord Elgin sailed east weighed down by a crystal chandelier, a musical table clock, numerous gold and diamond boxes, watches, rings and pistols. He also packed over 1,300 yards of silks, velvets, brocades and satins to clothe the Turkish court and promote British trade. The total cost of such largesse came to £7,000 (maybe £700,000 today).[11]

In return, the Elgins received an even more dazzling array of gifts. Mary Elgin was given a diamond ornament to wear in her hair, known as an aigrette, modelled as the 132-gun Ottoman flagship *Sultan Selim*.[12] Her husband received a beautiful horse, a traditional diplomatic gift, together with silks, Kashmir shawls, weapons, gems and diamond boxes. With great ceremony, Lord Elgin was also cloaked in a rich fur-lined pelisse, or robe of honour, an integral ritual of such occasions. But all these baubles were as nothing compared to the greater gift Elgin was eventually granted in 1801 when, at the height of his love affair with the British, Selim issued a *firman* enabling the British ambassador to strip sculptures from the Parthenon at Athens and ship them back to London.

From his spies in Paris, the sultan had heard as early as May 1798, even before their fleet of warships and transports sailed from Toulon, that the French were planning an expedition against Egypt. French officials in Paris and Constantinople vigorously denied the rumours. They were playing for time, hoping that the sultan would come to welcome an invasion of a territory so troublesome to him. Ostensibly governed by an Ottoman pasha, real power in Egypt lay with the Mamelukes, former slaves who over the centuries had forged a powerful ruling elite. Fiercely independent and rebellious, the Mamelukes had caused endless problems for the Porte, forcing an Ottoman expedition to restore order in Egypt as recently as 1768.

Napoleon Bonaparte, the dashing young general who led the French force, convinced himself he was helping the Turks, dressing up his invasion as a liberation from Mameluke tyranny in a series of impassioned letters to the Porte. He also sent the sultan a diamond ring set with a miniature of himself in an act of brotherly friendship. However, the real aim of the Directory in Paris appeared to be to threaten British interests in India (and to keep France at war abroad to suppress dissent at home). Securing an overland route to the Far East would disrupt trade and pave a way for a full invasion of India, the jewel in the British crown. French overtures were already being made to Tipu Sultan, the Tiger of Mysore, to form an alliance to help drive the British out of India. Despite these wider strategic goals, Bonaparte also wanted to explore, map and catalogue the hidden treasures of Egypt. It was said he dreamed of creating an enlightened new Islamic state in the spirit of the French and American revolutions. He even studied the *Koran* on the voyage out, appearing at breakfast in his flagship *L'Orient* in turban and robes and vowing to convert to Islam when he had conquered Egypt. Propelled by this vision and a burning personal ambition, Bonaparte evaded Nelson's warships in the Mediterranean before landing in Egypt unopposed on 1 July. After routing the Mamelukes at the Battle of the Pyramids, he installed himself in a palace in Cairo, in confident expectation of the grateful thanks of the sultan. Instead, on 13 August, he heard that his fleet, his lifeline to Europe, had been destroyed by Nelson at Aboukir Bay, near Alexandria. Badly shaken, Bonaparte was philosophical about this disaster. 'So, we are now obliged to accomplish great things,' he told his crestfallen officers, 'and accomplish them we will.'[13] He still expected the sultan to accept his occupation of Egypt, and took comfort from a promise made by French foreign minister Charles Tallyrand that he would travel in person to the Porte to sell the invasion to the Turks. But, unknown to Bonaparte, the Machiavellian Tallyrand had stayed in Paris, hoping and expecting his rival would die in the sands of Africa.

The invasion of Egypt placed Selim in a quandary. French diplomats in Constantinople had repeatedly assured him, possibly believing it themselves, that the real target of the massed French fleet was far-off England. When the invasion, and their deceit, was confirmed, they trusted to old ties of friendship to protect them. The attack on Egypt was a gross violation of Ottoman territory, but France was also the Porte's closest ally, supplying vital military expertise and equipment during Turkey's recent wars with Russia. The decapitation of the King of France had alarmed Selim – as it did every crowned head in Europe – but he was known to be in sympathy with many of the intellectual aims of the revolutionaries. They had been welcomed at Constantinople, where they wore tricolour cockades openly in the streets and, to the horror of a British patriot like Spencer Smith, had planted a Tree of Liberty outside the French embassy.

With public feeling in Turkey running high, the Grand Mufti issued a *fatwa* authorising holy war against France. Yet still Selim hesitated to act, handicapped by his Francophile ministers and the caution of his precarious position. He restricted French access to the Seraglio, but little else. Less constrained, Spencer Smith worked feverishly behind the scenes to stir up trouble for the French. He proposed an unheard-of alliance between Britain, the Porte and its old nemesis Russia to fight the now common enemy. The sultan acknowledged this radical idea, issued a *firman* granting the British fleet assistance in the Levant, but still bided his time on ratifying the treaty. Yet Smith was confident of winning him over. Writing to Nelson just two days before the Battle of the Nile, he reported that the shock in Constantinople at the invasion of Egypt had 'matured into positive enmity' against the French.[14]

Then everything changed. On 16 August, a week after sailing from the shambles in Aboukir Bay in a local dhow laden with beans, Lieutenant Thomas Duval of *Vanguard*, Nelson's dispatch safely tucked in his coat, reached Scanderoon, now İskenderun, near Aleppo in Syria, 'a little paltry place, in the midst of a swamp'. Here Duval 'delighted' the Turkish governor with news of the victory before forwarding it by letter to the British consul at Cyprus. Then, after swapping his uniform for Arab robes and hiring camels and guards, the intrepid Duval continued overland to India. With the Red Sea in enemy hands, he headed out across the desert to Baghdad, where the ecstatic Ottoman pasha ordered him back into uniform and, despite the scorching heat, clothed him in a robe of honour. He then gifted Duval a boat to carry him down the Tigris to the Persian Gulf, where a sloop met him for the voyage to India.[15] Finally, on 21 October 1798, just ten weeks after leaving Nelson, Duval reached Bombay and a hero's welcome from the embattled British community.

Duval's epic journey lit a fire across the Levant. His news confirmed the report from Rhodes and finally pushed Selim into decisive action. He issued a *firman* declaring war against 'those faithless brutes the French'.[16] 'God be praised,' he scribbled on the report of the battle, 'I am pleased. God willing, may they all be damned. Make it known to the British ambassador.'[17] The sultan's Francophile Grand Vizir, his prime minister, was instantly sacked and, lucky to keep his head, thrown into a prison with the French ambassador and his staff. 'The *Rubicon* is happily passed,' declared a triumphant Spencer Smith, who now received Nelson's triumphant dispatch addressed to Francis Jackson. Within days, Smith's proposed treaty between the Ottoman Empire, Russia and Britain was confirmed. Russian warships started arriving in the Bosphorus, with Russian admiral Feodor Ushakov going ashore to discuss joint operations against the French with the Capitan Pasha, head of the Ottoman navy. Remarkably, Selim then made a surprise visit to the Russian flagship himself. The highly decorated Russian admiral had been the scourge of the sultan's navy during the recent conflict between their countries, but now he was warmly welcomed to Constantinople and presented with a 'snuff box richly set with diamonds'.[18] It was agreed that an Ottoman fleet under Turkish admiral Abdul Cadir Bey would join with the Russians to expel the French from the Adriatic, where they occupied the Ionian Islands of Zante, Corfu and Cephalonia threatening an invasion of the Balkans. A smaller force of tenders, corvettes and gun boats would sail in support of the British blockade of Egypt, with the Porte favouring Nelson's idea of a land campaign through Syria to liberate Egypt rather than a landing by sea.

Spencer was delighted, watching as the hated Tree of Liberty was uprooted and his rival French merchants and diplomats rounded up and interned. He was now at the centre of things: meeting the sultan's ministers, going aboard the Russian flagship to meet Ushakov in person and, above all, bursting with 'an honest pride that HM'S mission has not been backward in keeping pace with the gallant admiral on *Terra firma*'.[19] He then heard he would be joined in his diplomatic mission by his brother, who was returning to Turkey. Back in London, fame and favour had combined to make Sidney Smith not only joint minister in Constantinople but also commander of all British naval forces in the Levant.

The sultan was captivated by the exploits of Nelson at the Nile and wanted to reward him in traditional Ottoman style. The day after the British victory was confirmed, the sultan personally ordered a 'fine fur and a superior *çelenk*' to be sent out to the admiral.[20] The reward of a *çelenk* – phonetically 'Chelengk' in English – for bravery on the field of battle was a long-established Ottoman custom. Usually a simple turban ornament cut from a silver plate, unadorned with gemstones and crested with three, five or seven plumes, depending on the award; for Nelson Selim selected a deluxe version from his personal treasury, one smothered in diamonds. Rumours that the sultan was sending presents to Nelson washed around the diplomatic quarter at Pera for days before Spencer Smith was told officially during an audience with the Ottoman foreign minister on 8 September. Smith had taken an Arabic translation of Nelson's Nile dispatch to the meeting, together with an explanatory sketch of the action, 'such as my experience taught me to be necessary for a nation of beings who judge only by the senses'. Whilst poring over the drawing, the ministers were interrupted 'in a dramatic way' by a messenger carrying a parcel from the sultan.[21] The courier produced a flowery letter of congratulation addressed to 'our much esteemed Friend Admiral Nelson' which promised 2,000 sequins for the men who had 'bled' at the Nile. As a sequin – a small gold coin used throughout the Levant – was worth 9 shillings, the bounty was estimated at about £900 (or £80,000 today). British casualties at the battle were 218 killed and 677 wounded, so assuming the sultan intended the money for the injured survivors only, each man would receive £1 6*s* 5*d*. However, it is not known whether, when or how this money was ever distributed.[22] Hearing that women were also present in the British ships during the action, ferrying water to the gun crews and attending the wounded, Selim sent them presents too, although at least two had since died of wounds (and a third given premature birth in shock).[23]

In his excited letter to London reporting the meeting, Spencer described how the messenger had then taken from his parcel:

> a superb aigrette (of which the marginal sketch gives but a very imperfect idea) called a Chelengk, or Plume of Triumph, such as have been upon very famous and memorable successes of the Ottoman arms conferred upon victorious (Musselman) Seraskers (I believe never before upon a disbeliever) as the *ne plus ultra* of personal honour as separate from official dignity.

It was indeed a most extraordinary and luxurious object, far more exotic, unusual and precious than other Chelengks Spencer must have seen before in Constantinople. It was whispered in diplomatic circles that the jewel had been taken personally by the sultan from one of his own turbans and was worth almost £1,000 (perhaps £100,000 today). Next, the messenger unwrapped a magnificent red robe of honour lined with sable fur 'of the first quality worn at this court', valued at a further 5,000 dollars. Finally, there was a diamond box 'of the usual ministerial kind' for Smith himself.[24] The messenger asked Smith to seek royal permission in England for Nelson to wear the Chelengk 'on his joyous head and to put on the fur'.[25]

Smith was struck 'dumb' when the presents were revealed:

> I did, however, at last contrive to find words to thank the Grand Signior in the name of the King my master; in that of my valiant fellow subjects; of his Majesty's ministers; and on my own account.

Familiar with Ottoman culture and its tradition of present-giving, Smith saw at once the exceptional nature of the sultan's gifts, explaining to his superiors back in London that, 'it can hardly according to the ideas annexed to such insignia here be considered as less than equivalent to the first order of Chivalry in Christendom.' Seeing the Chelengk as a military decoration comparable to the British Order of the Bath would make it easier for the king to agree, Smith conjectured, 'for the admiral's wearing the *Chelengk* upon his cockade'.[26] He described the jewel as a 'blaze of brilliants crowned with a vibrating plumage', an effect he tried to convey in the sketch he added to his letter back in Pera. His drawing shows an oval mass of tightly packed stones mounted on a bow and topped by five plumes. However, the jewel's most extraordinary feature, Smith enthused, was the 'radiant star in the middle turning upon its center by means of watch work which winds up behind'. A painting of the Chelengk by a Turkish court artist, on hand-burnished paper and highlighted with watercolour, confirmed the accuracy of Smith's hasty sketch. It showed each of the plump, 'brilliant' diamonds in the jewel and revealed that the star in the centre was enamelled in blue.

Whilst Smith completed his dispatches, Kelim Efendi was summoned from the sultan's divan to carry the presents out to Nelson. Accompanied by a small retinue, he was to go aboard a Turkish corvette and head for Egypt where he was expected to find Nelson (but discovered instead an irritable Captain Hood). In the ten days before Kelim embarked for his voyage, however, the çelenk Smith had seen at the palace, and had sketched and so excitedly reported to London, was substituted for a newly made jewel: a bespoke diamond aigrette of even more magnificent proportions, created by Selim especially in Nelson's honour. This last-minute exchange would cause endless confusion as to the true nature of the sultan's gift.

3

THE AMBASSADOR'S WIFE

Naples, Italy, September 1798

Sir William Hamilton was closing a letter to the foreign secretary when he heard the excited female voices, the soft patter of running feet on cool tile floors and the rustling of silks as the women all pressed for a better look with the telescope. The panoramic view of the Bay of Naples from the balcony of the Palazzo Sessa was breathtaking. Ahead in the shimmering distance was Capri, to the right the rocky heights of Posillipo, to the left Sorrento and further off the brooding smoking bulk of Vesuvius. Below lay a ribbon of palazzi sweeping along the edge of the water, their awnings panting in the midday sun.

Cornelia, who had kept vigil by the telescope for days, had spotted a small British ship far, far out in the bay. From his study, Sir William called for someone to row out and greet the stranger. As the embassy boat drew towards the brig, the women at the palazzo could clearly see through the glass an officer on the deck, his epaulettes glinting in the sun, madly gesticulating as if describing 'the blowing up of some ships and the sinking of others'.[1] It could mean only one thing, but everyone held their breath until Capel arrived at the palazzo to confirm the victory in person, his youthful face flushed with exertion and excitement. Lady Hamilton was hit 'like a shot' by the longed-for news, theatrically falling to the floor 'apparently dead' before composing herself to tell the queen.[2] Before rushing Capel and his lieutenant, William Hoste, to the Palazzo Reale to see the king and queen, Sir William added a hasty, joyful postscript to his abandoned dispatch. 'This moment Captain Capel arrived here in his Majesty's ship the *Mutine*,' he scrawled, 'with the glorious news which he carries to England.'[3] It was 4 September 1798 and since June, when Nelson's squadron had swept past Naples, this deeply divided city, threatened with rebellion and French invasion, had been on edge for news. Now it had arrived, the Bourbon royal family led the wild celebrations of their working-class *Lazzaroni* supporters while their Jacobin and intelligentsia opponents brooded and bided their time. At the palace, eager to impress the queen, Emma had burst out with the news before Capel could speak. Marie Carolina was ecstatic. 'Oh, brave Nelson, oh God bless and protect our brave deliverer,' she cried, 'Oh Nelson, Nelson, what do we not owe you. Oh, victor, saviour of Italy. Oh, that my swollen heart could now tell him personally what we owe him.'[4] Capel, son of the Earl of Essex, was bemused by such histrionics, reporting to Nelson that, 'I am totally unable to express the joy that appeared in every body's countenance and the bursts of applause and acclamations we received, the queen and Lady Hamilton both fainted, in short sir they all hail you as the saviour of Europe.'[5]

Capel's young lieutenant was less surprised by their reception in Naples. Hoste had met Emma with Nelson back in 1793, soon after he entered the navy. For an impressionable young boy meeting a famous woman at the height of her beauty, it was an experience he was hardly likely to forget. Nor had Nelson, who had maintained an occasional but warm correspondence with the Hamiltons since that first meeting. In recent months, Sir William, who now boasted of having spotted Nelson's future stardom, had been in frequent anxious contact as the admiral scoured the empty seas for his foe. Emma, too, had written, sending letters of encouragement, urging the admiral to victory. She was now 33 and growing plump on marsala and macaroni. But her great beauty – projected across Europe through prints and paintings – was undimmed, even perhaps at its zenith as its innocence turned to knowing maturity. Her energy and verve fizzed through the drawing rooms of Naples and the dim corridors of the Palazzo Reale. Raised in poverty, Emma prized luxury. Once powerless and abused, she also craved power. Her looks had carried her into the aristocracy, but it was her keen intelligence which had made her confidante to the Queen of Naples.

Now that Nelson's victory was confirmed, Emma wanted to share his glory. She grabbed Capel and Hoste as they left the palace, thrusting them into a carriage hastily bedecked with ribbons to clatter around the city proclaiming the news to ragged cheers. She tied a bandeau proclaiming 'Nelson and Victory' around her head and spat on Admiral Blanquet's captured sword, carried by a bemused Capel, taking it from him and waving it at the crowds. Soon, she declared, she was 'be-Nelsoned all over' with anchor earrings and a navy blue, gold-anchored decorated shawl. The triumphant tour ended at the opera house, where Sir William's box provided Emma with the perfect stage for a patriotic performance. The exhausted British officers finally returned to their ship after midnight, gazing back in wonder at the Palazzo Sessa, now lit, it was said, by a thousand lights in celebration. In a letter for Nelson, who was still sailing away from Egypt in *Vanguard*, Emma described how the Neapolitans were 'mad with joy' at his triumph, that 'not a French dog dare shew his face'. Yet the many French sympathisers and their Jacobin supporters had simply been driven indoors, fearful of events but biding their time.[6]

The next day, Capel set off for England laden with letters and the Nile dispatch, travelling overland to Manfredonia on the Adriatic coast, continuing from there by boat to Trieste to avoid French-occupied Italy, then onwards to Vienna and across Europe to the Baltic ports and home. Meantime, dizzy with the attention and sudden promotion, Hoste took command of *Mutine*, remaining a while longer as the guest of the Hamiltons. They put him up at the palazzo, dressed him in fashionable new clothes and entertained him 'with the most distinguished attention'.[7] One day a messenger arrived from the royal palace with a note for Hoste from the queen, together with a beautiful diamond ring which now became a treasured family heirloom. There was also 200 gold guineas, wine and meat for his ship's company to share.

The feting of Hoste was just a foretaste of what awaited Nelson. Knowing the hero was heading towards them, the Hamiltons began making preparations. 'A pleasant apartment is ready for you in my house,' the kindly ambassador wrote, 'and Emma is looking out for the softest pillows to repose the few wearied limbs you have left.'[8] Weakly, Nelson offered to stay in a hotel, but when he arrived at Naples, he gratefully accepted the best bedroom in Palazzo Sessa, on the upper floor with panoramic views of the bay and a constant cooling breeze scented by the pine forests which cradled the city. The prospect of living under the same roof as Emma made him tremble with a feeling he could not yet admit. He brought with him his secretary and, for Emma, a black Nubian slave girl liberated from a French prize, whom she renamed Fatima and adopted as her maid. Nelson was an unprepossessing sight: his mutilated and emaciated body was wracked with fever and his shorn head showed the still livid, weeping scar of his wound. But beneath the constant ministrations of his hostess, who plied her hero with asses' milk and fed him her fears for the future, he slowly regained his strength and health. He also fell in love.

After attending to her patient, Emma organised parties for him, laying on a spectacular ball for 1,800 people to celebrate Nelson's 40th birthday on 29 September. Thoughtlessly, she sent his wife back in England poems lauding her hero with a gushing account of his reception in Naples. She took Nelson for an audience with the queen and dinner with the kingdom's English-born prime minister Sir John Acton, who filled the admiral's aching head with Neapolitan fighting talk. Early in October, this new sense of mission propelled him back to sea to bolster the blockade of Malta, where the French were now besieged following an uprising by the inhabitants.

Having encouraged wild speculation about the lavish rewards Nelson would receive after his victory – her own extravagant suggestion being a statue of solid gold in the middle of London – it was Emma who sent the admiral the first details of the rumoured gifts from the Sultan of Turkey. These reached her through her husband's diplomatic channels after Nelson sailed for Malta, and they offered a glittering prospect. 'Your present,' she scrawled breathlessly, 'is a pelicia of Gibelini with a feather for your hat of dymonds large and most magnificent and two thousand sechins for the wounded men and a letter to you from the Grand Signior, God bless him.' A frigate was expected from Constantinople any day bearing these exotic gifts. Zibeline was the softest sable fur and Emma was bursting with sensual anticipation at the thought of the feeling of the robe against her own naked skin. She purred:

> How I shall look at it, smell it, taste it and touch it, put the pelice over my own shoulders look in the glass and say *vivo il* Turk; and by the express desire of his Imperial Majesty you are to wear these Badges of Honner, so we think it is an order he gives you for you are particularly desired to wear them; and his thanks to be given to all officers, God Bless, or Mahomet bless, the old Turk – I say no longer Turk but good Christian.[9]

The next day she wrote again, her excitement spilling over after hearing the rumour that the sultan had plucked the promised jewel from his own turban, 'to decorate you, and which is a sign of sovereignty'. She could hardly wait to meet the 'good turban'd soul' bringing these gifts to Nelson so she could convince him that English women, thought cold and frigid in the east, could be just as passionate, sensual and expressive as their Turkish counterparts.[10] More soberly, Sir William Hamilton, to whom Spencer Smith in Constantinople had addressed his report on the presents, described them to Nelson as a 'Zibeline Robe and Herons Feather aigrette set with Diamonds'. A famed art collector, he was as intrigued as his wife by the presents, happily indulging her excitement and remarking that Emma was 'delighted with the idea of our soon doing homage to you'.[11] Sir John Acton quipped that, 'The Admiral is now equal to a Bashaw [Pasha] with three tails', meaning the highest rank in Ottoman society below the sultan himself and distinguished by the use of three horsetails on the bearer's standard.[12]

But there was still no sign of the eagerly awaited Turkish corvette when Nelson returned to Naples from Malta in November, and it was forgotten in the sudden press of events. He had been drawn into a plan, hatched by a hawkish cadre within the Neapolitan court, to launch a pre-emptive strike on the French army in the occupied territories of northern Italy. Naples and France were not officially at war, but with the French rolling down through Italy, it was hoped this act of aggression could be portrayed as self-defence. In truth, the Queen of Naples wanted to wreak revenge on the killers of her sister, the French Queen Marie-Antoinette, whilst culture-mad Sir William Hamilton simply wanted to clear his beloved Italy of these French 'ragamuffins'.[13] The mood in the city was tense, with the people on a war footing. King Ferdinand IV had procrastinated for weeks, fearful of failure. But egged on by his queen and the Hamiltons, encouraged by the ever-aggressive Nelson and hoping an attack would trigger his defensive pact with Austria, he gave the go-ahead to proceed. On 23 November, Ferdinand led his army in person over the border of his beleaguered kingdom towards Rome. Meantime, Nelson, fired up by this mad endeavour, took a squadron up the coast to Leghorn (now Livorno) to establish a beachhead in Tuscany.

Far from home and with few orders to obey, dreams of operating on a larger stage now fired Nelson. He sailed just as the first reactions to the Battle of the Nile filtered back from England. Once again it was the well-informed Sir William Hamilton who notified him of his first award, having heard how Captain Capel, after delivering his dispatches to the Admiralty, had rushed to the Guildhall in the City of London with the vanquished Blanquet's sword. The Mayor and Aldermen had immediately voted a presentation sword for Nelson in return. 'Lady Hamilton is delighted,' he crowed, 'that by a glance of her eye the City of London give you a fine sword in return for the one she spit upon.'[14] However, after weeks of speculation on his reward from the English king, the Hamiltons were then shocked to read in the newspapers that Nelson had been made only a baron by George III, the lowest rung of the English peerage. Furious, Emma declared, 'If I was King of England I would make you the most noble puissant *Duke Nelson, Marquis Nile, Earl Alexandria*, Viscount Pyramid, Baron Crocodile and Prince Victory, that posterity might have you in all forms.'[15] 'I will renounce my country,' she vowed, 'and become either a mamluk or Turk.'[16] And yet Emma also played on this royal slight, using it to cement Nelson's new loyalty to the King of Naples, who, in contrast to his own ungrateful monarch, had heaped praise and presents on the touchy admiral. Emma quickly calculated that the insult created the perfect conditions for keeping Nelson at Naples, which she played on in a cleverly worded letter to Nelson's wife, Fanny. Sir William, she wrote, 'is in a rage with [the] ministry for not having made Lord Nelson a viscount, for sure this great and glorious action, greater than any other, ought to have been recompensed more. Hang them I say.'[17]

The French were unprepared for Ferdinand's sudden attack, and without engaging his army fell back ahead of his rapid advance to gather their strength and regroup. On 29 November, the king, stunned by his own success, entered Rome unopposed and headed straight for comfortable lodgings at the Palazzo Farnese. The daring plan, which he now took credit for, had so far exceeded all expectations, but very soon it fell apart. The Austrians did not take his bait and join the unprovoked attack, and although Nelson did secure Leghorn, he roughed up the friendly Tuscans so much that he squandered their goodwill. A week after Ferdinand's triumphant, palm strewn entry to the Eternal City, France declared war and the king was on the run back to Naples, in appalling conditions of winter with the enemy at his heels.

By mid-December, despite desperately keeping up appearances with the usual balls and fêtes, the royal family was secretly planning an escape to Sicily. Emma was tireless and impressive amid the growing chaos, drafting passenger lists and overseeing the secret packing of countless cartloads of royal treasures, art works, bullion and jewels to be smuggled aboard the waiting English ships. These now included *Alcmene* carrying Kelim Efendi and the sultan's jewel, which, after sailing from war-torn Egypt, had anchored in Naples bay on 14 December.[18] Everyone was panicking, 'I however,' Emma later recalled:

> began the work myself and gradually removed all the jewels, and then 36 barrels of gold to our house, these I mark'd as *Stores for Nelson*, being obliged to use every device to prevent the attendants having any idea of our proceedings.

Fretting about his own precious collections, which Nelson offered to send back to England in *Colossus*, Sir William estimated the value of this royal stash to be at least £2.5 million (perhaps a quarter of a billion pounds today). Over 270 wooden kegs, 'said to contain money', were loaded in the newly arrived *Alcmene,* riding at single anchor for a quick escape.

With public order falling apart, and the weather deteriorating, the evacuation was set for Friday, 21 December. At ten that evening, Nelson and the Hamiltons, feigning normality but with rapidly beating hearts, attended a reception hosted by the Turkish efendi at his palatial lodgings ashore. Emma remembered:

> I had to steal from his party, leaving our carriages and equipages at his house, and in about fifteen minutes to be at my post, where it was my task to conduct the Royal Family thro' the subterranean passage to Nelson's boats by that moment waiting for us on the shore.[19]

In fact, frozen by fear, the king and queen had at first refused to leave. So Emma, wrapped in a Kashmir shawl given her by Nelson, was pulled out alone to *Vanguard* waiting in the bay. With a posse of seamen brandishing cutlasses and pistols, Nelson then went back up the dark passageway, one of the many which crisscrossed the city beneath its streets, to fetch the royal family and compel them to follow him to his ship and away to safety.

4

THE HERO

Naples, Italy, September 1798

The 'band of brothers' started to arrive at Naples. First Troubridge and Ball in *Culloden* and *Alexander*, then, early on 22 September, the victor of the Nile himself appeared when *Vanguard*, her masts wrenched off by wind and war, limped into the sweeping bay under tow from *Thalia*. Like bees to honey, small craft funnelled towards the broken flagship with its heroic cargo. Two richly decorated barges led the colourful swarm three leagues or more out to the crippled ship. One flew a large royal standard and carried the Bourbon King of Naples and his eldest daughter, but it was the other, with the British ambassador and his wife aboard, which came alongside the steep wooden walls of the ship first. 'As the boat drew near to the *Vanguard*, Lady Hamilton began to rehearse some of her theatrical airs, and to put on the appearance of a tragic queen,' it was later said.[1] Looking down, Nelson saw Emma leap up in the boat, making it rock violently. 'Oh God, is it possible?' she cried out when she glimpsed the admiral among the crowd high on the deck above. 'With an oath', an officer ordered her to get on board quickly to avoid upsetting the boat. With her beaming husband, Emma climbed up the steps, where she burst into tears and, to Nelson's bemusement, 'fell into my arm more dead than alive'.[2]

Nelson had barely recovered his composure before the gilded royal barge pushed up, carrying the king within its plush interior. Ferdinand feared the French and they hated him. Crowned head of Naples and of the separate state of Sicily, together known as the Kingdom of the Two Sicilies, his Bourbon rule was an insult to their revolution; their principles a threat to his idle, self-indulgent life chasing women and animals. But he had dithered about what to do, his resolve undermined by his foreign minister the Marquis di Gallo, a French stooge. Nelson's unexpected victory had lifted the weight of indecision from his shoulders, so now he wrung the admiral's hand, proclaiming him his 'Deliverer and Preserver'.[3] He demanded a tour of *Vanguard*, visiting the sick bay to see the wounded and taking a close interest in the hat Nelson had been wearing when he was wounded, reverentially touching it for luck.[4] Shredded by the impact of the shrapnel that had hit him, the hat was gifted to the Queen of Naples, who put it in a glass case, like a reliquary.[5]

For her it was a more personal, high-stakes game. Maria Carolina was the sister of Marie-Antoinette, whose head had been lopped off in the Place de la Révolution five years before, and in her worst nightmares she saw herself in a tumbril clattering towards the same grisly fate. With northern Italy, Malta and now Egypt in enemy hands, Austria in alliance with the French and the Turks known Francophiles, the Kingdom of Naples felt isolated and fearful, vacillating between appeasing and opposing the French. Nelson's victory had been heaven-sent, stiffening her husband's resolve and offering her opportunities for revenge.

As ugly as her husband, but more intelligent, Maria Carolina was the real power in Naples, working with Prime Minister Sir John Acton to tighten royal control in these dangerous times. She used Emma Hamilton as her confidante, flattering her opinions and manipulating her influence over her ambassador husband whilst extracting secret intelligence and promises of help. Unlike the queen, Emma was a ravishing and famous beauty, a sex bomb whom Maria Carolina could lob at Nelson to destroy any opposition to her schemes. So she was delighted to see the Hamiltons now scoop up the admiral and whisk him through the crowds to the Palazzo Sessa to rest and recover.

At first Nelson was resistant to the many temptations of Naples and the bountiful and obvious charms of his hostess. 'It is a country of fiddlers and poets, whores and scoundrels,' he stormed. The worst of them was the foppish Marquis di Gallo, who spent his time showing off his medals and playing with his many bejewelled snuff boxes.[6] Yet the sultry heat, the lavish tributes, the late-night partying and the suffocating physical attention of Emma soon swept away what Nelson called his 'rough element', and with it his modesty, his morals and much of his reason.[7]

In the first week of October, a messenger arrived in Naples from Constantinople to announce that the sultan had declared Holy War on the French: a crusade which chimed with Nelson's own fervent religiosity. The courier also brought the news, which Nelson excitedly relayed to his wife in England, that the sultan, 'has ordered me a rich jewel if it was worth a million my pleasure will be to see it in your possession'.[8] Before he could discover more, Nelson escaped the rich food, drink and idolatry of Naples to sail to Malta, where the local populace had risen in revolt and thrown themselves on the protection of Naples. The occupying French army had been driven behind the fortifications of the capital, Valleta. Hard to dislodge, Nelson resolved to starve the enemy out with a blockade. This was a complex and exhausting task which occupied all his time, yet he could not shake the tantalising thought of the jewel from his mind, probing Spencer Smith in Constantinople for more details. 'The Neapolitan Minister at Constantinople wrote to this Court that the Grand Signior had ordered me a present, as a mark of his approbation,' he wrote hesitantly. 'As I have received no official communication of this circumstance, I cannot notice it.'[9] But still it played on his imagination.

Whilst waiting for news of the sultan's jewel, Nelson read in an old copy of the *London Gazette* that the king in England had awarded him a peerage. He was polite in accepting the award, but he had hoped for greater. Just a year before, Admiral Jervis had been made earl after the Battle of Cape St Vincent, then Admiral Duncan was raised to viscount after Camperdown. Yet they had been in command of a fleet at the time of their actions, whereas Nelson had been leading a squadron under orders. It was a point of principle which the king rigidly stuck to (or, no fan of Nelson, hid behind). Technically correct, the inferior award rankled Nelson and was not easily forgotten. After the pawing adulation at Naples, it struck him as a sign of indifference in London to his exploits. 'I receive as I ought what the goodness of our Sovereign, and not my deserts, is pleased to bestow,' he wrote through gritted teeth to First Lord of the Admiralty Earl Spencer, 'but great and unexampled as this Honour may be to one of my standing, yet I own I feel a higher one in the unbounded confidence of the King, your Lordship, and the Whole World, in my exertions.'[10] Nelson's disappointment over his title was eased by pecuniary rewards: an annuity of £2,000 from parliament, another £1,000 a year from Ireland, plus a massive one-off payment of £10,000 from the East India Company (close to £1 million in today's terms).[11] In addition, the Turkey Company voted funds to award him silver, a gesture repeated by the grateful merchants of Lloyd's Coffee House in the City of London.

There was still no sign of the sultan's presents when Nelson returned to Naples after Ferdinand's madcap adventure into Italy. With the French in hot pursuit, the city was on the verge of civil war, with the Jacobins emboldened and in open revolt against the king. Preparations began in secret for the evacuation of the royal family and their treasure, with Nelson summoning ships from Malta and Leghorn to assist. Late on 13 December, amid this unfolding chaos, sharp-eyed Cornelia Knight, who had first spotted Capel arriving in September, noted the appearance in the Bay of Naples of 'the *Alcmene* (Captain Hope) with a Turkish Ambassador, interpreters, &c. bringing the diamond Aigrette, &c., for Lord Nelson'.[12] Almost forgotten in the pandemonium, Kelim Efendi had finally arrived. But far from the stately and dignified ceremonial he might have hoped for, the efendi's presentation of the sultan's gifts had to be hurriedly arranged. With his ship at single anchor, the next day, 14 December 1798, Hope put down a boat and had the Turks, clutching their precious parcels, pulled ashore. Landing at the mole, crowded with troops, noisy porters, scared evacuees and goods for loading, they were taken up to the Palazzo Sessa, struggling to find their legs after so many months at sea. There they found floors covered in loose straw and open wooden crates as Sir William's priceless collections were dismantled and his artworks listed and packed for shipping to England in *Colossus*.[13]

With time pressing, the Turks changed into their richly coloured ceremonial robes in the palazzo's first floor ante-chamber. This room, its walls now stripped of paintings, was decorated in voguish neo-classical designs with brightly painted pilasters and ceiling. It was where officials on government business, dealers proffering works of art and painters looking for patronage had all waited to be summoned by the ambassador in happier days.[14] From its windows, the Turks could see the wide expanse of the bay, now crammed with shipping, with Vesuvius looming beyond. Reports that they dressed in the ante chamber suggest that the presentation ceremony itself took place in Sir William's study, identified merely as the 'Next Room' in an inventory of the palazzo which disguised its obvious splendour. Usually strewn with papers, its walls were hung with priceless paintings – among them portraits of the 'late Grand Signor & Vizir' by Candido Vitali[15] – and every surface was cluttered with Roman vases, artworks and objects.

So it was in this luxurious space – the Turks lending a calm, dignified air to the bustle all around them – that Kelim's odyssey came to an end. After crisscrossing the Mediterranean, he had finally come face-to-face with the famed British admiral, who looked tired but impressive in his dress uniform. After some preliminaries and many *salaams*, a letter from the sultan's deputy grand vizir was solemnly read out, a dragoman translating for the English listeners:

> The Porte desirous of showing a good action has destined two corvettes to go and remain with your [fleet] and has sent with them Kiélim Effendi one of the favourite secretaries of the supreme divan who will present to you a *pelliccia* or sable skin

> and a *çelenk* or diamond feather, which the grand signor sends you merely as a proof of his approbation for the zeal and courage which with such ardour and valour you have shown in the service of your country. You will also receive the sovereign's full gift of two thousand zuechins to be distributed amongst the people and who were on board the ships and wounded in the action.[16]

With 'great gravity and dignity', Kelim offered the Chelengk to Nelson on a plush velvet cushion, 'after the Oriental fashion'. The admiral was then robed in the magnificent fur robe, or hilat, made 'of scarlet cloth, lined with the finest sable imaginable, and of inestimable value'.[17] The Ottomans presented large numbers of such garments to foreign guests but only the very highest dignitary or monarch received a robe lined with sable fur. Hugely valuable, in both prestige and in value, sable fur came from a type of marten found only in the remote depths of Siberia. Presents 'of less value' were then exchanged. These probably included a gold *zarf* (coffee cup holder), now in the collection of the National Maritime Museum, which was a traditional Ottoman gift to a foreign dignitary. There was also a precious snuff box 'said to have been sent me', Nelson noted, by Selim's mother, Mihrişah, the beautiful daughter of an Orthodox priest from the Caucuses. Known as the Valida Sultan, she exercised great power in the Ottoman Empire, almost ruling alongside her son. Nelson described her present as 'a nearly round box set with diamonds'. In other accounts it is listed simply as a rose – a flower loaded with meaning in Ottoman culture – suggesting the box was shaped as a rosette encrusted with gems.[18] The Valida Sultan also sent Kashmir shawls from India woven in vibrant colours with exotic patterns. Such beautifully soft and shimmering garments were the height of luxury in Europe, yet they had other uses too. Intended for his wife, Nelson gave the shawls instead to Emma to deploy in the performance of her celebrated 'Attitudes' when, semi-nude and with spellbinding artistry, she assumed the posture of figures taken from art and Antiquity, switching effortlessly and gracefully between roles. One female spectator noted how Emma used such shawls to assume her characters. 'She disposes the shawls so as to form Grecian, Turkish and other drapery, as well as a variety of turbans,' commented Mrs Trench, who saw a performance of the 'Attitudes' in Dresden: 'Her arrangement of the turbans is absolute sleight-of-hand, and she does it so quickly, so easily, and so well.'[19] This ability to slip between roles had propelled Emma through life, protecting her, almost to the end, from the many dangers of her fragile position. Like other men, Nelson was completely smitten by Emma's routine, pressing Spencer Smith in Constantinople to send more shawls, price 'no object'[20].

Nelson was unfamiliar with Turkish custom, admitting that, 'I am entirely unacquainted with any person at Constantinople.'[21] So the ceremony and presentation of his gifts by the Turks was surely slightly bewildering, as was the strange-looking jewel he now turned over in his hand. He warmly thanked the old scribe 'for the very able, dignified, and polite manner in which he has executed his mission'.[22] Nelson then reciprocated the sultan's gifts with presents of his own, mindful of Spencer Smith's advice that, 'it is an Ottoman etiquette which you must not omit to recompose a messenger of this sort in a way proportioned to his rank in life'. Smith suggested a spy glass – a favourite Western luxury for the inquisitive Turks – as a suitable gift for Kelim, albeit one made of silver not gold to satisfy the Porte's strict laws of sumptuary.[23]

That same evening, 14 December 1798, the Hamiltons hosted a supper for Nelson at the Palazzo Sessa attended by, among others, 'the son of a merchant of Birmingham', probably Thomas Bingham Richards, whose father was a prominent silversmith, goldsmith and gunmaker in the town. Just 17, Richards, who acted as his father's agent in Italy, had only arrived at Naples on 6 December following a tour of Sicily but now found himself pitched into a revolution. An interest in antiquities may have secured him a place at the Hamiltons' table. In a letter home, Richards reported that during the supper, 'Lord Nelson shewed us the presents the Grand Seignor had sent him'. With a professional eye, Richards assessed the jewel he saw revealing it to be quite different to the one recorded by

Spencer Smith in September, his letter revealing also the reason for the change:

> The Aigrette is a kind of feather, it represents a hand with thirteen fingers, which are of diamonds and allusive to the thirteen ships taken and destroyed at Alexandria, the size that of child's hand about six years old when opened; the center diamond and the four round it may be worth £1,000 each, and there are about 300 others well set.[24]

Moreover, the jewel was set with rose-cut not the more valuable brilliant-cut diamonds observed by Smith. Nelson must have known by now that the Chelengk shown to the British minister in Constantinople was not the jewel he had just received. Smith's original letter to the foreign office, with its sketch detailing a five-plume *çelenk*, had been sent to London on 8 September. However, on 3 October – after Kelim sailed with the replacement jewel – a copy of Smith's description had been issued in Constantinople urgently annotated by an unknown hand: 'The top should have thirteen fingers or sprigs in allusion to the thirteen ships taken.' It appears this amended version passed through the admiral's hands before it reached London on 3 November – weeks after the first description arrived – as Lady Nelson subsequently noted that it 'was sent me by Lord Nelson'.[25]

Despite the urgency of the evacuation from Naples, Nelson composed a thank-you letter for Kelim to carry back to Turkey and deliver into the hand of the sultan. In his note, Nelson thanked Selim effusively for the 'exalted mark of approbation bestowed on me by the Imperial Grand Signior, which I must ever attribute to his goodness, not to my desserts'. He then promised to 'always pray to the God of Heaven and Earth to pour down his choicest blessings on the Imperial head, to bless his Arms with success against all his Enemies, to grant health and long life to the Grand Seignior, and for ever to continue me his grateful and devoted servant.'[26] Nelson handed the letter to Kelim, together with a bundle of others for Spencer Smith, promising before parting that he would entrust the efendi's safe return to Turkey to his own stepson, Josiah Nisbet, in the sloop *Bonne Citoyenne*. This was intended as a personal tribute to the efendi, but it was also a convenient means of getting rid of Josiah, whose presence in the fleet was becoming awkward and embarrassing for Nelson. Emma had mothered the young man at first, as she had Hoste, but Josiah was an obstacle to her relationship with Nelson and becoming an adversary. It was said she now used her influence with Nelson 'to keep Mr. Nisbet always at sea'. A story was told how Josiah, after finding Emma and Nelson alone, had 'said in a manner too pointed to be misunderstood, "Pray, where am I to cruise next, my lady?"'[27]

With the French bearing down on Naples, rumours that the royal family was about to flee the city caused panic, looting and violent unrest. Jacobins started openly fighting royalists. Somehow, Nelson kept up the pretence to the very end. On the evening of 21 December, after giving the order to smuggle the royal family on board *Vanguard*, he joined the Hamiltons for a party hosted by the efendi at the palace of the Turkish embassy in Naples, possibly arranged as a diversion. During the evening, they all slipped away in the dark to meet a waiting boat for the long haul out to *Vanguard*. With the Hamiltons safely aboard his flagship, Nelson and the boat, joined by others from *Alcmene*, returned ashore, where, using the secret tunnel, he slipped into the palace to collect the terrified royal family. By dawn on 22 December, the king and queen, their children, grandchildren, dozens of attendants and most of their ministers were cowering miserably in *Vanguard*, prevented by foul weather from sailing. Crammed into the hold were their hurriedly packed possessions, but they kept their jewels and money close about them. Nelson probably entrusted his jewel, and other valuables, to his querulous servant, Tom Allen. Originally a ploughman from Norfolk, Allen was 'an excellent specimen of the untutored and undaunted British sailor', with a fierce hatred of foreigners and, perversely, of rowing boats. This self-styled 'Wally de Sham' (*valet de chambre*), with his comforting local accent and prejudices, had been with Nelson since 1793, witnessing, before they parted company ahead of Trafalgar, 'fourteen skrimmages and fifteen reg'lar engagements'. Wounded three times himself, once uncomfortably in the 'privates',[28] Allen even claimed to have saved Nelson's life at the Nile, recalling how he had sewn a pad into the brow of the admiral's new and ill-fitting hat before the action to make it more secure and comfortable. This pad, he asserted, had lessened the impact of the shrapnel which struck and wounded Nelson, preventing more serious injury or death.[29]

In the chaos of the flight from Naples, Kelim and his retinue, now risen to fourteen with additions from the Turkish embassy in Naples, were hustled back to *Alcmene*, lying low in the water groaning with refugees and gold.[30] Confused by the turn of events, the Turks clung to Nelson's promise that his own stepson Captain Nisbet would soon take them home in *Bonne Citoyenne*. Hopes were raised on 23 December when *Alcmene* finally made sail, only to be dashed again when the ship anchored further out in the bay to be out of reach of the shore batteries. That same day, a seaman fell from the topgallant yard and was killed, a gloomy portent for the superstitious passengers.[31] They were then forced to watch as *Vanguard*, flying the Bourbon standard and the admiral's pennant, led a squadron of overcrowded ships and transports including, to their dismay, *Bonne Citoyenne,* out of the bay and towards Sicily. *Alcmene* remained at single anchor a further week, with Nelson having ordered Captain Hope to burn any Neapolitan ships left behind before they fell into enemy hands. Not until 2 January did Hope consider it safe to weigh anchor and follow *Vanguard* to Sicily.

One witness to the burning of the ships at Naples, 'the most magnificent spectacle ever exhibited', was Pryse Lockhart Gordon, a young officer in the army on an eventful tour of Italy with his friend Lord Montgomery, an invalid. They had also been evacuated to *Alcmene*, where Gordon had found 'a curious *mélange* of fellow emigrants', including three cardinals, various bishops, English tourists and the exhausted Turks. Kelim was a 'fine old fellow' and 'much more intelligent than the Christian prelates', although his health had suffered grievously after so many weeks at sea. Gordon was given coffee and invited to join the efendi on deck, where they sat companionably on cushions drinking sweetly sticky Maraschino in small crystal glasses and smoking perfumed tobacco, prepared by Kelim himself, in 'superb Turkish pipes mounted in amber'. Peter Ritor, the Greek dragoman, told Gordon this ceremonial offer of coffee and tobacco by the efendi was 'the greatest compliment he could pay'. The next morning, Gordon was again fetched by the dragoman and, to his surprise, taken to Kelim's cabin – a luxury in the packed ship – where he found the old man anxiously preparing to pray. The reason for his abrupt summons became quickly obvious, and with his pocket compass Gordon identified the direction towards Mecca, the efendi then swivelling around on his knees before 'counting his beads and whispering his prayers'. When he had finished, Kelim 'washed his hands and perfumed his beard and mustachios' before calling again for coffee and tobacco. Gordon was handed a beautiful pipe as a present for his help, carved in jasmine wood and set with amber. In return, Gordon offered the efendi a smoky brown quartz stone known as a Cairngorm from his native Scotland, growing embarrassed when the delighted Turk took it to be a more precious topaz. After carefully noting down Gordon's name and age, Kelim invited him to join his entourage for the voyage home to Turkey:

> where he would lodge me and show me every attention in his power; and as he was to have an English frigate to convey him thither, which would remain a short time, I might return in it, and have the opportunity of seeing *Stamboul*, the finest city in the world.[32]

It was an invitation Gordon hoped to accept, yet no one could be sure what still awaited them all at Sicily.

5

THE ADMIRAL'S WIFE

Suffolk, England, October 1798

Frances Nelson was in Suffolk when the express arrived. Hearing the news, Admiral Sir Richard Hughes, an old friend who lived nearby, rushed over to congratulate her. 'I found with her,' he reported to Nelson, 'your Worthy Brother the Clergyman, and one or two more of her Relations, together with a young lady, the sister of your Captain, I was received in the politest manner by the agreeable circle, and they seemed well pleased with my apparent joy on the subject of my visit.'[1] He spoke of Patty Berry, whose concern for her brother Edward – missing since sailing with Nelson's dispatch and now presumed captured or killed – dampened the celebrations.

Letters of congratulation poured into Roundwood, the house Fanny had found for her husband near Ipswich, which he had not seen and would never live in. She had been there just a few months, her only companion a portrait of her husband by the artist Lemuel Abbott, its paint still fresh and odorous and 'my sincere friend in your absence'.[2] Her letters to Nelson were full of domestic chit chat and titbits of social gossip. Her experience as a widow and single mother, then as the wife of a naval officer away for months on end, had made her resilient and self-reliant. She had a reserve which made her appear aloof to her neighbours and often arrogant to her family. She was economic, frugal even, with money and hardened against the unscrupulous ways of tradesmen. A good housekeeper, she watched every penny, buying second-hand silver plates and fussing over her husband's seagoing belongings, often to his annoyance.[3]

Above all, Fanny was level-headed and sensible, wearily used to fortune's wheel. Worried for the safety of her husband and her son Josiah, she seemed unimpressed by the dramatic news. Emma would claim that Fanny never 'asked him a single question relative to that glorious victory which had so astonished the world'.[4] Yet her concerns were those of a wife and mother, not of a lover. With Captain Berry's equally anxious sister Patty a guest in her house, Fanny would not indulge in wild celebration. Patty's fears were realised when she heard not only that her brother had been wounded at the Nile but that *Leander*, the frigate carrying him and Nelson's dispatch down the Mediterranean, had indeed been captured and Berry taken prisoner.

Living on the outskirts of Ipswich, Fanny could hardly fail to see, or hear, the effect the news had on the nation. The countryside around rang to the sound of bells and gun salutes. Overnight, she too became a reluctant celebrity, with dances, songs, even ships named in her honour. On 16 October, she attended an all-night dance and supper in honour of her husband at the Assembly Rooms in the town, with Admiral Hughes proudly leading her in on his arm. For weeks she had been tormented, 'almost killed' she told her husband, by the contradictory and often alarming reports in the newspapers of his defeat, victory or even death.[5] Fearful of further loss and bereavement, the strain had made her ill. Previous actions had taken a heavy physical toll on Nelson, and suggestions he had again been wounded were vague and troubling. Fanny was unlikely to be carried away by the partying and eulogising of her husband. But as Mary Lockhart, sister of Fanny's dead first husband, now shrewdly remarked, 'you really will now require more than common principles to withstand all that I hope in God await you.'[6]

Fanny relied on her brother-in-law Maurice Nelson, a bureaucrat at the Navy Office, and Nelson's agent Alexander Davison for news on her husband's health and whereabouts. It was Maurice who reported the award of his brother's barony, and like the rest of the family Fanny was dissatisfied, 'mortified' was her word, at the apparent royal snub.[7] Swallowing his disappointment, Nelson sent his wife a letter telling her, now that she was a peeress, that, 'I scarcely need state the propriety of your going to court. Don't mind the expense. Money is trash.'[8] He ordered her to, 'Support my rank and do not let me down.'[9] Such offensive remarks surely horrified Fanny, who could remember how she and her husband had carefully but contentedly eked out an existence in Norfolk on his half-pay before the outbreak of war. Like the wives of many naval officers, she had a better grasp of money than her husband, who for so much of his life led an insulated existence in a ship far from home.

Living in rented properties until the recent purchase of Roundwood, the Nelsons had few possessions: he had been at sea since the age of 13 and she had lived overseas in the West Indies on her family's plantation. Nevertheless, those few years spent together in Norfolk during the peace were the happiest of their marriage. They had wanted for nothing, except suitable gowns for Fanny to wear to the houses of the local aristocracy, such as the Walpoles at Wolterton and Cokes at Holkham. At that time, Nelson had been unimpressed by wealth, believing it was often acquired dishonourably or dishonestly. Only their lack of a child cast a long shadow. Now it appeared from his letters that Nelson's quiet humility and good sense was being washed away by vanity.

Admiral Lord Hood, a loyal old friend, volunteered to escort Fanny to the Drawing Room at St James's Palace when she returned to town, although it was the Countess of Chatham, wife of a former First Lord of the Admiralty, who presented her to the queen. Elegantly dressed in silver and white, Fanny 'was received with the greatest respect by the Royal Family and Nobility who greeted her with the liveliest emotion of congratulation'.[10] Admiral

Lord Keith was also at the palace that day, taking leave of the monarch before sailing to assume command of the Mediterranean fleet from Earl St Vincent, news which made Fanny hopeful of her husband's quick return. In the days following the battle, Nelson had assured his wife he would be in England as early as November. But writing from Naples a month later, there was no mention of him coming back, only of his tumultuous reception in the city as '*Nostra Liberatore*' and, repeatedly, of the talents, charms and generosity of Lady Hamilton, 'one of the very best women in this world' and 'an honour to her sex'. Insensitively, Nelson reported that Fanny's son Josiah 'likes Lady Hamilton more than any female'.[11] Emma Hamilton needed no introduction. Like every other well-informed person in England, Fanny knew the story of her rise from obscurity to wife of the ambassador in Naples; she also knew of her scandalous reputation as an aristocratic plaything and sexual temptress. Nelson had met Emma before, on a previous visit to Naples in 1793, and had admired her then as an 'honour to the station' occupied by her husband Sir William Hamilton. Fanny suspected, rightly, that Nelson had enjoyed dalliances before, so such expressions of praise for Emma, coupled with stories carried home by returning officers, were unsettling. More alarming still, Fanny started receiving unsolicited letters from Emma herself, reporting in an over-familiar manner on Nelson's improving health and, with inappropriate intimacy, on her own growing friendship with Josiah. 'I love him much,' Emma wrote in December, 'and although we quarrel sometimes, he loves me and does as I would have him.' She also prepared Fanny for the disappointment of not seeing her husband anytime soon, as the King of Naples, by now campaigning in Rome, had:

> urged of my Lord Nelson to be as much at or about Naples as he could, not only to advise and consult with her Majesty (who is regent) for the good of the common cause, but in case of accident to take care of her and her family.

This was news Nelson had yet to break to his wife himself.[12]

On 20 October 1798, the *London Gazette* published details, released by the Foreign Office, of the Sultan of Turkey's gift of a 'superb diamond *Aigrette* (called a *Chelengk*, or Plume of Triumph) taken from one of the Imperial Turbans, to be sent to Admiral Sir Horatio Nelson, together with a Pelice of sable fur of the first quality'. The *Gazette* also printed a translation of the deputy Grand Vizier's letter to Spencer Smith requesting permission of the King in England for Nelson to wear the awards.[13] News of the presents caused great excitement and curiosity in England. This was the first time Fanny heard about the jewel, as her husband's letter revealing the gift himself could not have reached her yet. The *haute couture* gown she wore to Court suggests Fanny had an interest in fashion, but a lack of money meant she owned few jewels and possibly no diamonds. Portraits show her wearing only modest pieces: a coral bead collar in one, simple gold earrings in another, a pearl necklace in a third. For a dance, she lent her niece Charlotte Nelson pearl earrings from her own jewel case and made her a wreath of wild flowers.

Fanny was so excited and proud of her husband's unusual award that when she dined at Lord and Lady Inchiquin's in December she 'shewed them a drawing of the Aigrette sent by the Sultan to Lord Nelson after the victory of the Nile'.[15] The public would have to wait until January 1799, however, before an 'exact representation' of 'Lord Nelson's Aigrette', taken from Spencer Smith's sketch, was reproduced in the fashion press.[16] Meanwhile, they could enjoy satirist James Gillray's less than respectful but sharply insightful caricature of the admiral, entitled 'The HERO of the NILE'. Published on 1 December, this print portrayed Nelson standing on his quarterdeck wreathed in gun smoke, displaying the captured sword of the defeated French admiral which had since been delivered to the Mansion House by Capel. His diminutive figure with tatty uniform coat and threadbare stocking is draped in the heavy, rich sable pelisse whilst his hat sports an outsize aigrette loaded with gems and topped by an extravagant feathered plumage. Nelson is portrayed as a comic character taken from the opera, or pantomime, not the battlefield. In previous drawings – 'Extirpation of the Plagues of Egypt', published on 6 October, and 'John Bull taking a Luncheon', published on 24 October – Gillray had admired the hero, showing him as a warrior and national hero. But news of the awards being heaped on Nelson by dubious foreign potentates and rumours of his growing vanity were too tempting for the satirist to ignore. Gillray sharpened his pen, and with 'The HERO of the NILE' treated the admiral like the much-maligned Prince of Wales, a favourite target. Nelson is mocked as a ludicrous figure bowed down by gaudiness and self-importance. The vignette below the caricature displays a bowdlerised version of Nelson's ostentatious new coat of arms, replacing the cross on the shield with a stocking purse bulging with the admiral's inflated government pension. Looking like nothing less than a pair of grossly pendulent testicles, the purse alluded to salacious rumours of the hero's infidelity and his rapacious sex drive. The print suggests the admiral already had a reputation in elite circles for sexual misdemeanour. For the first time, it also broadcast the sultan's jewel to a popular audience, making it the admiral's instantly recognisable trademark on the many prints which followed, regardless of the accuracy of the portrait.

Gillray's caricatures were produced and distributed from a print shop in St James's Street, near where Fanny lodged and shopped when in town. Published a few days after she attended Court, she could hardly have failed to see this biting satire of her husband in the shop window or have misunderstood its meaning. Gillray was a popular artist with a large following, and the risk to her husband's reputation was obvious. Keenly interested in his own public image, Nelson frequently asked his wife to send him the latest caricatures and prints of himself.[17] He preferred the gentler art of Piccadilly printseller Samuel Fores to the biting Gillray, standing godfather to Fores's son, although Fanny may still have sent 'The HERO of the NILE' out to him as a warning. It may also have tipped her into the dramatic decision to cross war-torn Europe and join her husband at Naples to discover what was going on.

Letters from her husband were becoming shorter, infrequent and infused with a dangerously disaffected tone. Captain Saumarez, safely back from Egypt, found her 'very impatient for letters from our gallant Admiral'.[18] On 7 December, before taking the coach to Bath, she stormed into the house of Nelson's agent, Alexander Davison, 'in good health but very uneasy and anxious' he reported to Nelson, but 'begs me say, that unless you return home in a few months, she will join the Standard [a 64-gun British warship] at Naples. Excuse a woman's tender feelings, they are too acute to be expressed.'[19] Nelson knew this was no idle threat. As soon as it reached him in Sicily, he responded by urging his wife not to pursue 'a wandering sailor', assuring her that 'nothing but the situation of affairs in this country has kept me from England'.[20]

He was too late. The revolution in Naples prevented Davison's letter reaching him until April, by which time Fanny had already embarked on then abandoned her quest, as a newly discovered document reveals. On 14 February, it was reported that *Penelope*, a 38-gun frigate, had returned to Portsmouth after taking Lady Nelson to Gibraltar and back.[21] Only a VIP with highly placed friends at the Admiralty could have travelled into a war zone for personal reasons in a Royal Navy ship. *Penelope* had left England on 3 January, with the lack of surviving letters from Fanny in the following weeks confirming her absence. By 21 February, she was back in Bath thanking Davison for the gift of some china. Presumably Earl St Vincent, Nelson's outgoing chief in the Mediterranean and an old friend to them both, had reassured her in Gibraltar that her husband would soon be returning home. She would also have heard there about the tumultuous events at Naples and the dangers of travelling further. Her husband's letters had been brief and circumspect, both for security reasons and to spare her feelings. Writing to her just a few days before evacuating the royal family from Naples, he had made no mention of the mayhem around him, only of the debt he owed the Hamiltons, 'with the exception of you and my dear father the dearest friends I have in this world'.[22] Soon there was talk in the press that Nelson had been betrayed or, worse, cynically used by the King of Naples. The *Morning Chronicle* deplored the loss of Naples, blaming Neapolitan cowardice and incompetence. 'Are these to be the fruits of our brilliant victories?' it thundered.[23]

Her voyage to Gibraltar and renewed promises from her husband that he would be in England by May 1799, or June at the latest, placated Fanny, but only for a short time. Pursuing her husband into the Mediterranean showed her depth of feeling and proved she was determined not to surrender him without a fight. By the spring it was obvious that Nelson was not coming home any time soon. As more officers from the Nile campaign returned to England with their scandalous stories, the true nature of those 'affairs' and the real reason for his delay was becoming all too apparent. Fanny complained bitterly to Davison that Nelson was 'a Slave to the State' and, to her shame, that his relationship with Lady Hamilton had been openly discussed when she attended Court again in June.[24] Soon *The Times* was comparing Nelson and Emma to Mark Antony and Cleopatra, blaming those 'perfidious Gods' Cupid and Venus, who 'have in all times spread their smiling snares for the first of mankind. Heroes and conquerors are subdued in their turn … what will not the Eye effect in the bosom of a Hero!'[25]

Friends rallied round, leaking to the newspapers, probably with Fanny's connivance, an affectionate letter from Nelson to her dated the year before. It was a well-meaning gesture which backfired when the *Observer* commented that, 'It is hardly fair to exhibit such characters, if we may use the term, in *dishabille*.'[26] The gossip and waiting took a heavy toll on Fanny's fragile health. In April 1799, she was bled of some 80oz of blood (five milk bottles worth) and now frequently sought the revitalising waters at Bath or Tunbridge Wells. She was accompanied by Nelson's frail father, Edmund, who anticipating his son's return, now started at every knock on the door. 'I should very much like to spend a few months in a warm climate,' she pleaded, suggesting she might winter at Lisbon or join her husband in Sicily.[27] Feeling alone and vulnerable, she was easy prey for a fraudster, later jailed, who charged her 12 guineas for fake news of her husband.[28]

Her husband's letters were more infrequent now; hers were still chatty but becoming strained. Nelson was becoming embittered against his own king, government and rivals like Sir Sidney Smith, who had appeared in the region to usurp his command. Whilst demanding all the trappings of his new status as a peer of the realm – a house, carriage and servants – he also bemoaned his lack of money and, a growing preoccupation this, his rising debts.[29] 'These jewels give not money, meat or drink,' he complained, 'and from the various circumstances of my having much more expenses than any commander in chief without any one profit it has been a heavy money campaign to me.'[30] The letters were shorter too. He blamed his health and his workload, but it was now obvious to the Nelsons, long before they met again, that their marriage was in crisis.

6

THE RIVAL

Constantinople, Turkey, January 1799

On 6 January 1799, the day after articles of the treaty between Britain, Russia and the Ottoman Empire were signed, Captain Sir Sidney Smith's ship *Tigre* moored in the Golden Horn below the Seraglio. Smith had left England two months earlier on 'a secret expedition with a detached squadron', having been summoned to the Admiralty as soon as Nelson's victory was confirmed.[1] It was given out that his 80-gun French prize was laden with gifts for the Emperor of Morocco, a country Smith had previously visited and which Britain was courting as an ally.[2] In fact, the fourteen wagon loads of ship models, naval paintings and three-pounder brass guns - adapted for carrying by camel for campaign in the desert – were secretly intended for the Sultan of Turkey.

Until now, Smith had been perhaps the most celebrated officer in the Royal Navy, with operettas penned in his honour, bestselling prints after his portrait and women falling at his feet. The reason for so much adulation was Smith's near-miraculous recent escape from prison in Paris, where he had been incarcerated following a daring boat mission to cut out a French privateer. 'The first lion of the day', Smith was also celebrated for his fire-raising exploits at Toulon in December 1793 when, in a haul to equal the Battle of the Nile, his men had burned or sunk fourteen French warships.

The king was his greatest admirer, inviting Smith to the palace to hear all about his amazing adventures.

Short, with a markedly large head topped with a mop of curly black hair, Smith cut a Byronic figure. He was now also dogged by ill-health, having 'suffered much during his imprisonment', according to a concerned friend.[3] Yet, like Nelson, he had enormous self-belief, with maverick views and a wilful disregard for his own safety. Unlike Nelson, however, he was well-connected and admired at Court. Back in 1792, this 'odd, eccentric man' had been invested with the Swedish Order of the Sword for his endeavours as a volunteer in the Swedish navy during its war against Russia.[4] The foreign knighthood had earned Smith opprobrium from his fellow officers in the Royal Navy – many of whose friends had died fighting as mercenaries on the other side – but the warm regard of the king, who supported the struggle of the Swedish monarch. In 1793, as clouds of war gathered in Europe, George III agreed to send Smith to Constantinople to gather intelligence on the failing Ottoman Empire. There Sidney had joined his brother Spencer at the British embassy, volunteering for the Turkish navy as a cover for his spying.

Now Smith was heading back to Turkey. With Ottoman-controlled Egypt occupied by the French, long-neglected relations with the sultan had to be improved to prevent his alliance with the enemy. No one was better qualified for this delicate task than Smith, who knew Turkey and the young sultan, spoke fluent French and possibly some Turkish too and was a battle-hardened naval officer. Having faced General Bonaparte at Toulon, Smith was also anxious to confront and defeat his old adversary. But he was given a confused, double role. His cousin, Foreign Secretary Lord Grenville, dispatched him on a diplomatic mission as joint minister in Constantinople beside his brother Spencer. At the same time, First Lord of the Admiralty Earl Spencer ordered Smith, Nelson's whereabouts and wellbeing since the Nile being then unknown, to 'take command of such of his Majesty's ships as he may find in those seas unless, by any unforeseen accident, it should happen that there should be among them any of his Majesty's officers of superior rank'.[5] Such vague and ambiguous orders would inevitably cause problems later. On 21 October 1798 Smith was ordered 'To put to sea without a moment's loss of time'.[6]

He sailed a week later, pausing at Gibraltar to deliver dispatches to Earl St Vincent, commander-in-chief of the Mediterranean. St Vincent, an officer of the old school, did not like the flamboyant and over-confident Smith. He liked Smith's dual assignment still less, telling Nelson that, 'I foresee that both you and I shall be drawn into a *tracasserie* about this *gentleman*, who, having the ear of *ministers, and telling* his story better than we can, will be more attended to.'[7] The earl warned Smith that his unorthodox appointment as diplomatic minister and commanding naval officer in the Levant would upset Nelson. Smith had expected to meet the admiral at Syracuse in Sicily to explain the complex situation in person, but at Malta he learned from Captain Ball that Nelson was already at Naples, so he penned a conciliatory letter instead. 'It shall be my study to shew your lordship,' he wrote, 'and all other officers superior to me, whom I may chance to meet in the service, by a ready obedience to their orders, that this arrangement will not affect the subordination necessary in the service, which I have it as much at heart to preserve, as any officer in it.' Wisely, Smith glossed his letter with extravagant praise for Nelson's recent triumph: 'the most perfect naval victory that ever was gained by any country in any age', he enthused.[8] Unfortunately, in the chaos unfolding at Naples this well-meaning attempt at soothing Nelson's bruised ego failed to reach the admiral for weeks, leaving Smith to endure a prolonged period of hostility.

The sultan was delighted to see *Tigre* moored below his palace, ordering, reported Smith, 'a *very ample* supply of fresh meat, vegetables, fruit and wine!!! To be sent on board every day for the consumption of the *ship's company*'.[9] During an exceptional private audience with Selim in the his 120-gun flagship, Smith presented the gifts from London, seeking in return, and this was a typical

Smith gesture, the release into English custody of forty-six French prisoners captured at the Battle of the Nile whose fate might otherwise have been very grisly. Selim was especially interested in the prints of naval actions and the portraits of famous British admirals which Smith offered. Noticing this, Smith urgently sent back to London for the latest images of the Battle of the Nile 'and the best likeness of Lord Nelson to be sent out as soon as they are published'.[10] He then hosted a dinner in *Tigre* to celebrate the triple alliance of Turkey, Russia and England, and had the brass guns, designed for the campaign to liberate Egypt, hauled up to the Seraglio to be demonstrated in front of the thrilled sultan, who showered the British gun crews with gold sequins.

Twelve shipwrights brought by Smith from England now set to work building gun boats for the Turkish fleet. Over the heads of his efendi, the sultan appointed Smith 'Marine Minister' in his Divan, giving him a squadron of ships and authority over all Turkish naval forces.[11] Together they planned an amphibious landing in Egypt launched from Rhodes, whilst harassing Bonaparte from the sea with gun boats manned by Albanian mercenaries. Unable to field an army capable of defeating the French in battle, Smith designed a special forces war to erode the enemy's resistance. Keen to avoid bloodshed, Smith also worked up a plan giving the French safe passage home, what he called a *pont d'or*, if they agreed to abandon Egypt. Unlike Nelson the avenger, Smith liked to pose as a knightly figure in the chivalric mould of his great hero, the Elizabethan Sir Philip Sidney, for whom he may have been named by his romantic-minded father. Yet he faced difficulty almost immediately: first, the capture off Syria of Osman Hadgi, a 'feudatory officer of the Imperial Court'[12] sent with transports to supply the Turkish force heading for Egypt, jeopardised the military campaign; then Nelson, piqued at Smith's command in his region, flexed his authority and ordered his rival away from Constantinople to support the British blockade off Alexandria.

Sailing off the coast of Egypt, Smith quickly learned that although the Battle of the Nile had cut Bonaparte's supply lines, it had not dented his ambition. After capturing and securing Cairo and crushing resistance by the Mamelukes, the general had taken his army across the Sinai desert and was now heading north through Syria towards Constantinople. Gaza then Jaffa had quickly fallen, the latter amid appalling scenes of bloody massacre. By the middle of March 1799, Bonaparte was gazing at Acre, the historic Syrian port and stronghold of the fearsome Djezzar Pasha, Ottoman governor of the Levant from the Nile to Turkey. A former powerhouse of the medieval Knights Templar, the old city with its crumbling walls appeared defenceless. But to his dismay, Bonaparte saw *Tigre* lying at anchor in the bay below Acre's crusader fort, Smith having sailed from Alexandria with a small squadron of ships to intercept the enemy. For a second time, the two men were pitched against each other as Smith rallied a defence against Bonaparte's siege guns. For two months he cajoled, inspired and led 'The Butcher' Djezzar and his rag-bag army of Albanians, Syrians, Bosnians, Turks and Kurds into enduring constant bombardment and the enemy's frequent assaults. Many times Smith was seen on the ramparts of the fort, sword in hand as piles of French bodies mounted in the ditches below him to be defiled and decapitated by the enraged defenders. He survived two assassination attempts, countless attacks and the suffocating heat, stench and disease of the besieged city. Yet, 'never was Sir S. so merry, nor did he ever utter such *Bon Mots*,' recalled one amazed observer, 'as in the very thick of it.' At the height of the siege, old Djezzar was seen sitting on a bag of rice at the entrance to the ruins of his palace, his sword and trademark tomahawk at his feet. Lying all around him were dozens of severed French heads:

> arranged by him like cabbages in a market: his secretary on one side writing the names of those who brought them in: the cashier on the other side paying 50 piasters for each; while he was cutting with a pair of scissors a kind of plume, called 'Chelengk' out of a thin plate of silver, which he himself placed in their respective caps.[13]

In peaceful times, Djezzar liked to cut paper into colourful flowers to give as presents, now he used his skill to craft these crude badges of honour.[14] He knew the inspiring effect of a Chelengk to his embattled troops and how it could motivate its wearer and the men around him in the desperate defence of his city. The impact of a single Chelengk was worth more than many blows from his bloodied Shamshir sword.

On 20 May, Bonaparte finally despaired, calling his shattered army away back to Egypt. Acre would be the limit of his Eastern adventure, or, as Smith described it in a jubilant letter to Nelson, 'The plain of Nazareth has been the boundary of Bonaparte's extraordinary career.'[15] The general's thoughts started turning again to France, where there were new worlds and people to conquer. But his defeat stung, and the wound inflicted by Smith felt deep and lasting. Their confrontation at Toulon, Smith's escape from Paris and now their duel at Acre had made it personal. 'That man made me miss my destiny,' Bonaparte would say in exile years later, a tribute he never paid Nelson – or the Duke of Wellington.

When Smith returned triumphant to *Tigre*, he found a pile of old letters from Nelson steaming with indignation at having him command ships in his region. Smith's unorthodox joint role as a minister and naval officer had, as St Vincent foretold, infuriated Nelson, who stuck rigidly, even doggedly, to official procedure (when it suited him). Having spoken with St Vincent in person at Gibraltar and written politely to Nelson on arriving in the Mediterranean, Smith was puzzled and shocked by the admiral's outburst. Exhausted and bloodied by the siege, in his weary reply he searched 'in vain' for an explanation:

> unconscious as I am of ever having had a thought, or a wish, but to appear correct in the eyes of my immediate commanding-officer, and having made it my study to do that which you would approve. I hope your Lordship will set me right in future, rather in the form of a friendly and fatherly admonition, than with the severity I at present experience at your hands.[16]

In a candid letter to his patron Lord Grenville back in London, Smith blamed a 'paroxysm of jealousy' for Nelson's behaviour, 'which his Lordship I trust now sees to have been a mere sensation from his extreme sensibility'.[17] The well-connected Smith also complained to his 'old friend' Sir William Hamilton about Nelson, criticism which fell on deaf ears.

Nelson had reason to be jealous. The defeat of Bonaparte in Syria had matched, many said exceeded, his own victory at the Nile, and it was greeted with wild enthusiasm in England and Turkey. There was astonishment that Smith, with just a handful of men, had defied Bonaparte's formidable army. The sultan wept when he heard the news, which came to him with sack-loads of severed ears taken from the corpses of French soldiers. He titled Smith 'The Valiant'[18] and ordered a Tartar messenger take him a diamond jewel and sable fur 'similar to those bestowed on Lord Nelson'.[19] Like Nelson's, Smith's presents travelled with the imperial appeal 'that permission and power be granted him by his Court to attach this aigrette to his forehead, radiating with glory, and wear the pelisse, as testimonies of the zeal and ardour which he has displayed'.[20] The king in England was unlikely to refuse. Already his fervent admirer, George III went in person to Parliament to speak of Smith's heroic endeavours at Acre, praising his 'skill' and 'heroism'.[21] Smith would get a pension of £1,000 a year for his achievement, but no peerage as the battle again fell outside the conventions for elevating a naval commander after a fleet action. The City of London compensated with a beautiful presentation sword, while the cash-strapped Turkey Company, having just completed a large silver cup for Nelson, ordered another lavish trophy.

Smith heard of none of these awards for months, having sailed to Rhodes immediately after the siege of Acre to rejoin the Turkish army being assembled for the invasion of Egypt. It was there that he received the jewel and sable-lined pelisse sent by the sultan. Familiar with Ottoman custom, Smith was more sensitive to the privilege and esteem of these awards than Nelson, and the respect they commanded in the Islamic world. Based on hearsay, the press back in England valued Smith's jewel at 8,000 guineas (close to £1 million today): a similar sum to the price attached to Nelson's.[22] The only image of Smith's Chelengk, which he would illustrate on his coat of arms, shows it to be the highest-ranking 'seven plume' type, very similar to those worn by the sultan himself.

Selim had promised a silver Chelengk in return for every decapitated French head brought back to him from Egypt. But the Turkish landings at Aboukir Bay, still littered with the burnt-out hulks of French warships, ended in bloody defeat, with the loss of thousands of men and the chaotic flight of the survivors back to Cyprus. To prevent a massacre of the Christian population cowering on the island, Smith pinned his jewel to his hat, using its authority to quell the bloodlust of the Turkish troops. In gratitude, the Greek Orthodox Church on the island appointed Smith Grand Prior of the Knights Templar in England, presenting him with an elaborate gem-set gold cross worn by Richard the Lionheart when he was Grand Master of the Order back in the twelfth century. In this strange way, Smith's Chelengk, that sparkling emblem of Islamic authority, won him a prized relic of Christendom. The Knights Templar had long ago been disbanded, but the cross played on Smith's romantic imagination, feeding his lifelong interest in freemasonry and medieval cults. He was still wearing it next to his heart when he died peacefully in bed forty years later.

After winning plaudits on the battlefield, Smith now exercised his dwindling diplomatic powers. Before departing the coast of Egypt following the Turkish repulse, Smith, having nurtured excellent contacts among the local tribes, leaked reports to the occupying army of military defeats and political unrest in France. After proclaiming a great victory at Aboukir, these rumours may have finally tipped Bonaparte into abandoning his Eastern adventure. Sensing a greater prize back in Paris, Bonaparte slipped away from Egypt, evading Smith's watching warships. He left his demoralised, diseased and mutinous army behind in the hands of General Jean-Baptiste Kléber. Highly experienced and popular with his soldiers, the bluff Kléber, the son of a peasant who had risen through the ranks, saw Bonaparte's escape from Egypt as a betrayal. He had been highly sceptical of the mad enterprise from the outset. 'That bugger has deserted us with his breeches full of shit,' he raged at his officers. 'When we get back to Europe we'll rub his face in it.'[23] With Bonaparte gone, the French army faced a perilous future as the sultan, smarting from the failed landings, had dispatched a powerful Turkish force of some 80,000 troops through Syria to Egypt, which Kléber feared his weakened army would find impossible to resist. The pragmatic Kléber was now willing to negotiate the peaceful evacuation proposed by Smith before the siege of Acre.

Smith knew that Nelson fiercely opposed any settlement with the enemy. But believing he acted with the approval of London, and the support of the sultan, he secretly opened peace talks in *Tigre*. A treaty was signed on 24 January 1800 at El Arish, about 100 miles east of the Nile delta, which the sprawling Turkish army had now reached, slaughtering the French garrison. The deal confirmed a truce giving the French three months to gather their forces, arms and baggage at the Egyptian ports for embarkation and safe passage to France before returning Egypt to Ottoman control. Delighted with the outcome, Smith sent Frederick Maitland, youthful commander of the sloop *Cameleon*, back to England with the treaty and his dispatches. Forty years later, this same Maitland would capture the Turkish guns given to Queen Victoria. But Smith's well-intentioned effort at peace was short-lived and quickly overtaken by events far away. On his return to Paris, Bonaparte had seized power in a coup, ushering in a new and more dangerous phase of the war with Britain. To allow Bonaparte's abandoned army in the east to return intact to Europe was now inconceivable, with London reverting to Nelson's policy of annihilation. In Constantinople, too, Smith's influence was waning, undermined by Lord Elgin, who had arrived as the new ambassador to outrank the Smith brothers at the embassy. Elgin had met with Nelson at Palermo on his journey out to the Porte, and had since been assailed with letters from the admiral demanding the complete extermination of the French in Egypt. The ambassador fed these demands to the sultan, further undermining Smith's treaty. 'At all risks of giving offence,' Nelson implored Elgin, '*not one Frenchman should be allowed to quit Egypt*.'[24] The sultan had at first been bewildered by the sudden and unexplained shift of power in the British embassy, but Elgin's smooth aristocratic manner won him over. Behind his back, Elgin complained bitterly about Smith to London then, without his knowledge, sent a secret envoy to the Turkish camp in Egypt urging immediate attack. The grand vizier did not hesitate, steering his massive force towards Cairo to engage the French. Furious at Smith's apparent deceit, Kléber took his much smaller but better disciplined and trained army out of the city, bent on revenge. The two armies clashed at Heliopolis, where the outnumbered French, fired up by Kléber's furious rhetoric, repulsed then routed the shambolic Turks. The grand vizier himself only narrowly escaped capture, with Smith taking all the blame for Nelson and Elgin's disastrous strategy. The Convention of El Arish lay in ruins in the bloodied sand, together with Smith's reputation. Although he escaped official censure and a court martial – it was agreed he had acted in good faith – Smith was stripped of his command in the Levant and sent back to his ship. His brother Spencer was recalled to London from Constantinople, bitterly resentful of his treatment at the hands of Elgin. He entered parliament before securing a quieter diplomatic posting in Stuttgart. Later, his wife was arrested by the French, and after her dramatic escape, and a shipwreck, had an affair with Lord Byron, who found her 'very pretty, very accomplished and very eccentric'.[25] The humbling of the Smiths made Elgin triumphant, but Nelson was silent and with the French still entrenched in Egypt it was not the last that either man would hear of Sir Sidney Smith.

7

THE FIRST KNIGHT

Palermo, Sicily, December 1798

Nelson had seen many seas, but none as cruel as the one he faced escaping Naples. Packed with terrified refugees, *Vanguard* reeked of vomit and excrement as the ship lurched crazily through the towering waves. One of the young princes died in Emma's arms, while Sir William cowered below waiting to blow his brains out if the ship foundered. Only when they reached the safety of Palermo in the gloom of Christmas Eve 1798 did he put the pistols down. Exhausted and missing his collections, Sir William found chilly lodgings with his wife and Nelson to brood over his losses in Naples. His gloom only deepened when he then heard that *Colossus*, carrying his most precious objects, had been wrecked near England. For Nelson, the greatest shock was now learning that 'a piece of my command is lopped off' by Sir Sidney Smith, his junior officer, who had been appointed over his head to command the British naval forces in the eastern Mediterranean, and with a larger ship too.[1] Worse still, London had made Smith joint minister with his brother Spencer in Constantinople, granting him the political clout Nelson longed for. He responded to this perceived insult by sending sarcastic letters about 'abler Officers' and 'the Swedish Knight' to his commander-in-chief Earl St Vincent before losing his temper altogether, '*I do feel*,' he stormed, '*for I am a man*, that it is impossible for me to serve in these seas, with the squadron under a junior officer – could I have thought it!' Of all the officers in the Royal Navy, Smith was perhaps the most like to Nelson: with an ego, flair and taste for publicity to match. He lacked only Nelson's pathological hatred of the French, despite his spell in the infamous Temple prison in Paris. Smith's career had dogged the admiral. To date, his exploits had caught the imagination as much, if not more than Nelson's, and even now, after the Battle of the Nile, it appeared that Smith remained the Admiralty's, the king's and the public's favourite. What more did he have to do? He had had enough. Feverishly picturing a conspiracy forming against him in London – 'it is all of a piece,' he exclaimed bitterly - Nelson offered his resignation. 'Pray grant me your permission to retire,' he implored St Vincent, 'and I hope the *Vanguard* will be allowed to convey me and my friends, Sir William and Lady Hamilton, to England.'[2]

Furious at Nelson's treatment, and fearful of losing him, Emma tried to undermine Smith by writing to Earl St Vincent about him in highly disparaging terms. She feared the damaging impact of Smith's sudden appearance on her friend's fragile self-confidence, influence and health. 'Your Ladyship's diverting description of S.S.S. is very just,' the earl replied. 'I remember him exactly the figure you have so ingeniously delineated. It was unfortunate for him that foolish young women in England did not feel like your Ladyship, for they really ran after him and turned his head.' St Vincent simply could not understand 'the very unaccountable influence' Smith had over the government in London, 'of whom he has taken entire possession, insomuch that they put unlimited confidence in all he utters, however extravagant and incredible, has made him the important figure he now exhibits'. *Soi-disant* is how the earl described Smith: self-deluded. 'I trust, your Admiral,' he finished, 'who is in every sense of the word, a hero, will laugh at this *modern Mahomet*, taking care to put a strong hand on him when necessary.'[3]

It was in this grim mood of feeling slighted and defeated that Nelson's triumphant year ended. Only Emma, with a resilience and reserves of energy lacking in the lackeys and hypochondriacs all around them in Palermo, remained upbeat and irrepressible. She busily fixed up ramshackle accommodation and a household of sorts at the baroque Palazzo Palagonia. She was impressive and irresistible, and when Sir William took to his bed feeling ill, Nelson took to hers. Believing his career over after the debacle at Naples, and facing an uncertain future, he was feeling militant and devil-may-care. Far from home, having sex with Emma was an antidote to months of physical pain, insult and emotional turmoil.

With Naples occupied by the French, who had declared the city capital of the radical Parthenopean Republic, the king and queen festered on Sicily, gaming, hunting and sowing counter-revolution in the guise of a holy crusade. Nelson stayed too, in strange limbo after the chaotic activity of previous weeks. This lethargy bred a poisonous and spiteful atmosphere, and a damaging sense of unreality as he sat night after night watching Emma gamble his money away. 'Good Sir William, Lady Hamilton, and myself, are the mainsprings of the machine, which manage what is going on in this country,' Nelson declared, echoing the clockwork mechanism of the sultan's jewel whirring on his hat.[4] His acceptance of the freedom of Palermo, only the second foreigner since the Sun King Louis XIV so honoured, further inflated his burgeoning ego. By a quirk of this Bourbon family grant, then Britain's enemy, allowing him to be addressed as 'Most Excellent'. Pryce Gordon was astonished by Nelson's boasting when he eventually reached Palermo with Kelim Efendi and the Turks in *Alcmene*. After mooring in the bay on 5 January 1799, Captain Hope took Gordon with him to the Palazzo Palagonia to report the burning of the remaining ships in Naples. Before they could do so, however, they found themselves in a bizarre ceremony 'got up with considerable stage effect' for Emma's introduction, 'her raven tresses floating round her expansive form and full bosom'.[5] Nelson appeared impatient, exchanging 'significant' glances with Emma and insinuating that *Alcmene* had lingered in Naples too long. He then turned to Gordon and asked him, 'Pray Sir, have you heard of the battle of the Nile?' Astonished, Gordon assured the admiral that he had, and had often toasted its success. Nelson continued:

> *That* battle, Sir, was the most extraordinary one that was ever fought, and it is unique, Sir, for three reasons: first, for its having been fought at night; secondly, for its having been fought at anchor; and thirdly, for its having been gained by an admiral with one arm.[6]

This extraordinary boast might be attributed to Nelson's tiredness and irritability, yet Gordon claimed that the admiral made the exact same speech to the Lord Mayor when he collected the City of London sword over a year later.

Before evacuating Naples, Nelson had promised that his own stepson, Josiah Nisbet, would convey Kelim safely back to Constantinople in *Bonne Citoyenne*. Josiah was an embarrassment to the admiral, who would be glad to see the back of him. As they were now conveyed across the bay from *Alcmene* to Josiah's waiting sloop, the Turks were hailed by slaves, all Ottoman subjects, incarcerated in the Portuguese man-of-war *Principe Real*. Their faces pressed through the ports of the ship, the cries of the slaves were so distressing that Kelim sent back an appeal for their release. Feeling awkwardly obliged, Nelson, a firm upholder of the rights of property – including of slaves – petitioned the Portuguese commander Marquis de Niza, 'as a friend, as an English admiral – as a favour to me, as a favour to my country – that you will give me the Slaves'.[7] The marquis acquiesced to the unusual request, allowing twenty-four slaves to be pulled across to *Bonne Citoyenne*, their blessings to their English saviour ringing out across the harbour as their names were added to the sloop's already crowded muster book.

Josiah sailed on the tide around midnight on 10 January with his stepfather's command 'not to permit any irregularities to be committed by any person who may go ashore' – by which he meant drinking and whoring – ringing in his ears.[8] The ship weighed anchor too soon for Pryse Gordon to join the voyage to Constantinople as an honoured guest of the efendi, as he had hoped. At their last meeting, Kelim had presented Gordon and his friend Lord Montgomery with a bale of perfumed Turkish tobacco and no less than fifty various tobacco pipes. In return, the Scot gave the Turk a pair of pistols with silver inlay and a blunderbuss. They parted with regret, Gordon vowing to visit Constantinople one day and to meet again the cosmopolitan efendi with his love of smoking, drinking and graceful habits 'of a man of rank'.[9]

By 30 January, *Bonne Citoyenne* was off Gallipoli in the Dardenelles, reaching Constantinople three days later where Josiah fired a twenty-one-gun salute beneath the Seraglio. At 9.30 that evening the ship moored beside Sidney Smith's ship *Tigre*, and the efendi and his attendants were taken ashore, together with an officer with Nelson's dispatches for Spencer Smith and the Porte: Josiah lacking the confidence to deliver them himself.[10] Their adventure was finally at an end. The Turks had been afloat almost continuously for over four months, having travelled to Egypt, then Naples and Sicily before heading home. They had sailed into a war zone and a revolution, endured storms and illness before finding Nelson and safely delivering the sultan's jewel. Kelim Efendi had completed his mission, and when he stood before his sultan to recount his extraordinary journey, and to deliver Nelson's fulsome letter of thanks, it is to be hoped he was given a jewel of his own.

The triumphant arrival of Kelim Efendi at Constantinople was sketched for Spencer Smith. When he returned to England, Smith passed the drawing to marine artist John Thomas Serres for completion and publication as a print. The picture shows *Bonne Citoyenne* moored below the Seraglio at the Artillery Quay, where a large crowd has gathered to greet the Turks after their long journey. The quay itself is laden with guns awaiting shipment for the campaign to recover Egypt. The deck of *Bonne Citoyenne* is jostling with the figures of the freed slaves, who line the rails anxious to begin their new lives ashore. Behind the sloop looms *Tigre*, firing a salute of welcome as the ship's barge is pulled ashore, with Sir Sidney Smith clearly visible sitting in the stern. His brother's ministerial skiff has already arrived, having made the short crossing from Pera, and is now empty as it gently rides the tide lapping the quayside. The lone figure nearby may be Spencer Smith waiting for his brother. Flying from the mainmast of *Tigre* is the broad pennant of a commodore, the rank senior to captain for an officer commanding a squadron. Smith's orders from London were far-reaching, but had not included such an official promotion. Josiah reported this *faux pas* to his stepfather when he returned to Palermo in March. As expected, it provoked an outburst which Nelson vented at Earl St Vincent during a letter of complaint about 'Captain Smith's parade and nonsense – Commodore Smith - I beg his pardon, for he wears a Broad Pendant – has he any orders for this presumption over the heads of so many good and gallant Officers with me?'[11] Hastily, the earl replied that, '*He* (that is Sir Sidney) has no authority whatever to wear a distinguishing pendant, unless you authorise him, for I certainly shall not.'[12]

Back in Sicily, Captain Hope of *Alcmene* was rewarded for bringing the Turks and the royal treasure safely away from Naples. Before Hope sailed for Gibraltar, the King of Naples gave him a sparkling diamond ring together with 100oz in silver coins to be shared out among his boat crews.[13] Hope carried with him dispatches and confided in Admiral Lord Keith, who had since arrived in the Mediterranean to assume his command, the first hints that Nelson was 'making himself ridiculous with Lady Hamilton [and] idling his time at Palermo when he should have been elsewhere'.[14] These damaging rumours were fuelled by Nelson and Emma's increasingly bizarre behaviour. Pryce Gordon, who remained in Sicily to explore the island, witnessed another extraordinary scene when a Turkish naval officer arrived carrying a letter and gift for Nelson from Tsar Paul of Russia. These had been sent to the combined Russian and Turkish fleet off Corfu as long ago as October, but no ship could be spared to deliver them to Sicily until now. 'With her usual tact',

Gordon wearily recalled, Emma insisted that Nelson change into full dress uniform, wear his pelisse and pin the sultan's jewel to his hat before greeting the envoy. She then theatrically threw open the doors of the reception room, revealing Nelson in all his glory to the Turk, who, 'the moment he caught a glimpse of his lordship's costume', threw himself prostrate on the floor, 'making the grand salaam'.[15] When he had recovered, he handed Nelson a letter in the tsar's own hand, together with '*une boite avec mon portrait enrichie de brillants*' ('a box with my portrait brilliantly enriched').[16]

Gordon was then forced to endure a noisy, self-congratulatory dinner hosted by the Hamiltons. Among the usual 'toad eaters' were more sceptical guests like Charles Lock, who was stuck in Palermo with his pregnant Irish wife, waiting to replace Sir William as British consul in Naples. Emma sat beside the Turkish officer, 'a coarse savage monster' who flirted with her and got drunk on rum ('which does not come under the prohibition of the Prophet', Gordon noted wryly). His words translated by 'Peter Ritor', the Greek dragoman who had remained behind in Palermo after Kelim Efendi sailed, the Turkish officer noisily boasted of murdering wounded French soldiers captured at sea leaving Egypt. He then dramatically raised a large sabre. 'With this weapon,' he cried, 'I cut off the heads of twenty French prisoners in one day! Look, there is their blood remaining on it!' Delighted, Emma took the sword and, as she had done with Admiral Blanquet's, pressed the bloodstained blade to her lips before passing it to Nelson.[17] Cecilia Lock was so shocked that she fainted and had to be taken out of the room, to jibes from her hostess that she was an Irish Jacobin. Appalled at this insult to his wife, Charles Lock launched a vituperative and damaging campaign against 'that superficial, grasping and vulgar minded woman' who was making Nelson 'the laughing stock of the whole fleet'. Lock also noticed that despite Sidney Smith's heroics at Acre, 'his praises here are little sung. His coming into these seas with Admiralty orders independent of Lord Nelson will never be forgiven him.'[18]

In an unctuous letter of thanks for his diamond and gold box, Nelson promised Tsar Paul that:

> The Invaluable gift of Your Portrait shall I assure you be cherish'd as the dearest drop of my blood and my constant prayers shall never cease being offered to the Almighty for your Imperial Majesty's health and success against the common enemy.[19]

Nelson also now added a codicil to his will, bequeathing Emma this box, together with the rose-shaped one gifted him by the Valida Sultan, 'as token of regard and respect for her every eminent virtues'.[20] It was unusual for Nelson to change his last testament without the immediate prospect of battle, with this being the first occasion Emma was mentioned in the document as a beneficiary. The bequests showed that since the evacuation from Naples their relationship had now reached a deeper and more intimate understanding.

The bejewelled and fur-bedecked figure which had struck dumb the Turkish officer was soon after portrayed by Sicilian artist Leonardo Guzzardi. Long thought to have been ordered by Sir William Hamilton, the painting was more likely paid for by the Queen of Naples. In happier days she had promised a portrait of the hero, making her son Prince Leopold vow to stand beside it every day to say, 'Dear Nelson, teach me to be like you.'[21] With the court now in exile, this task was given to Guzzardi, described at that time as a 'Celebrated Artist at Palermo, Portrait Painter to the King'.[22] Indeed, a full-length portrait of King Ferdinand by the same artist had been abandoned at the Palazzo Reale at Caserta when the royal family were forced to flee Naples.[23] Guzzardi had a strange and highly distinctive style, and despite the clutter of victory – a cannon, helmet and shield, and the battle raging in the distance – his portrayal of Nelson was disconcerting and unheroic. Standing on the quarterdeck of his ship, Nelson looks debilitated, almost haggard, his one languid arm gesturing towards the distant action. His face is gaunt and lined, the scar on his forehead vividly evident. His hat is awkwardly pushed back, as much to display the wound as to ease its pain. The empty eyes betray exhaustion and stress, and something else, less easy to discern: a coldness which could be despair, or cruelty. They are eyes which had seen too much. The focus of the theatrical staging, perhaps a reason for the portrait itself, is the jewel pinned to the admiral's hat and, thrown over a chair behind him, his fur-lined red pelisse. And yet, the jewel portrayed by the artist is a strange amalgam of the undelivered Chelengk described by Spencer Smith in Constantinople and the version with thirteen plumes seen by Thomas Richards after its presentation to Nelson at Naples. This suggests that Guzzardi, like so many artists to come, did not see the jewel itself and was working from jumbled accounts and hearsay.

Guzzardi's portrait is one of the least familiar but most interesting and revealing of all the many representations of Nelson. It is a curiously foreign-looking picture to English eyes, transfused with the crazed world of wartime Palermo, which was projected to a wider audience through the smaller copies Guzzardi made for the Hamiltons, for Nelson to send the sultan in Constantinople, and for members of the Egyptian Club. It was updated by the artist as the admiral garnered more awards before eventually finding a wider audience through prints. The original full-length version was framed in carved gilt wood inscribed in English and Italian: *Mi Lord Orazio Nelson, erva del secol nostro, a ninno secondo, forte, invetto, terore de' rebelli, destrutore degli empi, difensor de' re, a tutti caro, questa cittude e il regno, l'ama, loda ed ammira.* Lord Horatio Nelson, hero of the age, surpassed by none, unconquered, a terror to the rebellious, destroyer of the perverse, defender of kings, dear to all, this city and the whole kingdom, love, praise and admire him.[24]

Friction with Sidney Smith, caused by ambiguity over their respective roles, was further darkening Nelson's mood at the time the painting was completed. Distance and the difficulty of communication made his situation worse. It took time for London to reassure him, as he bluntly told Spencer Smith, that 'it never was intended to have any one in the Levant separate from me'.[25] Yet actions always spoke louder than words for Nelson, and reports of Sidney Smith's valiant defence of Acre shifted, in public at least, his low opinion of his flamboyant rival. He now wrote:

> Be assured, my dear Sir Sidney, of my perfect esteem and regard, and do not let anyone persuade you to the contrary. But my character is, that I will not suffer the smallest title of my command to be taken from me; but with pleasure I give way to my friends, among whom I beg you will allow me to consider you.[26]

There was no rancour when Nelson then heard that the sultan had also sent Smith a Chelengk, or '*Aigrette*', as he now called his own jewel too. He sent a generous letter of congratulation, but there was perhaps a tinge of disappointment that such a rare Ottoman award was no longer uniquely his own.[27]

Admiration of his rival was swept away, however, by the chance of his own redemption for the disaster at Naples. Remarkably, a Bourbon counter-revolution in the guise of a holy crusade was gaining ground in the abandoned kingdom. Nelson sent a squadron from Sicily in support of the insurgency, while the Russians allied with the Austrians and pushed down from the north of Italy. By June, this so-called 'Army of the Holy Faith' was at the gates of Naples, sparking a loyalist uprising in the city by the working class *Lazzaroni* against their Republican rulers. The much-heralded Parthenopean Republic was doomed when the French then withdrew their army to counter the threat in the north, leaving the defence of the city to a small garrison of troops supported by Jacobin sympathisers.

With a large enemy fleet roaming the Mediterranean, Nelson had no orders to restore the monarchy at Naples. But believing Admiral Lord Keith, who had replaced the ailing St Vincent as commander-in-chief, could contain the threat at sea, he shifted his flag to the 80-gun *Foudroyant* and sailed for Naples to complete the restoration of the monarchy. He did so for sound reasons, encouraged by the Hamiltons, who accompanied him, but with disastrous consequences for his later reputation. These were dangerous, crowded waters. On 19 June, Lord Keith intercepted five French ships off Toulon, remnants of the fleet destroyed by Nelson at Aboukir Bay, which had been chased away from Syria by Sidney Smith and, low on supplies, were running for home. Keith sent a squadron of ships in hot pursuit, among them *Peterel*, a 16-gun sloop commanded by Francis Austen, twenty-five-year-old brother of novelist Jane. After a short engagement, the French ships were captured, when they were found to contain several high-ranking Turkish prisoners, among them Osman Hadgi, the young Turkoman sent by the sultan with transports for the army in Syria. Keith dispatched the prizes back down the Mediterranean, paroled the French captives and ordered the Portuguese corvette *Swallow* to carry the freed Turks back to Constantinople, calling at Naples with orders for Nelson on the way.

There was an uneasy peace when *Foudroyant* entered the Bay of Naples on 24 June 1799. The remaining Jacobins were holed up with a small French garrison in three forts, having agreed to a treaty brokered by a junior naval officer which gave them immunity and safe passage away from the city. Some had already been moved to waiting transports in the bay. The complex situation Nelson now faced pressed dangerously upon all his beliefs and prejudices, a rigid adherence to the rule of law coupled with his devotion to the Church and monarchy. These clashed with his loathing for insubordination and, above all, fierce hatred of rebellion and the French. He also arrived in the city pumped up by a queen back in Palermo hell-bent on revenge. Marie Carolina channelled her own hatred for the French and Jacobins through her 'deputy' Emma Hamilton, who, she saw, now held Nelson in thrall.[28]

In this fatal mood and in the face of opposition from his Turkish and Russian allies, Nelson tore up the treaty and handed the Jacobins over to the *Lazzaroni*, unleashing a wave of vile bloodletting with beheadings, burnings, even cannibalism. He ordered a rebel Neapolitan admiral to be strung up from the yard arm of a Royal Navy ship. The Tree of Liberty in front of the royal palace was torn down by his own officers, many of whom were swept up in the orgy of violence. Nelson called it 'Sicilifying my own conscience, and I am easy', but pursuing the queen's vendetta stained him and corrupted the heroic image.[29] Emma was even accused of taking bribes to save people from the scaffold, many of whom were then executed anyway.[30] The massacres contrasted foully with the feasting in *Foudroyant*. As 'justice (Italian fashion)' was meted out ashore, Emma played 'heavenly' music on a harp whilst opera singers drowned out the screams of people she had lived among for years.[31] On 1 August, the first anniversary of the Battle of the Nile was celebrated afloat with trails of smoke and the stench of death hanging over the benighted city. A barge was converted to a Roman galley. 'On the oars were fixed lamps and in the centre was erected a rostral column with my name,' Nelson told his wife, 'at the stern elevated were two angels supporting my picture.' He continued, 'An orchestra was fitted up and filled with the very best musicians and singers. The piece of music was in great measure my praises, describing their distress, but Nelson comes, the invincible Nelson and we are safe and happy again.'[32]

The day after the macabre celebrations, ignoring Keith's order to reinforce the defence of Minorca, Nelson took the Hamiltons back to Palermo, leaving a military junta behind in Naples to purge the city and prepare for the full restoration of the monarchy. Their triumphant return to Sicily triggered a frenzied fresh round of extravagant gift-giving and wild partying. The king and queen gave gold boxes to Nelson's captains and a 'thumping' canary-coloured diamond to Sir William Hamilton. Emma was showered with jewels and expensive gowns. Safely back in Birmingham, Thomas Richards, who had marvelled at Nelson's jewel over dinner in Naples, designed a medal for the famed Matthew Boulton to strike in celebration of the restoration of the Bourbon king. Yet all this glitter failed to hide the tarnishing of reputations. As one disgusted French émigré remarked, 'Luxury and intrigue reigned in one of the Two Sicilies, while drunkenness and violence were reigning in the other.'[33] The royal family then hosted a grand fete, where crowds worshipped a life-size wax effigy of Nelson with almost religious fervour. A party of heavily armed Turkish officers looked on in 'rich and unique attire' before such a serious brawl broke out with the local Italian men that they returned afloat vowing to sink the first Neapolitan ship they came across.[34] The hero himself, crowned with laurel, appeared beside veteran Russian admiral Feodor Ushakov, who had brought his squadron to Sicily after driving the French out of the Ionian Islands. Nelson had a low opinion of the Russian, who outranked him, believing he had 'a polished outside, but the bear is close to the skin'.[35] He was also wary of Russian intentions in the Adriatic, feeding his concerns to the Admiralty in London to undermine his ally. Ushakov was the senior naval officer in the region, a sainted figure in his own country, and like Nelson and Sidney Smith had been rewarded by the sultan with a Chelengk. Nelson grumbled that he felt 'encircled by Turks & Russians', but their use to his campaign was 'not worth the *6d*'.[36] Not to be outshone, he tried to upstage the Russian admiral at the fete by wearing a magnificent sword gifted to him by the King of Naples, which had descended in the Bourbon royal family as a prized heirloom. 'The expressions which are usually employed to denote true gratitude' Ferdinand had written, with unusual humility:

> are neither adequate nor satisfactory to the extensive sense of what I know myself indebted to you, and of what is deeply engraved in my heart. Permit some marks of my gratitude which cannot wound your just and elevated delicacy may be presented to you in my name; my August father at his departure left to me with these Kingdoms a sword as a symbol of their preservation, which duty he imposed on me, to you my lord, I consign it in remembrance of the obligation I then contracted, an obligation which you have put it in my power to satisfy by the manner in which you and your brave followers have fulfilled the duty enjoined you to deliver Naples and the Fortresses from the enemy, who retained them, and have supported my steps for the reestablishment of order and tranquillity. To your magnanimous sovereign my excellent ally, and to your generous nation I owe a sign of my unbounded gratitude, which may at least in part attest a sentiment that will not cease, my lord, but with your affectionate Ferdinando R.[37]

Once owned by the Sun King, the hilt, pommel and candy twist grip of the sword now in Nelson's hand were entirely studded with brilliant diamonds, which flashed in the flickering torchlight of the palace gardens.

The king's further reward was richer still. In addition to presenting his treasured sword, Ferdinand made Nelson a Sicilian duke and granted him 35,000 acres of unprepossessing land clinging to the side of Mount Etna. The new duchy was named Bronte after the ramshackle town at its heart. Seized from a medieval hospital, the land was a blend of volcanic lava fields, woods, streams and orchards, with a ruined castle, small abbey, thousands of feudal inhabitants and many debts. Emma said later that Nelson had hesitated to accept the gift. He was wary of its likely cost and had an innate prejudice against foreign titles, which had made him mock the 'Swedish knight' Sidney Smith. Only the tempting prospect of a rental income of £3,000 a year and a personal appeal from the king made him relent. 'Do you wish that your name alone should pass with honour to posterity,' Ferdinand had exclaimed, 'and that I, Ferdinand Bourbon, should appear ungrateful?'[38] Childless, Nelson may also have been persuaded to accept the duchy by the terms of its grant, which allowed him to choose his ducal successor. He proposed his father Edmund as heir, then in succession his brothers and nephews.[39] Memories of the great estates in Norfolk made Nelson dream of becoming another Coke or Walpole, and he was well aware he was the first British admiral to become a duke, a feat which rivalled the elevation of John Churchill to Duke of Marlborough after the Battle of Blenheim. The Queen of Naples' personal gardener was dispatched to cultivate the duchy, and the admiral wistfully pictured himself living out his days 'under the shade of my great chestnut tree at Bronte where the din of war will not reach my ears'.[40] Emma had now replaced Fanny in these daydreams, and Nelson saw her there with loyal friends like his flag captain Hardy, who was offered 100 acres and an apartment in the ducal residence at Maniace. Hardy accepted the land but, fearing scandal, wavered about living under the same roof as the admiral and Lady Hamilton.[41] That storm was about to break.

8

THE MISTRESS

Palermo, Sicily, October 1799

A year after the battle, the Nile kept giving, loading Nelson's diminutive figure with still more decorations. The King of England had sent his official gold medal to jangle next to the one the admiral earned at Cape St Vincent, while Nelson's agent, Alexander Davison, made rich by the victory, spent £1,200 (maybe £100,000 today[1]) on medals for all the men at the action. At Nelson's request, deluxe versions of Davison's medal in gold were presented to George III, Sir William Hamilton, the King of Naples, the tsar and the sultan. As Davison had earned £8,000 in commission from the battle – three times Nelson's prize money – he could well afford the gesture. He then went further and ordered a silver centrepiece for presentation to his valuable friend, designed as a column surrounded by three lions 'copied from the celebrated Egyptian lions at Rome … emblematic of British Generosity and Valour', and topped by a figure of Britannia holding a model of the Chelengk.[2]

In October 1799, Nelson sent a list of all his 'official' Nile awards, together with a heavily glossed 'Sketch of my Life', to the *Naval Chronicle*. Conceived as a 'General and Biographical History of The Royal Navy', this new and bestselling serial was the brainchild of former naval, now royal chaplain James Stanier Clarke and John McArthur, a purser in the Royal Navy known to Nelson.

Always with his eye on self-promotion, Nelson willingly prepared a souped-up memoir for McArthur's enterprise, trusting to the editor's 'pruning knife' if it was deemed too lengthy.[3]

Still more presents continued to arrive in Sicily long after Nelson's list had been submitted to the *Naval Chronicle*. On 1 November, a Turkish ship moored at Palermo carrying a special envoy from the sultan called Abdurrahaman. Alongside dispatches from Constantinople, he handed Nelson, in the admiral's words, 'a diamond star; in the centre, the Crescent and a small star'.[4] The star, the accompanying letter explained, was a further gift from the generous sultan 'to be attached and suspended to your glorious collar'.[5] It was offered in gratitude for the safe return to Constantinople of Osman Hadgi, the Turkoman agha captured by the French in Syria. After his rescue by Lord Keith's squadron off Toulon in June, Osman had been shipped to Naples, where, despite the escalating violence and chaos ashore, he had been looked after by Nelson, who arranged his voyage back to Turkey. Delighted to see his aide safely home, the sultan had summoned Spencer Smith for advice on how Nelson should be rewarded for this further service to the Porte. Selim wanted to send the admiral another pelisse, jewel and money, but Smith politely pointed out difficulties with this idea. He explained the 'inutility according to European Costume' of wearing a fur pelisse for a naval officer like Nelson, whilst a precious jewel was insufficient as a 'public and popular token' of the sultan's pleasure. Smith was concerned that the diamond jewels given to Nelson and to his own brother Sidney were difficult to wear with uniform and inadmissible as official decorations to European eyes.

Picking up a suggestion of Captain Samuel Hood, Smith proposed the 'adoption of some device that might serve to perpetuate the memory of Lord Nelson's present service towards the Ottoman nation, 'a sort of *Civic Crown* to serve as the pendent to the Triumphal one he had gained under the form of the Chelengk, and which like that might be worn with a British uniform'. Selim loved this novel suggestion. He charged Smith with designing 'some suitable ornament' which could be repeated and worn as a decoration but was still precious and Ottoman in style. At first, the resourceful Smith trialled a version of the badge of the British Order of the Bath, replacing the three crowns at its centre with the Sultan's personal cypher, his *Tughra*. However, enamelling the complex *Tughra* on the badge was 'found too difficult for the state of the arts at Constantinople'. So Smith proposed instead copying the recently adopted naval ensign of the Ottoman navy – a star and crescent on a red background – onto a gold medal worn as a badge on a red ribbon to match. An enameller was found in the Seraglio able to complete this simpler design.

Selim was enchanted, but not understanding Smith's aim to create an Ottoman order of chivalry to match the Order of the Bath, felt the medal failed to 'meet the Turkish ideas of richness in point of show'. He insisted that diamond rays be added, their tapered shapes matching the plumes on the Chelengks, to create a more impressive bejewelled star for the highest rank of the new order. As a possible concession to the Royal Navy and to avoid a clash with the star of the Order of the Bath, the enamel for the diamond star was changed from red to blue. The result was a hybrid between an Ottoman jewel and a European military decoration, and unlike the precious Chelengks, 'a more convenient and appropriate reward for European auxiliaries than mere articles fit only for sale or a museum'.[6] The star and its medal could be replicated for future European recipients, particularly as the Porte was now allied to Britain and Russia. Almost by accident, Spencer Smith and the sultan had instituted the first Ottoman order of chivalry as there was no previous tradition of such awards in any Islamic culture.

Smith now named the order. In a letter to Nelson, he explained that the star – which he called a 'rich diamond ornament' – 'has been adapted to the form and purpose of a Badge of Knighthood; and as such I comprehend your Lordship is expected to employ it. I have suggested that it may be entitled the Order of the Crescent.' He hoped that Nelson:

> will long live to display, with honest pride, these genuine Badges of Merit, and that after the one and the other have successively passed through my hands, I may again see them united upon the person of the *First Knight of the Crescent.*[7]

The press was quick to pick up the significance of the new award, news of which reached England before Nelson in Sicily. 'The Porte is beginning to imitate the practices of other Courts, with respect to military distinctions and awards,' the *Evening Post* observed in late October 1799:

> Hitherto the Shelengk, or diamond aigrette, was the prerogative of the turban granted to such Seraskiers or Commanders who had performed splendid actions; and only the extraordinary circumstances of the present war could have occasioned it to adorn the heads of three Christian heroes. But it was not expected that this innovation would suggest the idea of a new Order, that of 'The Crescent' with the ensigns of which his Highness has decorated Admiral Nelson. They consist of a sun of precious stones, set in blue enamel, within a crescent of brilliants.[8]

This was the jewel Abdurrahaman now handed Nelson at Palermo. After close inspection, Sir William Hamilton gave it his seal of approval, noting with satisfaction that, compared to Nelson's aigrette, the star was 'set in the European fashion'.[9]

Nelson was thrilled with this further exotic decoration. Taking Smith's cue, he styled himself 'First Knight of the Imperial Order of the Crescent', pinning the diamond star, he told the grand vizir, 'on my coat, on the left side, over my heart'.[10] In a tactless letter to the Admiralty, Nelson informed his superiors that he displayed it 'over the Star of the Order of the Bath', giving his Ottoman order precedence over his English one.[11] The king was furious when he heard. It took another two years, and Nelson's victory at Copenhagen, before he granted permission for the admiral to wear the Ottoman diamond star officially on his uniform.[12]

Later this same rewarding month, Nelson took possession of a 'very massy and elegant gold-hilted Sword, and a beautiful Cane, enriched with diamonds' sent by the Greek population on the beleaguered Ionian island of Zante, recently liberated from the French. The gifts came with a letter thanking Nelson for saving Zante 'from the horrors of anarchy; and prayed that his exploits might accelerate the day, in which, amidst the glory and peace of thrones, the miseries of the human race would cease'. In truth, the islanders owed their freedom more to the Russians and Turks than the Royal Navy. But Zante was an important hub for the Turkey Company's valuable trade in currants, and Spiridon Foresti, the British consul on the island, was among Nelson's greatest admirers. The sword was inscribed *Phario Victori Zacynthus*, and the cane, a traditional accessory for a seaman, was 'set round with all the diamonds that the Island could furnish'.[13] The women on the island had wanted the cane to be more 'richly ornamented with jewels', but a single row was all they could muster. Nelson was touched, thanking them for a present 'valuable ten thousand times more than any gold or diamonds'.[14] He sent the cane to his elderly father to be preserved as a family heirloom.[15]

'Highly flattering', too, was the delivery in December by emissaries from Constantinople of a sketch of the Battle of the Nile, together with a drawing of Nelson. For the sensitive admiral, the 'curious present … marks I am not in the least forgotten'.[16] In fact the portrait, now lost, confirmed Selim's continued high regard for Nelson, as making images of foreigners was frowned upon in Islamic culture. This touching gift of a portrait of Nelson contrasted with those of the Tsar of Russia, the King and Queen of Naples and the King of Sardinia, all of whom had given the admiral portraits of themselves. In his letter of thanks to the sultan, Nelson recognised 'the extraordinary high honour conferred upon me' by the giving of presents 'more valuable than gold or jewels'.[17] To Spencer Smith he observed that, 'A handful of diamonds comes naturally from the hand of a great Monarch, but this drawing, made probably for the occasion, could only come from an affectionate, amiable disposition.'[18]

Finally, from the Balkans came a sword, gun and silver flask from Ali Pasha of Ioannina, a much-feared Ottoman warlord eager to curry favour with the British admiral.[19] Nelson was fascinated by this legendary pasha, who terrorised swathes of latter-day Greece and Albania. Tales of his cruelty abounded. Lord Byron, who met Ali in 1809, was awed and impressed, calling him, 'a remorseless tyrant, guilty of the most horrible cruelties, very brave, and so good a general that they call him the Mahometan Buonaparte.'[20] Ali had earned Nelson's admiration for his massacre of an isolated French garrison at Nicopolis near Preveza in Epirus (then in Albania, today Greece) weeks after the Battle of the Nile. Before their own execution, the few survivors were forced to parade the decapitated and salted heads of their comrades through the streets of Ioannina. It was said that Nelson 'would have embraced the "Hero of Epirus" in person on the shores of Nicopolis, had he not been taken away by other important matters'.[21] As elsewhere, he could ignore the barbarity of an unsavoury despot and overlook his crimes to secure a vital ally and 'staunch friend to the English'.[22] He asked London to send Ali a pair of pistols in return for his own high-status presents, and corresponded warmly with the devious and criminal pasha.[23] Ali told Nelson he treasured his letters:

> as precious memorials of the greatest, and most illustrious person that ever graced this or past centuries in a noble military career, and showing such valour and such wisdom and discernment never before known and at the same time such prudent conduct in political affairs, that all must wonder and be pleased with.[24]

Nelson denied without conviction that his head was being turned by such unsavoury adoration. He assured Davison:

> These presents, rich as they are, do not elevate me; my pride is, that at Constantinople, from the grand seignior to the lowest Turk, the name of Nelson is familiar in their mouths; and in this country, I am everything which a grateful monarch and people call me.[25]

However, those around him were horrified at the change in the admiral. 'They say,' Mary Elgin told her mother, 'there never was a man so vainglorious (that's the phrase) in the world as Lord N. He is now completely managed by Lady Hamilton.'[26] The worst of these rumours had been confirmed on Mary's arrival in Sicily before she continued to Constantinople with her husband. 'It is really humiliating to see Lord Nelson' she reported. 'He seems quite dying, and yet as if he had no other thought than her.' While her husband and Sir William Hamilton chatted about antiquities, Mary examined Nelson closely. She was shocked to find him looking so old and stooped – he was barely 41 – with no upper teeth and a whitish film over both eyes. In startling contrast, Emma was a 'whapper' smothered in jewels and heavy make-up. Mary was disgusted by the suffocating atmosphere of idolatry, sycophancy and adultery pervading Palermo. 'I never saw three people made such thorough dupes of as Lady Hamilton, Sir William and Lord Nelson,' she exclaimed.[27]

Nelson was protected by a small coterie of fiercely loyal friends like Hardy and Troubridge, but his behaviour disturbed the tight-knit ranks of the Royal Navy as rumours rippled out from Palermo. It was said his relationship with Emma and his apparently wilful disregard of Lord Keith's orders 'mortified and disgusted' his fellow officers, rubbing the gilding from their victory at the Nile. 'There was a mutiny among them,' recalled Count Roger de Damas, a royalist who had escaped France and joined the King of Naples's army, 'and Nelson, whom they would have obeyed implicitly in a battle, was treated by them everywhere else without any of the respect of consideration that were his due.'[28] The count was biased against the English admiral, but his candid account explains the growing resentment Nelson felt towards his superiors and the siege-like mentality he adopted with Emma. Always more comfortable with his junior officers and men – a consequence of his fragile ego and modest upbringing – Nelson now nurtured younger, uncritical acolytes like William Hoste, the young captain who had carried news of his victory to Naples.

Hoste was present when Nelson was summoned to an awkward meeting with his commander-in-chief, Admiral Lord Keith, at Leghorn in January 1800. Keith dragged Nelson off to the blockade of Malta, where their tetchy relationship deteriorated still further. It hardly helped that before meeting the dour Scot on his flagship, Nelson had 'arrayed himself in his paraphernalia of stars and diamonds'.[29] Keith had no time for such fripperies in the middle of a war. Writing to his wife after a Turkish officer arrived with letters from the sultan, the admiral noted with some irritation how he had also been given 'a very handsome snuff box set in diamonds for which I have little use. I believe it valuable.'[30]

There was some success off Malta, including the capture of one of the French warships which escaped the Nile, but as soon as he could Nelson fled back to Sicily and to Emma. He pleaded illness and exhaustion, but his reasons for staying any longer at Palermo were already threadbare. The threat to the Kingdom of Naples had receded and the focus of the war had shifted westwards with Bonaparte.

The restoration of the monarchy in Naples brought reward for Emma too. The queen showered her with gems and jewels, sending two coach-loads of 'most magnificent and costly dresses' to her palazzo in Palermo. Among the haul were royal miniatures, diamond necklaces and earrings; even a diamond aigrette to rival her lover's. For a woman like Emma with a passion for jewels it was an astonishing windfall (valued by her at 6,000 guineas, or half a million pounds today[31]). There had been a time when her husband had given her jewels. 'Once indeed she so longed for diamonds,' Sir William had written in 1790, 'that, having an opportunity of a good bargain of single stones of good water and tolerable size,

I gave her at once £500 worth.'[32] But now, deeply indebted, he lacked the funds and inclination to lavish such treasures on his wife. He preferred to acquire rare antiquities for himself, declaring grandiloquently that, 'diamonds and precious stones may be found at market but such pieces of art can only be purchased when the opportunity offers and which is but seldom.'[33] When Sir William did gift Emma jewels, they tended to be hardstone gems intricately carved in the antique style with her portrait (Nelson adopted one as a fob to seal his letters). She wore these simple 'intaglio' gems in the paintings her husband ordered of her, carefully posed in Classical garb. Emma's beauty was so great, Sir William assured her conveniently, that it required no further adornment; it already shone translucently beside the thickly rouged and powdered ladies of the Neapolitan court.

Starved of diamonds, the royal bounty had an instant effect on Emma. At the string of parties, fêtes and receptions in Palermo which followed the suppression of the revolt in Naples, she appeared bedecked in silk and jewels, to the fury of Lady Elgin, who, having been advised by Emma to dress modestly, complained that, 'it is a constant trick of Lady H to make everybody she can, go undressed.'[34] Already growing fat, Emma now ballooned in size until one observer called her 'the fattest woman I've ever laid eyes on, but with the most beautiful head'.[35] The once beautiful girl, for so long the most precious object in her husband's collection, was becoming corrupted by sex, food, gambling, drink and avarice. Her appetites grew so large and her 'avidity' for presents so great that, it was said, she now grasped at other people's treasures too, 'by the common artifice of admiring and longing'.[36] As a wife she had little property she could call her own, but now that she had tasted wealth she wanted to grab it for herself. She was heedless to her husband's warning that if she continued a spendthrift, she would die a beggar.[37]

One simple jewel outshone them all, and this she rightly earned. In December 1799, Emma was instrumental in sending emergency relief to Malta. Despite their liberation from French rule, the people on the benighted island were starving under an embargo imposed by the King of Naples to prevent food shortages in his own troubled land. Nelson was willing to make sacrifices to restore to power the Knights of St John, the ancient order which had ruled the island for centuries until their expulsion by the French. 'The Emperor of Russia's magnificent box is ready to go to market,' he told a friend at the Navy Office, 'in order to assist in placing the Grand Master of Malta in his seat of government.'[38] The box was spared when Emma cajoled the queen into allowing a food convoy, and £10,000 cash, to be shipped to the island. Nelson encouraged Emma's bold request – his friend the Nile veteran Alexander Ball was now governor of Malta – then lobbied the tsar in Russia for her reward. Tsar Paul was Grand Master of the Knights of St John, so felt a personal connection to the islanders' plight. An admirer of Nelson, he obliged by appointing Emma a Dame of the Order of St John, sending her the distinctive insignia of a white enamelled cross beneath a coronet. 'It is with pleasure that I grant at your request,' Paul replied to Nelson, 'the cross of Commander to Captain Ball, and that of Chevalier to Lady Hamilton, which you will deliver to them accompanied by letters from me.'[39]

Plain and unadorned, the cross and its title were priceless treasures for Emma. 'I am the first Englishwoman that ever had it,' she declared, bursting with pride.[40] They carried status and rank, placing her on the same footing as the men around her laden with their sparkling orders and decorations, often ill-deserved. The daughter of a blacksmith, she was now allowed a coat of arms, which she arranged with the College of Arms back in England: three lions rampant beneath a Maltese cross. The Queen of Naples made Emma a copy of the cross in diamonds, sparking a craze in England. Yet Emma liked the tsar's simple gold one best, wearing it 'constantly … at her breast'.[41] 'She now has all the titles that can impress people,' commented a Swedish diplomat.[42] She asked permission to wear the cross outside Italy, so 'it is of use to me'.[43] She wore it for her next portrait, cutting her hair short and

John Spencer Smith in 1802 (© National Portrait Gallery, London)

Sultan Selim III wearing a sorguç turban jewel, after a portrait by Antoine Ignace Melling (1763–1831). (Author's Collection)

Spencer Smith's sketch of the Chelengk in the margin of his excited report to the Foreign Secretary in London just hours after first seeing the jewel at the Topkapi Palace in Constantinople. (National Archives, FO 78/20 f.22)

The Hero of Acre: Sir Sidney Smith wearing the Ottoman Robe of Honour sent after the siege by a jubilant Sultan Selim III. (Author's Collection)

Pryce Lockhart Gordon who befriended Kelim Efendi and was invited to Constantinople. (Author's Collection)

The handles of the silver dishes presented to Nelson by Lloyd's of London were designed as the Chelengk based on Spencer Smith's original drawing. (Author's Collection)

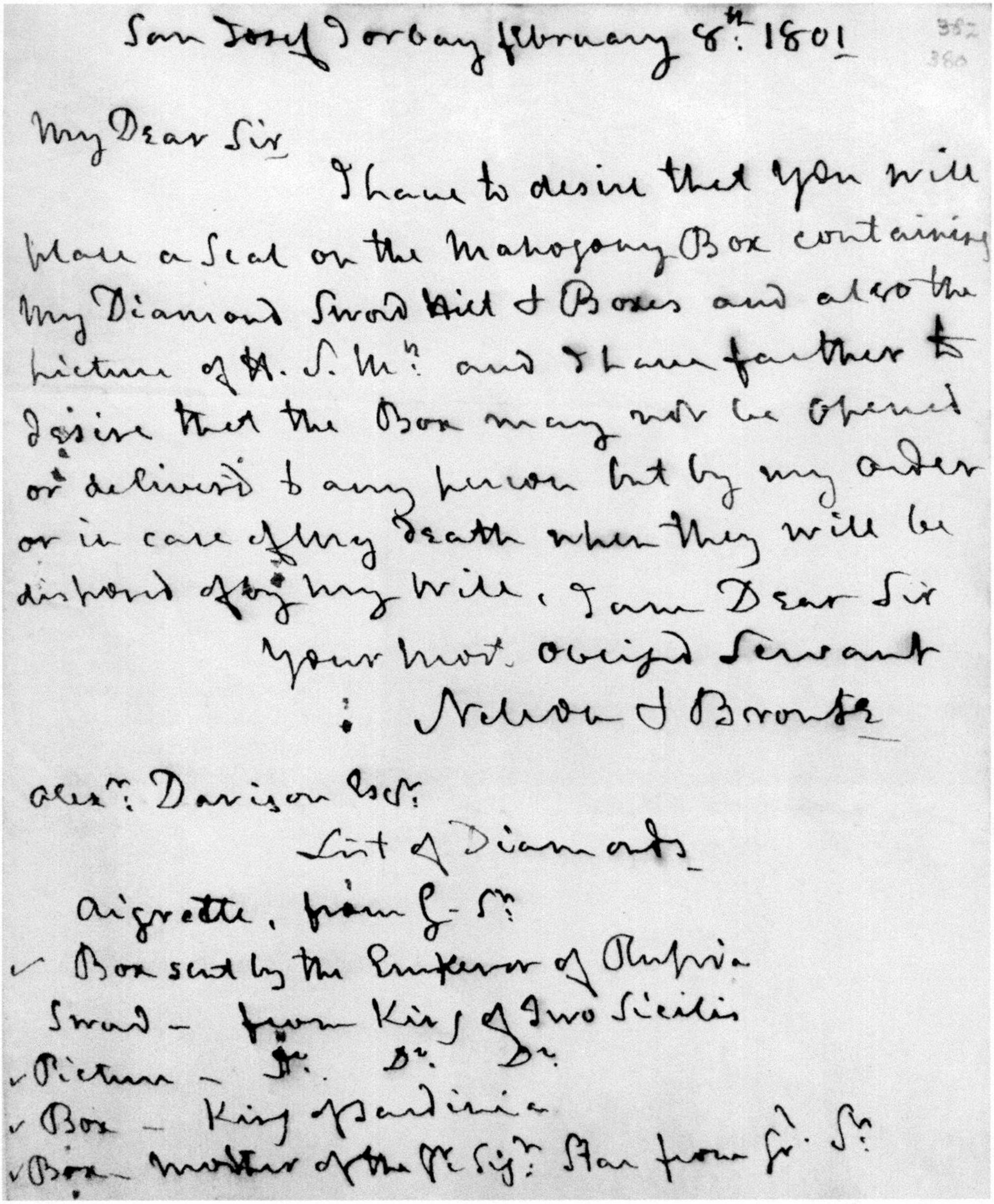

San Josef Torbay February 8th: 1801

My Dear Sir

I have to desire that you will place a Seal on the Mahogany Box containing my Diamond Sword Hilt & Boxes and also the picture of H. S. My. and I have farther to desire that the Box may not be opened or delivered to any person but by my order or in case of my death when they will be disposed of by my Will. I am Dear Sir

Your most obliged Servant

Nelson & Bronte

Alexr. Davison Esqr.

List of Diamonds

Aigrette, from G. Sr.

✓ Box sent by the Emperor of Russia

Sword – from King of Two Sicilies

✓ Picture – Do. Do. Do.

✓ Box – King of Sardinia

✓ Box – mother of the Gd. Sigr. Star from Gd. Sr.

Nelson's letter to his agent with a 'List of Diamonds' marked with items for sale. (British Library Add MS 34988 f.380; Author's Collection)

John Flaxman's massive monument to Nelson in St Paul's Cathedral shows the hero wearing the Sultan's pelisse to hide his disfigurement. (Conway Library, The Courthauld Institute of Art, London)

Monument to William, Earl Nelson erected by his daughter Charlotte in the church at Cricket using the money he had intended for a memorial in St Paul's Cathedral. (Author's Collection)

Nelson's orders, medals, boxes and other awards, including the King of Naples' sword, the Egyptian Club sword and a tantalising last glimpse of the pelisse. They were photographed at Cricket in 1889. Within a few years most of these treasures were lost forever. (Author's Collection)

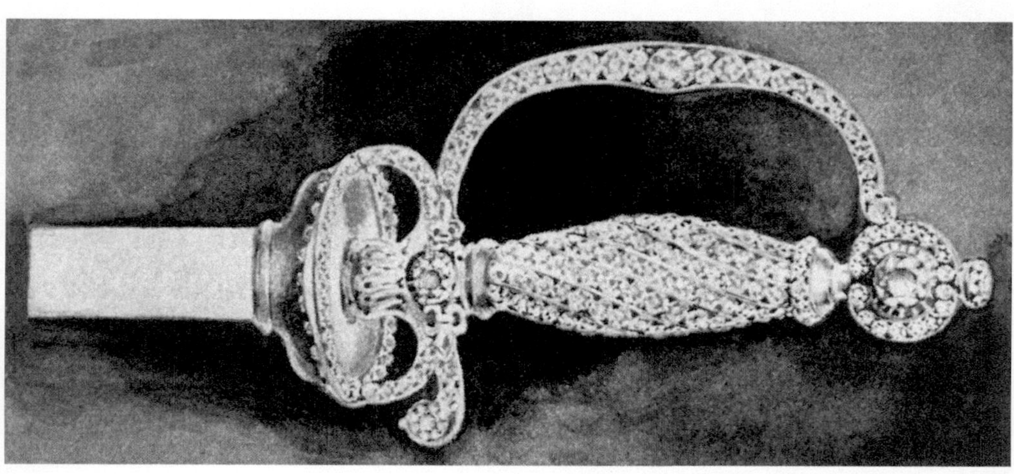

Drawing of the King of Naples' sword at the Royal Naval Exhibition in 1891. The diamonds had already been replaced by paste. (Author's Collection)

General Alexander Nelson Hood, 1st Viscount Bridport, 4th Duke of Bronte, who was forced to sell the sultan's jewel when he was swindled by his solicitor. Oil on panel by Rudolf Swoboda (1859–1914), before 1891. (Royal Collection Trust / © HM Queen Elizabeth II 2017)

The sultan's jewel in its display case in the Nelson Gallery at the National Maritime Museum, circa 1950. (© National Maritime Museum, Greenwich F4337)

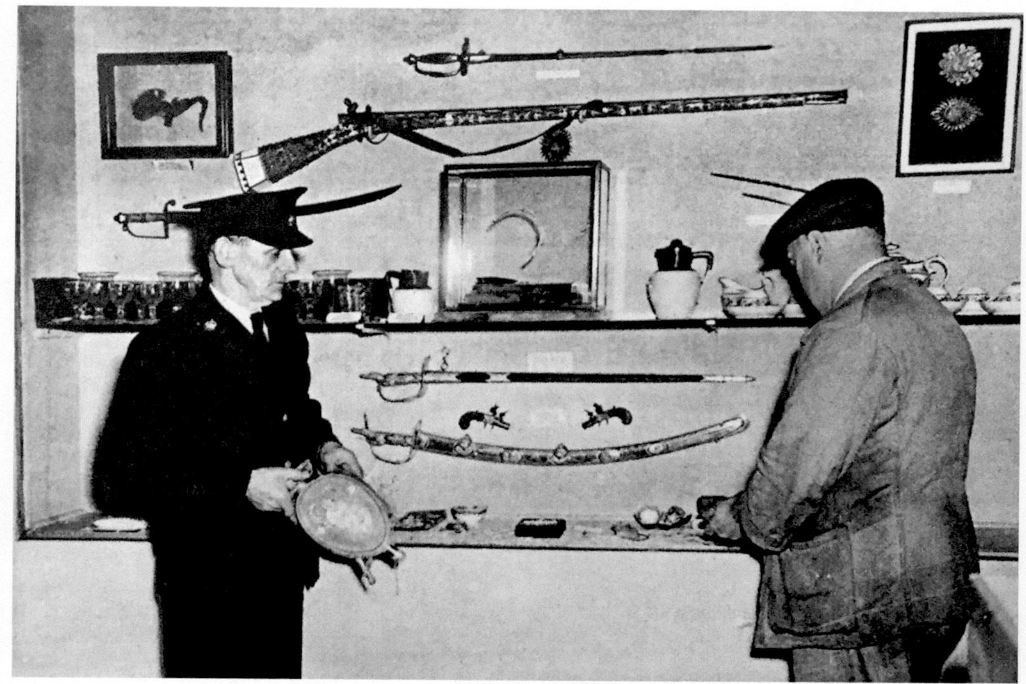

The empty case on 11 June 1951, with bemused wardens. One is holding Ali Pasha's canteen. (*Illustrated London News*)

The sultan's jewel as it appeared at the time of its theft from Greenwich, long after its flowerheads and clockwork mechanism had been removed by Charlotte Bridport. (*Illustrated London News*)

swapping her often provocative attire for a demure white gown lent by a member of her retinue. It was the last sitting Emma gave to any artist, and it was how Nelson now liked to see her and how she wanted to be seen, as sober, dutiful and respectable. He would keep the painting in his cabin: its modest image assuaged his guilt and eased the jealousy he felt at seeing the many sexually charged images of her youth. It hid the reality of Emma slipping roles again: from friend to lover, wife to mistress. Perhaps it was the realisation that Nelson would have to go home soon and the dreadful prospect of separation which finally overcame their fragile defences. By the warm Sicilian spring of 1800, Nelson and Emma were in a sexual relationship, leading, as they may have secretly yearned, to the birth of their child. In bed, Emma did things, Nelson exclaimed, 'which no woman in this world but yourself ever did': a tribute to her experience and a hint of his previous infidelities.[44]

For now, while Emma remained in Sicily waiting with Sir William for his diplomatic orders, Nelson stayed too, still weakly insisting his duty was to protect the Kingdom of the Two Sicilies. He dispersed his fleet around the Mediterranean, making occasional forays to sea himself, taking the Hamiltons on a cruise but in a lacklustre and tetchy sort of way, and to the despair of the Admiralty back in England. Everyone was in unhealthy limbo, acquiring bad habits, spending too much money, anxious for the future yet unwilling to face it. All the bloody excitement of putting down the rebellion in Naples had sunk into torpor. It was almost with relief when confirmation, dressed up as retirement but feeling like dismissal, finally came that Sir William had been recalled to London. His written summons arrived only just before his fresh-faced replacement, Sir Arthur Paget, appeared, whose piercing and unsullied gaze the ageing diplomat sought to escape. Nelson too could no longer ignore the clamour from friends and family to return home. Earl Spencer had shielded Nelson from the worst criticism at the Admiralty, and despite being silkily expressed, his meaning was obvious when he wrote in private, 'that you will be more likely to recover your health and strength in England than in an inactive situation at a foreign court, however pleasing the respect and gratitude shown to you for your services'.[45]

In the suddenly frantic preparations to leave Sicily, King Ferdinand pressed a miniature portrait of himself mounted with diamonds into the admiral's hand. He was also anxious to decorate Nelson in an official way for saving his kingdom. As the existing Neapolitan Order of Chivalry, the Order of St Januarius, was restricted to Catholics, the king hurriedly inaugurated a new order especially for his protestant hero. He called it the Order of St Ferdinand and Merit, in honour of his sainted ancestor Ferdinand the Great, Bourbon King of Castile, whose radiant image was depicted in Arthurian style on the new order's breast star and badge. Nelson was knighted in the order alongside Tsar Paul and the Russian Field Marshal Alexander Suvorov, who had brilliantly led his army over the Alps to expel the French from northern Italy. Suvorov bore a striking physical resemblance to Nelson, and there was much mutual admiration between them (although a pathological fear of mirrors spared the field marshal any vanity). However, even Suvorov eventually grew exasperated by Nelson's fixation with Sicily, telling him pointedly that, 'Palermo is not Cythere': a tart reminder that the city was not the mythological home of Aphrodite, Greek goddess of love.[46] Lesser officers like Hood, Ball, Hallowell and Troubridge were decorated in the second class of Ferdinand's new order. One quirk of the knighthood – Nelson's third, and the second inaugurated in his honour – allowed him to wear his hat with its sparkling jewel in the royal presence. But the order was instituted in such haste that there was no time to complete its jewelled star and badge before he sailed in June 1800.[47] These would be finished back in London, to Ferdinand's designs, by court jeweller Philip Gilbert, who had previously made Nelson's collar for the Order of the Bath.

The voyage home was complicated by the Queen of Naples' last-minute decision to accompany Nelson and the Hamiltons as far as Vienna so that she could visit her daughter, the Empress of Austria. Maria Carolina also seized at a chance to escape her boorish husband and his interminable hunting parties. The queen, her younger children, their entourage of servants and trunk-loads of plate, jewels, furniture and gowns added considerably to the discomfort in the overcrowded *Foudroyant*. Nelson's cabin was already full with souvenirs and trophies. The sultan's jewel, with his other jewels and gold boxes, were secured under the watchful eye of Tom Allen, probably in the same red leather box containing valuables discovered in Nelson's desk in *Victory* after he died.[48] But the masthead of *L'Orient* also had to be accommodated, together with the bulky carved wooden plume of feathers from the figurehead of French prize *Guillaume Tell*, the coffin made of *L'Orient*'s charred timbers presented by Hallowell, sundry captured weapons and the 8ft-high portrait of the admiral by Guzzardi. The uncomfortable conditions were made still worse, like the earlier flight from Naples, by a terrible storm which overtook *Foudroyant* near Elba. which threatened the destruction of the ship and everyone aboard. For a second time in his brief possession, Nelson's jewel escaped being lost forever in the waters of the Mediterranean.

Before departing Sicily, Nelson penned a final letter to Constantinople assuring Selim that:

> should the Enemy (which I do not believe) dare to send another Fleet to menace the Dominions of his Imperial Majesty, I shall hold myself ready, if I am thought fit for such a service, to come forth, and be the instrument of God's vengeance on such miscreant infernal scoundrels.[49]

Both Nelson and Sir William Hamilton sailed for home under a cloud of ignominy which they surely felt but never acknowledged. Each had overreached himself, exceeding their authority by becoming embroiled in the terrible events at Naples, and they faced accusations of insubordination, even of judicial murder. Moreover, they returned carrying the stink of sexual scandal, which only grew more pungent as they drew away from the debauched air of Palermo. To many, as they would soon discover, they had made fools of themselves and to their positions as admiral and ambassador.

9

THE GRAND TURK

London, England, October 1798

For weeks that summer there were confused reports of Nelson's fate. Alarming rumours of his defeat, even of his death, swirled around the press. It was not until 21 September 1798 that definite news of a sea battle off Alexandria was picked up in the Paris press and published by *The Times*. A few days later, the same paper carried a report from Spencer Smith in Constantinople telling of the French brig which had escaped a recent battle and fled to Rhodes. Confirmation of a great victory eventually came through diplomatic channels when Sir William Hamilton's account of Captain Capel's jubilant reception at Naples reached the Foreign Office on 2 October. The very next day, Capel appeared in person at the Admiralty after conveying Nelson's dispatch across war-torn Europe.[1] Admiral Duncan, hero of an earlier victory, immediately dispatched an express to Suffolk to reassure Fanny that her husband was safe but recovering from a wound. In triumph, Capel then carried the captured sword of the defeated French admiral Blanquet, the weapon kissed by Emma at Naples, to the Guildhall, along with Nelson's desire 'that the City of London will honour me by the acceptance of it, as a remembrance, that Britannia still rules the Waves'.[2] Blanquet's weapon was reverentially placed in a glass case, with the City responding in kind with a sword of its own to give the admiral. Expecting the hero home any day, it ordered him 'a rich chased gold sword with painted enamelled medallions and ornamented with brilliants' costing £210 (perhaps £20,000 today).[3] Missed by many among the jubilant accounts of the battle which filled the newspapers during those febrile days was the short notice that Sir Sidney Smith was hurrying to Portsmouth to join his ship and sail for the Levant.

News of the sultan's awards to Nelson appeared in *The Times* on 18 October with a translation of the letter sent by Selim after the Nile:

> This joyful event, therefore, laying this Empire under an obligation, and the service rendered by our much esteemed Friend Admiral Lord Nelson on this occasion being of a nature to call for public acknowledgment, his Imperial Majesty, the Powerful, Formidable, and Most Magnificent Grand Signior has destined as a present, in his Imperial name, to the said Admiral, a Diamond Aigrette (Chelengk) and a sable fur with broad sleeves; beside 2,000 Zequins to be distributed among the wounded of his crew.

The letter concluded with a humble request for 'the permission of the Powerful and Most August King of England, for the said Admiral to put on and wear the said Aigrette and Pelice'.[4] Readers puzzled by the peculiar sounding Chelengk were enlightened by a well-travelled correspondent in the *Evening Post* who explained that:

> The Chelengk is given to common janissaries who have distinguished themselves. It is in the form of a hand, with five fingers of silver and thin like strong brown paper. Some have three fingers only. Janissaries have frequently several for different acts of bravery. To pashas it is set with diamonds. The sultan wears one on the side of his imperial turban. It is always of great value; and no doubt that sent to Lord Nelson is worth 10,000l. sterling. It

> is equivalent to an Order of Knighthood, or *Order de Merite*. The admiral must wear it attached to the cockade of his hat.[5]

The newspaper welcomed the gifts in nautical terms, reporting, 'Lord Nelson will be so oppressed with honours, that it will hardly be in his power "to bear them all about him",' before adding, anticipating further glory, that, 'His uniform as Admiral, his robes as a peer, his Turkish *Chelengk*, with his fur pelice, will at least keep him *warm* during the winter.'[6]

The jewel created wonder. 'A monarch's aigrette decks the hero's brow of whom I sing,' poetised a Mrs Bayley.[7] But the public had to wait until January 1799 to see a picture of it. That month, the *Ladies' Monthly Museum*, a women's fashion magazine, enjoyed a scoop with the publication of an 'exact representation of the superb diamond Aigrette (called a Chelengk or Plume of Triumph) taken from the Imperial Turban, and sent by the Grand Signor, among other presents, to Admiral Lord Nelson'.[8] Copied from the sketch of the undelivered Chelengk sent to London by Spencer Smith, it is possible the image had been passed to the magazine by fashion-conscious Fanny Nelson, encouraged by her friends. The print certainly created a stir, with similar jewels fast becoming the rage among women and men. At a ball to celebrate Queen Charlotte's birthday that same month, 'The most distinguished insignia worn by Gentlemen was the Aigrette, or Plume of Triumph Button, taken from the drawing of Lord Nelson's superb Aigrette.' Oriental plumes were now '*tout à-fait nouveau*' ('everything that is new'), worn by the royal princesses and 'many persons of fashion'.[9] Ottomonia reached such a pitch that Lord Hartington and William Ponsonby even attended a ball 'as two tall young ladies, dressed in the last fashion, with diamonds, spotted muslin, and silver turbans and feathers'.[10] The craze spread quickly overseas, with a jeweller in Dublin advertising, 'Nelson brooches, Aigrettes, Anchors etc now so generally worn in London.'[11]

Unlike Nelsonian jewels, the *beau-monde* had long enjoyed wearing rich Turkish-style fur-lined pelisses: long for women, short and dashing for military officers. Despite rumours mischievously spread by the French press that Nelson had given his pelisse away to the Queen of Naples,[12] these luxurious garments, preferably in Turkish red, now gained a gloss of celebrity. Enterprising manufacturers like Shabner & Son, 'Robe and Riding Habit Makers to Her Majesty', based in Covent Garden, leapt on the vogue, promoting 'their Turkish Pelice, which for elegance in fitting the shape, is far superior to anything hitherto offered'.[13] The Battle of the Nile further fuelled an existing fashion for eastern dress, particularly of oriental-style turbans with plumed feathers, sometimes worn with the tall crowns of the Mamelukes. Even in sleepy Hampshire, budding novelist Jane Austen could not escape the fad. 'I am to wear a Mamalouc cap,' she wrote to her sister Cassandra in January 1799 ahead of a social function. 'It is all the fashion now, worn at the Opera, and by Lady Mildmays at Hackwood Balls.'[14]

British institutions competed to reward Nelson. At a meeting at their headquarters in Bishopsgate on 2 November 1798, the court of the Turkey Company resolved:

> that a piece of plate with a suitable inscription be presented to Lord Nelson and that his Lordship be requested to accept of the Freedom of this Company as a token of the high sense the Company entertain of the important advantages derived to the Levant Company by the late splendid victory obtained under his Lordship's command.[15]

Royal goldsmiths Rundell & Bridge on Ludgate Hill were employed to supply the 'piece of plate', a task they gave to thrusting young silversmith Paul Storr. Aged just 29, Storr had recently established a workshop in Piccadilly, where he was fast acquiring the reputation as London's leading silversmith. The magnificent silver cup he crafted for the company was a hybrid of the prevailing neo-classicism and the more massive, naturalistic style which would become Storr's trademark. Designed as a monumental 2fthigh urn, the cup had handles shaped as voguish winged Egyptian goddesses. The cover was embellished with crocodiles, representing the Nile, and symbols of naval victory. Encircling the cup were laurel wreaths framing the names of the captured and destroyed enemy ships, together with Nelson's newly embellished coat-of arms. Above the arms, also garlanded with laurel, was an engraving of the Chelengk taken by Storr from the picture recently published in the press.

Rundell & Bridge also gave Paul Storr the task of completing a service of silver tableware for Nelson from £500 voted the admiral by Lloyd's Coffee House, 'to be laid out in plate'.[16] Lloyd's was a hub for the merchants and insurance underwriters in the City of London who had most to lose from French maritime success. On the very day victory was announced in London, the coffee house had opened a subscription book for the bereaved families and battle-scarred veterans, eventually raising over £38,000. From Italy, Nelson had asked his agent, Davison, to spend his £500 grant on a practical and robust set of silver plates and serving dishes suitable for seagoing use by his officers. The pieces were plain and simply decorated with engravings of Nelson's coat of arms and a presentation inscription. The only extravagance was to order handles for the eight dishes modelled as the Chelengk. These added £21 to the cost, and were again modelled by Storr on the picture of the jewel then circulating in London.[17]

In April 1800, a 'Biographical Memoir of The Right Honourable Lord Nelson of the Nile' was published in the *Naval Chronicle*, adapted from the 'Sketch of my Life' sent by Nelson from the Mediterranean. Of most interest to readers was a list, with estimated values, of 'Presents to Lord Nelson for his Services in the Mediterranean, between October the First, 1798, and October the First, 1799.'[18] By issuing this statement, it appeared Nelson was seeking to price his victory in monetary terms. It was not behaviour likely to impress his monarch, fellow officers or superiors at the Admiralty:

From his King, and Country, a Peerage of Great Britain, and the Gold Medal	
From the Parliament of Great Britain, for his own life, and two next Heirs, per annum,	*£ 2,000*
From the Parliament of Ireland, not exactly known, but supposed to be the same as given Earl St Vincent, and Lord Duncan, per Annum	*1,000*
From the East India Company,	*10,000*
From the Turkey Company, a piece of plate of great value.	
From Alexander Davidson, Esq., a Gold Medal.	
From the City of London, a Sword of great value.	
From the Grand Seignior, a Diamond Aigrette, or Plume of Triumph, valued at	*2,000*
From the same, a rich pelice, valued at	*1,000*
From the Grand Seignior's Mother, a Rose, set with Diamonds, valued at	*1,000*
From the Emperor of Russia, a Box, set with diamonds, and a most elegant letter, value	*2,500*
From the King of the Two Sicilies, a Sword richly ornamented with diamonds, and a most kind and elegant letter,	*5,000*
Also the Dukedom of Bronti, with an estate, supposed, per annum	*3,000*
From the King of Sardinia, a Box set with diamonds, and a most elegant letter,	*1,200*
From the Island of Zante, a Gold Headed Sword and Cane, as an acknowledgement, that had it not been for the battle of the Nile, they could not have been liberated from French cruelty.	
From the City of Palermo, a Gold Box and Chain, brought on a Silver Waiter.	
Also the Freedom of the City of Palermo, which constitutes him a Grandee of Spain.	

To increase the sensational aspect of its publication, the memoir was illustrated with a specially commissioned portrait of Nelson arranged by editor John McArthur from Lemuel Abbott. Despite his chaotic lifestyle and a mental fragility which led him to the asylum and early death, Abbott enjoyed a solid reputation as a prolific and competent painter of portraits, particularly of naval officers. Nelson had sat for him twice in 1797 whilst recuperating from the amputation of his arm. From these sittings, Abbott had already produced at least four half-length portraits in oils for distribution among Nelson's family and friends. It was one of these which Fanny Nelson had gazed at with such anxious longing at Roundwood. In the paintings, the admiral is shown bare-headed - it was unusual for an officer to be portrayed in a studio portrait with a hat – and wearing his undress uniform with the Order of the Bath and naval gold medal for the Battle of Cape St Vincent. Prints of Abbot's portraits had been rushed out after news of the victory, but for the *Naval Chronicle* McArthur, with an eye on the popular market, specifically wanted a new image showing Nelson with the Chelengk. As it was rumoured Nelson wore the Chelengk with his dress uniform like a turban ornament, Abbott simply added a gold-laced hat to his existing portrait. The hat may have been borrowed by McArthur from Lady Nelson, with whom he was acquainted, but it made the admiral appear in the portrait to be wearing undress uniform with his full-dress hat.

For the Chelengk, Abbott did not copy the published drawing of the jewel used by Paul Storr for Nelson's silver and coat of arms. Instead, better informed, he used a version of the jewel taken from the portrait of Nelson by Leonardo Guzzardi. This suggests that prints of the Sicilian's portrait, or even a copy of the painting itself in the hands of an 'Egyptian Club' officer such as Captain Ball, who owned one, were available in London before the completion of Abbott's painting in March 1800. That month, McArthur tentatively sent his wife with the finished portrait to St James's Street to seek Fanny Nelson's approval for its publication. In a letter to her husband mentioning the visit, Fanny described the portrait as, 'your picture which Abbott has drawn for Mr McArthur with the chelengk', suggesting that publicising his jewel was always a prime purpose of the new painting.[19] Unaware the jewel had been exchanged, Fanny made sure to refer to her husband's jewel as his Chelengk; whereas Nelson never used this term for the jewel he received. Instead he called it his aigrette, a generic term for a head ornament taken from the French for the egret, a small type of heron whose brilliant white plumage often adorned such objects. In doing so, he was acknowledging that the jewel he received in Naples was not the Chelengk shown to Spencer Smith in Constantinople.

Before his painting was sent for engraving, Abbott hurriedly added the diamond star of the Turkish Order of the Crescent, received by Nelson in Palermo just a few weeks earlier. No one in London had yet seen this further decoration, and no image existed of it, so the artist relied on Nelson's description of 'a magnificent diamond star, in the centre of which on a blue enamel, is the Crescent and a Star'.[20] In his painting, Abbott understandably imagined the star to be circular, not oval; he also portrayed it as Nelson reported he wore it, 'over the Star of the Order of the Bath'. This prompted McArthur, mindful of the admiral's *faux pas*, to hastily caption prints of Abbott's portrait, 'as worn at foreign courts'.[21]

When it was published in the *Naval Chronicle* in March 1800, Abbott's portrait was trumpeted as, 'the only painting in this country that represents Lord Nelson's additional honours, viz: the plume of triumph and the patent of the Dukedom of Bronti &c.' It was printed alongside Nelson's new coat of arms, which since the Nile had been augmented with an image of the Chelengk as a heraldic crest. The article, together with juicy rumours that a sex scandal was engulfing the admiral in Naples, all further whetted the public's impatient desire to see Nelson back in England. But they would have to wait until a stormy day in November before Nelson's caravan rolled into town, having wound its way across Europe attracting headlines. Everywhere he went, Nelson's bizarre appearance as he stooped beneath the clattering weight of his jewels had provoked comment. In Vienna, haughty Lady Minto, using Eton schoolboy slang for an idiot, called the hero, 'a gig from ribands, orders and stars'.[22] A German newspaper vividly reported that, 'Admiral Nelson alone has a complete treasury vault on his body'; another shocked observer, after queuing for hours, described him as a 'miserable collection of bones … almost covered with orders and stars'.[23] The disparity between Nelson's obvious heroism and his vulgar display was striking and, further tainted by scandal and snobbery, was often recorded in highly negative terms, particularly by English tourists. Melesina St George, who met Nelson with the Hamiltons at Dresden, found him a 'little man, without any dignity', whilst Emma was 'bold, forward, coarse, assuming and vain', who 'puffs the incense full in his face, but he receives it with pleasure, and snuffs it up very cordially'. Emma was now in the habit of wearing Nelson's hat with its jewel openly in public, in bold defiance of propriety and naval etiquette. Still more extraordinary was Melesina's invitation to the Hotel Pologne to witness the performance of Nelson dressing for court, as if he was the Sun King. She counted him pinning no less than eight gold medals and diamond stars to his coat, topped by 'the large diamond feather, or ensign of sovereignty, given him by the Grand Signior'.[24] Even by the showy standards of her day, this was an astonishing haul, which Melesina found noteworthy for the quantity and its gaudy display. The sense of theatre was reinforced a few days later when Emma and her black maid, Fatima, the former slave rescued from Egypt, were discovered behind the scenes bawling at each other in thick accents laden with expletives, 'like Hogarth's *Actresses Dressing in the Barn*'.[25]

More gilding flaked off as the party neared England. Even the Chelengk lost some of its glitter in the softer northern light. Lady Minto dismissed it as, 'very ugly and not valuable, being rose diamonds', while in Hamburg a large diamond fell out of the sword gifted by the King of Naples.[26] But all the gold medals and bejewelled orders were in place when Nelson's carriage rolled into London on Sunday, 9 November, their glimmer lighting up the autumnal gloom. An enterprising publisher rushed out a print of the hero on his return weighed down with medals and carrying the promised sword from the Egyptian Club captains, which had arrived just before he left Sicily. Its hilt was pure gold and shaped like a crocodile, with the battle in miniature painted on its body.[27] Ordered by Captain Saumarez, this extraordinary weapon was rumoured to have cost the thirteen officers a total of 350 guineas (maybe £35,000 today). Nelson was excessively proud of this 'sword given me by the Captains of the Nile', showing it off to the children of the Queen of Naples on the voyage to Leghorn.[28] After the Battle of Copenhagen, he would use it to knight an officer on his quarterdeck at the behest of the king.[29]

Wisely, it was the gold sword from the City of London that Nelson took to the palace on 12 November, not his novelty Egyptian Club weapon. He had fretted for over a year about appearing at Court following his victory, writing to Sir Isaac Heard, Garter King of Arms, for guidance on how he should display the sultan's gifts. He was particularly concerned about showing the sultan's jewel. He would be bare-headed in the presence of the monarch, and with his disability he could not both carry his hat and kiss hands with the king. He anxiously enquired:

> As the Pelises given to me and Sir Sidney Smith are novel, I must beg you will turn in your mind how I am to wear it when I first go to the King; and, as the Aigrette is directed to be worn, where am I to put it? In my hat, having only one arm, is impossible, as I must have my hand at liberty; therefore I think, on my outward garment.[30]

Unsure of the answer, Heard queried the Home Secretary 'on what part about his person he may wear the *Aigrette*'.[31] As he neared England, Nelson wrote again, asking Heard, 'whether I may wear the Star of the Crescent and the Star of the Order of St Ferdinand and Merit, all of which at present adorn my coat. It is my wish to be correct in all these points'.[32] None of these foreign orders had received royal assent for wearing in England yet.

Regardless of any advice he was given, it went disastrously wrong for Nelson. Despite his misgivings, he did wear the jewel on his hat and the star of the Order of the Crescent on his uniform when he went to St James's.[33] It was a mistake to go to the palace flaunting foreign decorations, particularly as the Turkish star was still being worn above the Bath star on his coat. It was also whispered that accounts of massacres in Naples and rumours of the admiral's blatant sexual liaison with the wife of the British ambassador, a childhood friend of George III, 'shocked the King's morality'. Nevertheless, it was still surprising that the hero's greeting at Court was so 'singularly cold and repulsive'.[34] When they met, the king had made a curt enquiry after Nelson's health before turning his back to talk 'in great good humour' with an army officer. The royal snub was highly public and very painful. After two years of being worshipped by the crowd, the stark reality of his scandalous situation in London struck Nelson with sickening, bewildering force. Lady Elizabeth Foster was with Emma when Nelson returned from the palace and heard him say 'in a loud whisper, "I found St James's as cold as the atmosphere"'.[35] He was still brooding over the king's insult two months later when he confided the details of his humiliation to his friend Admiral Cuthbert Collingwood.[36] Like the Hamiltons, who had been absent from England for some ten years, Nelson was unprepared for the shift in public sentiment since his last appearance at Court back in 1797. With the dawning of the nineteenth century, attitudes against sexual impropriety were hardening, hastened by the rigours of war and the embarrassing behaviour of the Prince of Wales. Even old friends who understood him best, like Earl St Vincent, were astonished at the change in Nelson and the ludicrous figure he had become. 'Poor man,' the earl sighed after meeting Nelson on his return to England, 'he is devoured by vanity, weakness and folly. [He] was strung with ribbons, medals, etc., yet pretended that he wished to avoid the honour[s] and ceremonies he everywhere met with upon the road.'[37]

Emma shared the blame for the fiasco at the palace, having encouraged Nelson in his performance. Her appearance in London was as overblown as her lover's. With her luxurious hair, beautiful teeth and sun tan, Emma cut a glamorous and dazzling figure to a war-weary public. She tried to mask her pregnancy with high-waisted gowns and 'a kind of Turkish dress' which shrouded her in silk from neck to feet.[38] She fooled no one, with the press soon making sly comments that she was looking 'rosy', 'plump' or '*en bon point*'.[39] All these disguises were deployed ahead of Emma's long-dreaded introduction to Nelson's father and his wife in the lobby of a London hotel. After Trafalgar, both women fed accounts of this unhappy meeting to biographers. According to Emma, a visibly nervous Nelson, 'unconscious of crime, happily perceived not, in his beloved father, any symptoms of suspicion', but, 'at the obvious coldness of her ladyship, however, the warmth of his affectionate heart felt a petrifying chill, which froze for ever the genial current of supreme regard that had hitherto flowed with purity through the inmost recesses of his soul'.[40] Emma labelled her rival 'Tom Tit', a popular term for small, irritating people with a high opinion of themselves. Meanwhile, to Fanny, painfully aware of the rumours, it was:

> as if Lady Hamilton had lost all idea of propriety in the climate where she so long danced the circle of pleasure, the sober customs of England were treated by her with utter contempt; and she showed but too clearly a determinate plan to effect that fatal breach.[41]

Fanny then had to endure a series of public humiliations as Emma constantly sought to upstage her. For a visit to *The Mouth of the Nile*, a musical tribute at Covent Garden, Emma wore dazzling blue beside Fanny's lily white, with both women in fashionable turbans with plumes of feathers.[42] At dinner, Fanny was compelled by Nelson to hold a basin for Emma to be ill with morning sickness. Prevented by English laws and custom from forcing their divorce, Emma sought to drive the Nelsons apart 'by calumniating aspersions, and jealous insinuations', inciting the admiral to furious outbursts against his wife.[43] Hurt and bewildered, Fanny stayed strong and hopeful throughout the onslaught, searching her own conduct for fault. 'I love him,' she told Davison:

> I would do anything in the world to convince him of my affection. I was truly sensible of my good fortune in having such a husband. Surely, [if] I have angered him it was done *unconsciously* and without the least *intension.* I can truly say my wish; my desire was to please him and if he will have the goodness to send for me I will make it my study to obey him in every wish or desire of his and with cheerfulness. I still hope. He is affectionate and possesses the best of hearts. He will not make me miserable. I hope I have not deserved so severe a punishment from him.[44]

Now that Nelson was back in England, artists with an eye on the lucrative print market jostled for sittings. A request from John Hoppner to pose for a 'State' portrait for the Prince of Wales's gallery of military heroes at Carlton House could hardly be refused. Another flattering commission came from Norwich, which felt a keen pride in its local hero. The corporation paid £210 to William Beechey, an artist with links to Norfolk who had already painted Nelson's father, to produce an 8ft-high full-length portrait for display in the city's guildhall. The staging was similar to the Guzzardi picture, with Nelson on his quarterdeck, a French tricolour at his feet and the rigging above his head mimicking the drapery of the Italian portrait. Nelson was shown bare-headed, but he took his hat and jewel to the sittings, possibly at Beechey's request, and in the painting these are displayed on the sultan's pelisse draped across the taffrail behind him. A stickler for accuracy, Beechey's image of the jewel is the most reliable from Nelson's lifetime. The artist balances the Nile trophies with the sword captured by the admiral at the Battle of Cape St Vincent, which is propped against a gun draped with a Spanish flag. Nelson had given this sword to the city of Norwich after the action, so Beechey was compelled to include it. Known for his blunt manner, Beechey warmed to the Norfolk hero. He asked the admiral to stand godfather to his son and received the prize gift of the hat shown in his painting. Beechey later claimed Nelson, 'parted with it … as an old and tried friend, for he had worn it in many battles'.[45] Yet this could not be so. The hat in the painting is a full-dress version with gold lace, and very unlikely to be the hat worn at the Nile. As the King of Naples could testify, that hat had been shredded when Nelson was wounded and now resided in a glass case in the royal palace at Caserta.

Sculptor Ann Seymour Damer, a well-connected friend of the Hamiltons, was also given a battle-stained relic. She had pressed for a sitting with the admiral to complete a promised bust for the City of London. Nelson called at her studio several times in late November 1800, grateful to escape the clamour of his personal life. On the final visit, he gifted her his uniform coat, preserved from the Battle of the Nile:

> which I have never worn, nor even allowed to be brushed since, in order that my Naval as well as other friends may know from the streaks of perspiration and hair-powder which are still to be seen on it, the exertions which I made, and the anxiety which I felt, on that day to deserve the approbation of my King and Country.[46]

Nelson took his jewelled stars to the sitting, and, still smarting from the snub at the palace, sullenly ensured that Damer depicted them in approved fashion, with the star of the Order of the Bath pointedly displayed above the Order of the Crescent.

During this busy period, John McArthur was urging the admiral to visit Lemuel Abbott's Pall Mall studio, where the artist was struggling to update the portrait published in the *Naval Chronicle* earlier that year before he finally slipped into madness. Abbott, McArthur reported, had been busy 'finishing the Orders on your Lordship's Portrait', altering the Order of the Crescent from a circular to an oval badge and adding the star of the Order of St Ferdinand conferred on Nelson in April. He also added Ferdinand's diamond-set miniature picture on a ribbon around the admiral's neck, its only known representation.[47] No new sitting was possible, but Abbott might have seen these decorations at an exhibition of the admiral's awards hosted by the Admiralty in December. Viscount Palmerston saw them there and was most impressed by the 'fine presents of every kind', although he was struck at how 'shrunk and mutilated' the admiral himself appeared, a frequent comment of those who met him.[48] The sultan's jewel may not have been on display, however, as Abbott's jewel remained at odds with the version painted by Beechey. Taken from out-of-date sources and anecdote, Abbot's jewel had six plumes, whereas Beechey's, painted from life, had the correct thirteen: 'allusive to the thirteen ships taken and destroyed at Alexandria'.[49]

Before these new images of the admiral could be completed, the Nelsons separated: violently, according to Emma; amicably said supporters of Fanny. Roundwood was sold and Nelson walked out of the house his wife had taken in London. Their shared possessions were put into store under Nelson's lock and key. His life ashore now became unsettled as he shuttled between hotels and the houses of friends like the Hamiltons in Piccadilly and Alexander Davison in St James's Square. When Nelson was ordered back to sea in January 1801, it was Davison who took charge of his jewels and precious objects. Nelson gave instruction that these were to be placed in a mahogany box sealed with wax so it 'may not be opened or delivered to any person but by my order or in case of my death when they will be disposed of by my Will'.[50] He was plainly worried that his estranged wife might try to seize these valuable heirlooms whilst he was away. Cash-strapped, Nelson may also have deposited his jewels with Davison as collateral for a loan. The Prince of Wales would do similar when he entrusted a sealed box of diamonds to the same agent in 1809 in return for an advance of £11,000.[51]

Nelson attached a 'List of Diamonds' to his letter comprising his '*Aigrette from G Sr*', his diamond boxes from the tsar, the King of Sardinia and the Valida Sultan, his diamond star for the Order of the Crescent and his diamond hilted sword and miniature picture from the King of the Two Sicilies. He then escaped London for the sanctuary of his new ship *San Josef*, his prize from the Battle of Cape St Vincent. He would never see his wife again. In a final salvo, he sent her a series of bad-tempered letters complaining that various articles sent to Plymouth from their former home had been badly packed, damaged or forgotten altogether. Even the 'Turkey Cup' had suffered, despite having a robust fitted box, with the trident on its lid having been 'bent double from ill package'.[52] Fanny's tentative offer to travel to Devon to unravel the mess and nurse Nelson's damaged eye, which had flared up again, was brusquely dismissed. 'I only wish people would never mention my name to you,' he angrily fired back:

> Had you come here, I should not have gone ashore, nor would you have come afloat. I fixed, as I thought, a proper allowance to enable you to remain quiet, and not to be posting from one end of the kingdom to the other.

The meaning of her husband's words – to stay still and silent – was not lost on Fanny. 'I think you had better not mention my name and leave me to my fate,' she told Davison miserably. 'I am resign'd and trust to my god who has been a merciful father in many a difficulty.'[53]

Nelson's bitter words to his wife contrasted with the jubilation he had felt just days earlier that February, when Emma told him of the birth of their daughter. Having a child, and Fanny's attempts at reconciliation, forced him to think in practical terms about the future. Writing and re-drafting their final testaments was a preoccupation for officers departing on active service, and Nelson was no exception, adding many codicils to his will over the years. As early as May 1799, he had named Emma as a beneficiary of the pretty little diamond box gifted him by the Valida Sultan.[54] But now he drew up an entirely new document, granting Emma the full income from Bronte, rumoured to be £5,000 a year, and bequeathing her the picture of the King of Naples and all his diamond boxes 'lodged in a mahogany box, in the care of Alexander Davison Esq., St James's-Square, London'. Fretting that if he died these treasures might end up in the rapacious hands of Sir William Hamilton, as his wife Emma had no property rights of her own, Nelson put them in trust for her, with Davison as trustee.[55] The diamond star for the Order of the Crescent, gained in the heat of Palermo at the outset of their affair, was afforded special status. He assured Emma:

> The star I shall leave to you, not in trust, nobody would take that memento of friendship, affection, and esteem from you. May curses light on them if they did. The king's sword should go with the Dukedom and estate of Bronte; the aigrette also to my heirs, as a memento that I once gained a victory.[56]

The large diamond lost from the sword in Hamburg had since been replaced for £200, placing further strain on Nelson's already fragile finances (and causing him to regret waiving aside compensation of £800 proffered by his embarrassed hosts in Germany).[57] As an afterthought, he also left Emma 'my Turkish pelisse', suggesting she was already enjoying its use.[58]

Concerned that his stepson Josiah Nisbet might lay claim to his titles after his death, a fear mischievously conjured up by Emma, Nelson further ordered Fanny to send all his 'papers, parchment and freedoms' to his brother William for safekeeping.[59] Constrained by the need to invest £20,000 in an annuity for his estranged wife, there was little cash surplus to sustain his heirs – or Emma and his child, a baby girl they christened Horatia. Their future well-being and the need to make money now became Nelson's overriding concerns – down to the hour of his death.

10

THE DOCTOR

Norfolk, England, October 1798

William Nelson was tipped off about his brother's victory a day before Capel reached the Admiralty with the Nile dispatch. A friend glimpsed a letter from Nelson to Lady Spencer, 'informing her he had taken the whole of the French Toulon Fleet (2 ships excepted)'.[1] Lady Spencer, wife of the First Lord of the Admiralty and an ardent fan of Nelson, was 'half mad' with joy at the news. 'My heart is absolutely bursting with different sensations of joy, of gratitude, of pride, of every emotion that ever warmed the bosom of a British woman on hearing of her Country's glory,' she gushed.[2] William immediately hurried to Suffolk to be beside his sister-in-law Fanny and his father Edmund. He was 'not a little rejoiced' at the news, Fanny wryly reported.[3]

Born in April 1757, William was eighteen months older than the brother from whom he would eventually derive titles, a great fortune and notoriety. Spoilt as a child – it was said he was always given the 'largest Norfolk dumpling' in the Burnham Thorpe nursery[4] – William was the apple of his adoring parents' eye. It was he, not his brother Horatio, who was expected to restore the Nelson family to what their father Edmund considered its rightful place in society. Edmund had married well, as his wife Catherine was a great niece of Sir Robert Walpole, George II's prime minister, whose powerful interest had a long reach over his home county of Norfolk. Carefully nurtured, this patronage could open doors, secure jobs and win favours, even for distant relatives like the Nelsons. Edmund owed his ecclesiastical living at Burnham Thorpe to the Walpoles, who also worked smoothly behind the scenes to advance Horatio's naval career. But it was disconcerting for Edmund to survive on his wife's name, so first he, then his son William, grew fixated by titles and family heritage. Even before his brother's triumph at the Nile, William had been obsessing about which title the family would one day adopt, proposing Earl of Orford, a dormant Walpole title. Now that victory had come, he returned to this idea in a letter to his brother, 'not that I ever wish to see ye name of *Nelson* forgotten', he hastily added.[5]

Near in age, William and Horatio were close as children, a bond forged by the early death of their mother. Often tested by William's erratic behaviour, the sentimental strength of that relationship only grew with Nelson's rising fame. They had a special understanding which excluded their other siblings. Physically apart – William was heavy and boisterous, Horatio slight and quiet – the brothers shared the same characteristics of ambition, selfishness, kindness and arrogance to varying degrees. A practical difference lay in their education, although both were clever men. After similar schooling in Norfolk, William had gone to Cambridge University and Horatio to sea. Ordained in 1781 and appointed, again with Walpole help, curate of Little Brandon in Norfolk three years later, it seemed inevitable that William's life would follow his father's own quiet existence as a country parson. Yet he badgered his brother, recently appointed captain of the 28-gun frigate *Boreas*, to be taken on as a naval chaplain. He craved more excitement than a sleepy Norfolk village could offer him, or envied his brother's exotic life, perhaps seeing a chance to benefit from the powerful tide already propelling Nelson's fast-moving career.

But William lacked the stamina for a life afloat. After just four months in *Boreas*, William – tellingly nicknamed 'the Bishop' by the seamen – was heading home, too ill to stay at sea any longer. He returned clutching a payslip forged by Nelson, which claimed he had been in the service fifteen months longer than he really had.[6] This was a common fraud in the navy, but taking the risk showed the depth of Nelson's affection for his exasperating brother, with his mood swings and conceits. Their clear-sighted father blamed 'various passions' for his son's bad behaviour, 'first of all ambition, pride and a selfish disposition'.[7] It was obvious William was also becoming bitterly resentful of his successful and easy-going brothers-in-law, George Matcham and Thomas Bolton, a simmering rivalry which would have damaging consequences in future.

A naval career quietly dropped, William turned his attention to making the best of a duller, safer position in the Church by marrying Sarah Yonge, a cousin of the Bishop of Norwich. She was almost ten years older than the rector: a small, obliging woman who gossiped and schemed. Nelson called such people 'country town tabbies'.[8] Obsessed by class and manners, 'Norfolk Sally' was the perfect companion for her overbearing husband. She polished his ego, fuelled his ambition and stoked his pomposity. She gave him two children, Horace and Charlotte, but her advancing years became an issue for a man anxious to build a dynasty. In 1797, William was appointed to the richer living of neighbouring Hilborough. From here, the couple watched the astonishing rise of Nelson. When he lost his arm in action in 1797 it was William who had tended to his brother, acting as his amanuensis whilst Nelson adapted to writing with his left hand.

Even before the Battle of the Nile, William had been pressing Nelson to use his growing influence to secure him a position at one of the great English cathedrals, 'the larger the income the better'.[10] He followed the health of other clerics with covetous self-interest, especially the very elderly ones. When the victory was announced, he stepped up this unedifying campaign for preferment, prompting their sister Catherine Matcham, well used to his wiles, to complain that William 'thinks the *mitre* is very near falling upon *his head*. Now he will be *very great* in his own eyes. Poor fellow, he had his good qualities, though he has an odd way of showing them.'[11] Nelson appealed directly to Lord Eldon, the

Lord Chancellor, on his brother's behalf, but to no avail. In a field crowded with competing political interests, William never did achieve the episcopal prize, although he did secure a Prebendal stall at Canterbury Cathedral, a valuable sinecure with little spiritual function. However, his satisfaction at gaining the position was tinged with concern at its likely cost, 'as from the situation I am now in I am in some measure obliged to give dinners and good wine, it is required and expected of me in ye double capacity of Prebendary of Canterbury and Lord Nelson's brother'.[12] Status came at a price, as Nelson also discovered with his titles.

Like the rest of his family, William anticipated a high honour for his brother after the battle. Had not Admiral Duncan been made viscount and Jervis an earl for less resounding victories? But there was a problem. After the Battle of Cape St Vincent, Nelson had refused a baronetcy, pleading poverty. Instead, he had coveted the glittering star, collar and sash of the Order of the Bath (a baronetcy came with no baubles). 'If my services have been of any value,' he told an aide, 'let them be noticed in a way that the public may know me or them.'[13] Sensitive to issues of class, there was also pleasure in knowing, as Nelson told William, that 'chains and medals are what no fortune or connection in England can obtain'.[14] The king granted Nelson's wish, but he also remembered the rebuff. Now, with the far greater victory at the Nile, George III archly proposed giving Nelson money, and no title at all. The decision caused havoc in official circles. The government, mindful of public opinion, had already strongly hinted that the admiral would be given a viscountcy, at the very least. But the king blocked the idea. After some furious backpedalling in Whitehall, he grudgingly granted Nelson a barony, the very lowest rank of the peerage, making him Baron Nelson of the Nile and of Burnham Thorpe in the County of Norfolk. All this manoeuvring over titles and honours further soured the already difficult relationship between the hero and his monarch.

One gratifying benefit of the Order of the Bath was the right to add supporters to the knight's coat of arms. Not for Nelson the usual unicorn, gryphon or greyhound as displayed by the aristocracy. He had requested a sailor 'trampling on a Spanish flag' and 'the British lion tearing the Spanish flag the remnants hanging down and flag in tatters'.[15] For his crest, Nelson chose the stern view of *San Josef*, his Spanish prize at Cape St Vincent. These were the arms of a showman, and raised eyebrows at the College of Arms. Now that the admiral had taken a step on the lowest rung of the peerage with his triumph at the Nile, he had opportunity to further embellish his coat of arms, a task he willingly delegated to his brother William. 'It cannot, I know,' Nelson wrote from Palermo, 'be in better hands.'[16]

William relished the task of redesigning arms which might be his own one day. With no children of his own, Nelson's rightful heir was his father, the Reverend Edmund Nelson, followed by his eldest brother Maurice, an unassuming bureaucrat at the Navy Office. But Maurice had recoiled at the prospect. 'I now declare to you that William may have all the honours to himself,' he confided to his sister-in-law Fanny. 'I move in too humble a sphere to think of such a thing.'[17] So when William consulted with Garter King of Arms Sir Isaac Heard on his brother's coat of arms, he did so with an eye on his own future use. After discussion, he agreed to the flowery additions of a seascape representing Aboukir Bay and symbols of victory such as palm fronds and the French flag clasped in the lion's jaw. As an inspired finishing touch, Heard suggested adding the Chelengk. On 3 November 1798, he went to Lord Grenville's office to copy Spencer Smith's sketch of the jewel to be placed above Nelson's coat of arms as an additional heraldic crest. Completed in December, Heard's finished design inadvertently showed the original, undelivered Chelengk. Moreover, it was highlighted in blue suggesting the Turkish watercolour of the Chelengk – the only surviving source for this telling detail – had also arrived in London, possibly forwarded by Nelson to his wife who may have shown it to the Inchiquins when she dined with them this same month. The drawing came into the possession of her son Josiah Nisbet who, estranged from his step-father, gave it away. It was all highly theatrical – and wickedly lampooned by

Gillray in his caricature *Hero of the Nile* – but it was also a brilliant piece of self-branding which delighted Nelson in distant Italy.

The new coat of arms demonstrated that this was a family rising fast. From Palermo, Nelson indicated he now wished to live among the mansions of the *beau monde* near Hyde Park in London, with a 'neat carriage' and 'good servants'.[18] Shocked by such extravagance but eager to please, Fanny procured for her husband a 'new chariot' costing £342 (about £30,000 today). 'Nothing fine about it,' she observed, 'only fashionable.'[19] Although Fanny described the vehicle as a chariot – a simple carriage with cutaway body and two forward-facing seats – the high cost suggests she purchased the latest model of coach with a full body, facing seats and doors to be emblazoned with Nelson's splendid and soon-distinctive coat of arms.[20] A door panel survives and shows the carriage was painted a trendy yellow.[21] The livery for the coachman and footmen who would ride the coach was also enthusiastically designed by William. 'I cannot say that I am a competent judge,' he suggested with false modesty:

> However, my idea is this. The coat lined with yellow and yellow button holes, the collar and cuffs black velvet the same as at present, only it should have a standing collar, the waistcoat yellow, and I think there should be shag breeches the colour of the waistcoat, the coat, and coat and waistcoat pockets and collar should be embroidered with a worsted lace composed of the colours of the livery with the cross which composes part of [the crest] worked upon it, one or two gold epaulets as [you] please on the coat and a gold laced hat [that is] my general idea, I have only seen Lord Walpole's full dress which is something in this manner; the buttons should have either the aigrette or San Josef crests upon them.[22]

Nelson paid for William's son Horace to go to Eton, less for the schooling than for the upper-class company. He developed a warm affection for his nephew, his possible future heir, sending him presents and gently joshing letters. Fanny considered Horace thoroughly spoilt, unable to admit her husband treated him like the son he so desperately desired. The education of his niece Charlotte was entrusted to Fanny, who approved of a school found for her in leafy Chelsea called Whitelands. William then insulted their sister Susannah Bolton, who was married to a wealthy Norfolk squire, by insisting that her sons Tom and George should also 'be brought up gentlemen'. He pressed her to enter them in the navy, where Nelson's powerful interest could drive their rapid promotion.[23] Despite his mother's qualms, 12-year-old midshipman George Bolton was duly sent to join his uncle in the Mediterranean. The boy's death on the voyage out must have embittered Susannah against her elder brother and his constant cajoling. Even Nelson admitted that, 'My brother has a bluntness, and a want of fine feelings, which we are not used to; but he means nothing.'[24]

In public, William's relationship with his sister-in-law Fanny was respectful but distant. With no young children of her own, she had taken on the care of Nelson's ageing father, earning his family's gratitude. The return of Nelson to England with the Hamiltons, however, brought years of resentment boiling to the surface. The ease with which Emma's poison infected William suggested it was acting on his existing dislike of Fanny and their mutual loathing. In a letter to her husband, Fanny described William as, 'the roughest mortal, surely, that ever lived'.[25] A proud, reserved woman who could appear haughty, Fanny had too often shown impatience with her provincial-minded in-laws. Furthermore, William's wife Sarah Nelson now became Emma's unlikely soulmate, flattered by the attention, overwhelmed by the gushing emotion and naively ignorant of its true purpose. 'You and I liked each other from the moment we met,' Emma confided, 'our souls were congenial.'[26] Sarah was disgracefully complicit in Emma's campaign to discredit and denigrate 'Tom Tit'. Years of living with William and his petty jealousies had ruined her. Emma easily exploited this weakness to make Sarah a willing accomplice in the humiliation then complete defeat of her rival. Nelson encouraged the friendship, paying for Sarah to stay with Emma as her companion when he sailed for the Baltic.

Worse was to come. With his brother away, William started to make clumsy advances on Emma, encouraged by her flirting and betraying the same sexual drive as his wayward brother. 'Your image and voice are constantly before my imagination, and I can think of nothing else,' William wrote to Emma in February 1801.[27] Then, a few months later:

> comes your roguish, waggish letter, on a Sunday morning (amidst all my meditations for the good of my parishioners) about love, courtship, marriage, throwing the stocking, going to bed, &c – quite shocking to write to a country parson, who can have no idea of such things.[28]

Such behaviour simply worsened the rifts in the family. The Boltons, mourning their son, were awkwardly ambivalent, whilst the Matchams stayed loyal to Fanny. She reported 'terrible' and then 'violent' quarrels between William Nelson and George Matcham over the matter.[29] Sir William Hamilton tried to be dispassionate, hiding his true feelings and watching events with a wry humour. He found William Nelson ludicrous. News of Nelson's victory at Copenhagen in April 1801 made William, he joked, 'more extraordinary than ever. He would get up suddenly and cut a caper rubbing his hands, every time that the thought of fresh laurels came into his head.'[30] Yet even in 'high spirits', Alexander Davison remarked, William kept up his 'grumbling disposition'.[31] The family expected an earldom for this further triumph, and anything less, in Davison's opinion, would be 'degrading'.[32] Instead, they had to settle for a viscountcy, which, in a nod to his likely heir, Nelson named Hilborough after his brother's parish in Norfolk. 'I hope Revd. Sir will be satisfied with the new patent,' Nelson told Emma, 'as it is taken from Hilborough on purpose to please him, and if I leave none, he must breed stock from his own place.'[33]

The king also extended Nelson's existing barony with a special remainder so that if the male line failed – an unthinkable calamity for William, whose son was heir – the title could descend to the sons of Nelson's sisters Susannah Bolton and Catherine Matcham. Accordingly, Tom Bolton, the eldest of these nephews, now received almost as much attention as Horace Nelson. Nelson offered to pay for his education, and Tom and Horace acted jointly as Nelson's 'Esquires' at a ceremony for the Order of the Bath at Westminster Cathedral in May 1803. However, William believed making Tom an heir deserved more gratitude. 'Mrs Bolton made no remarks nor seem'd in the least elated or pleased,' William grumbled to Emma:

> Indeed to say the truth there appears a *gloom* about them all, for what reason I can't devise, unless they are uneasy *Tom Tit* does not share in it, to whom I verily believe and think they are secretly attached, they did not deserve to have a *chance*.

He continued in similar vein:

> I wish it had gone to Charlotte and her heirs male, but I hope to God it will be a long time before it leaves the *true Nelson* line and that the young *Baron* and Duke (who is now writing by my side) will raise up posterity, and cut all the others out.[34]

Hearing from Emma, who loved to stir things up, that Nelson had indeed considered pressing for Charlotte's sons to be included in the inheritance of the title, William vowed to see it done, 'if he is made an Earl'.[35] Meantime, he clung to the forlorn hope – Sarah was now over 50 – that he might still have another son and 'keep the line of the Nelsons in the true name and blood, without being obliged to go to others to assume a name which scarcely belongs to them'.[36]

The succession uneasily settled, William returned to a familiar theme. 'Now we have secured the Peerage, we have only *one* thing to ask,' he reminded Emma, 'that is, my promotion in the Church, handsomely and honourably, such as becomes Lord Nelson's brother and heir apparent to the title. No put off with beggarly stalls.'[37] William revelled in his status as heir to his famous brother.

When William Pitt, or 'Billy Pitt' as he called him with over-familiarity, bowed to him at the Senate House in Cambridge during the 1802 general election, he could hardly conceal his joy, sidling up to the former prime minister to offer some words of advice.[38] Even Sarah grew weary of her husband's constant pestering for titles and offices, telling him that, 'Your brother does all he can that I do know, so that I *wish* you would never say a word about it.'[39]

There was no mention of Nelson's stepson Josiah in the succession, although both his mother Fanny and Nelson's father Edmund believed he had a moral claim on the title. Recalling the violent scenes in Naples between Nelson and Josiah, Emma seized upon this threat to drive a further wedge between Nelson's family and his wife Fanny. In a letter to Sarah Nelson, she directed her ire at Edmund. 'Would your father have seen,' she railed, '*his own* flesh and blood set *aside* for who? For Nesbit's, the doctor's son, a villain who many times called the glorious Nelson villain and that he would do for him.' She accused old Edmund of conspiring with Fanny, '*against the saviour of his country* and his darling, who has risen to such a height of honour, and for whom? A *wicked false malicious* wretch who rendered his days and nights miserable ... 'tis a bad bird befowls its own nest.'[40] Nelson weakly defended his father, blaming dementia. 'My poor father is led now he does not know what he does,' he told Emma. Outwardly, Nelson remained dutiful, but when his father died he did not stir from London to join his family at the Norfolk graveside. Guilt, a dread of death, fear of meeting Fanny and concern that his celebrity risked turning the quiet country funeral into a circus all played a part in his decision. The real reason was the woman sitting beside him as he wrote to inform Davison of the death of 'my poor dear father'. Before this sad note was dispatched, Emma snatched it up and added a request that Edmund's vacant parish be given to Nelson's former chaplain in *Vanguard*, Stephen Comyn, a loyal and forgiving friend from Naples days.[41]

With Edmund in his grave and England at peace, there was nothing to keep William and Sarah from joining the Nelson roadshow for a tour of the west of England and Wales. The purpose of the journey was Sir William's desire to inspect his estates in Pembrokeshire, inherited from his first wife Catherine. He also wished to see progress at Milford, a sleepy port he owned and which his nephew, Emma's former lover Sir Charles Greville, was energetically trying to develop as a naval base, a long-held dream of the heavily indebted Sir William. On a previous visit there, Sir William had seen 'houses rising up, like mushrooms, even in these difficult times'.[42] Impressed, he had promised to secure Nelson's priceless endorsement for the project. He was more than willing now to use the celebrity of his wife's lover for commercial gain. Sir William planned to return to Wales, not only with the admiral in person but with the large portrait of Nelson painted by Guzzardi in Sicily, which he intended to display at Milford as a tourist attraction and as a clever piece of branding for the port.

Sarah Nelson was in ecstasies at the prospect of the holiday, which was timed to arrive at Milford for the anniversary of the Battle of the Nile on 1 August 1802. Young Horace was taken out of school for the trip, with the party travelling in two coaches with a handful of servants and the picture safely stowed. Tracked by local newspapers, large crowds greeted the cavalcade everywhere they went. The Matchams met them at Oxford, where Nelson received an honorary degree and the Freedom of the City in yet another gold box. William was also awarded a doctorate in Divinity to join the one granted, after his lobbying, by Cambridge University the previous year. His insistence on being addressed as the 'Doctor' caused his brother much amusement. Hearing of William's Cambridge award, Nelson had told Emma that, 'His being a Doctor is nonsense, but I must write tomorrow and congratulate him or else the fat will be in the fire.'[43]

Milford was reached on 29 July, where the Nelsons and Hamiltons were lodged in the newly built Packet Hotel at the heart of the harbour development. Charles Greville had stage-managed a series of events to welcome the hero and exploit his fame. An annual fair was inaugurated, and at a banquet in the hotel the Guzzardi portrait was unveiled and gifted to the town, 'for the perpetual gratification of visitors'.[44] Nelson then spoke dutifully in support of the port, comparing it to the beautiful sweeping harbour of Trincomalee in Ceylon.

That Sir William was even willing to consider parting with Nelson's portrait suggests a growing frustration at his situation. Before the tour, he had complained to Greville of 'the nonsense I am obliged to submit to here, to avoid coming to an explosion'.[45] He had already consigned a picture of Emma for sale at Christie's, which, furious, Nelson had bought back in secret. Now the admiral was forced to watch as his own image was hung over the fireplace at the Packet Hotel, injecting the colour and heat of the Mediterranean into its windswept view of the Irish Sea. But the picture never achieved its goal of making Milford a port to rival Portsmouth. With interest in Nelson fading after Trafalgar, the painting was taken down and put in a cupboard to mould away until 1849, when it was salvaged and placed in the boardroom of the Admiralty in Whitehall, where it remains.

Nelson, Emma recalled, 'often mentioned his progress through South Wales to Milford, as an affecting contrast of the genuine enthusiasm of natural character, to the cold expression of ministerial approbation by which his reception had been marked on his return from the Mediterranean'.[46] Newspapers started to compare the tour to a royal procession: unfavourably so for a monarch disabled by bouts of madness and hidden from his subjects. Others echoed the critics of the earlier journey across Europe, calling Nelson's appearance 'pitiable'. After Milford, the travellers unhurriedly looped back to London through the humming industrial heartland of England. At Worcester, Nelson ordered a service of porcelain in psychedelic 'Old Japan' style, a hugely popular pattern which he made his own by adding his heraldic devices to the decoration, the Chelengk crest updated since his return from Italy to more accurately portray the jewel he had actually been given by the sultan. Then to Birmingham for a tour of the factories, where a highlight was meeting the famed but ailing Matthew Boulton, mass-producer of coins and Nelsonian medals. Time, too, to see again young Thomas Richards, designer of one of those medals and refugee from Naples, at his father's 'toyshop' in the High Street. No doubt several purchases were made from the tempting array of luxury goods on offer. After a courtesy call on Earl Spencer in Northamptonshire, the tourists were back in London by early September. Nelson was revitalised by the affection of his countrymen but growing weary of his celebrity. Having courted publicity with his decorations and portraits, he now complained to Emma that he hated to be 'stared at'.[47] The pressure of fame was growing onerous now that he craved seclusion with his lover.

A looming confrontation with Sir William was avoided by his timely death a few months later. Emma and Nelson were at his bedside as the old ambassador died, genuine grief mingled with realisation that their life together was now simpler, if still more financially stretched as Sir William had left them his debts, but his estates to Greville. William and Sarah supported Emma in the days which followed, visiting her at Merton Place, the house she shared in Surrey with Nelson, and at Clarges Street, her rented property in London. Here the doctor and his wife gawkily mingled with Emma's colourful friends from the theatre and fringes of the aristocracy, who found them 'very strange looking-people', meaning boring, unfashionably dressed and provincial.[48] There was barely any contact with Fanny now. She had appeared defiantly at Court in January 1802, 'dressed in the most simple but elegant stile … with a beautiful plume of Paradise and Ostrich feathers', but she was not sent tickets to the fete in Ranelagh Gardens, where the family gathered following the service for the Order of the Bath.[49] Gallantly, Earl St Vincent and Captain Saumarez offered her their tickets, but Fanny declined, causing the *Morning Post*, a critic of Nelson's behaviour, to lament, 'that her Ladyship should be indebted to strangers for an attention due to her from a much nearer quarter'.[50]

When Nelson returned to sea, William and Sarah took Emma bathing in Southend, a favourite pursuit she had acquired in Italy, which helped a skin condition, possibly psoriasis caused by nerves.

Emma also stayed for long spells with the Nelsons at Canterbury, duetting in the cathedral with her friend Mrs Billington, a celebrated opera singer. 'Shall I sing an anthem for the benefit of the County Hospital, Mr Dean?' she bawled down the aisle. 'The Dean, affecting deafness, returned no answer, and her Ladyship understood him.'[51] It was said that, 'the inhabitants of Canterbury were not a little surprised at the appearance of such visitors in the house of one of their reverend dignitaries.'[52] But smitten by Emma and glowing in the sheen of her celebrity, William was impervious to such barbs.

The Reverend Doctor was again by Emma's side to welcome his brother home in August 1805, staying close throughout Nelson's last days in England, many of them spent happily at Merton Place. There were streams of visitors, boisterous family dinners, shooting parties and games. The holiday mood shifted sharply with the news, anticipated by Nelson, that the French and Spanish enemy fleets had combined at Cadiz for an unknown mission. With Bonaparte, now emperor, massing his troops at the Channel ports, an invasion of England was feared. Nelson was summoned and ordered back to his latest flagship *Victory* to face the threat.

With uncharacteristic sensitivity, William took Sarah and his children away from Merton, leaving the lovers to enjoy their last precious days together. He was not there to bid farewell to his brother on 13 September, yet he still loomed large in the premonitions now haunting Nelson. After missing a chance to engage the enemy earlier that summer, Nelson had told William, half in jest, that, 'If I had fallen in with them, you would probably have been a Lord before I wished; for I know they meant to make a dead set for the Victory.'[53] As he headed for battle, he recalled this dark humour in a letter to Emma, telling her that, 'My brother hopes I shall meet the enemy's fleet that somehow or other he may be a Lord.'[54] Then he was gone, leaving Emma to go to Canterbury to drink tea and eat macaroni and curry with the doctor and his boring friends. 'It is *so dull*,' she complained.[55] All everyone could do now was wait.

11

THE INVASION

The Smith brothers had worked hard as joint ministers in Constantinople to steer the Sublime Porte to an alliance with Britain rather than siding with Turkey's old friend France. So they were horrified to hear that London had appointed the urbane Lord Elgin over their heads as ambassador. Sidney Smith bitterly complained that the news, 'paralysed the action of those we had to deal with by making them feel that much of what was in hand might be to be done over again'.[1]

The sultan was bewildered too. He had heaped more presents on Sidney Smith after the Convention of El Arish, which offered the French free passage home if they returned Egypt to Ottoman rule. He had knighted Smith in the newly instituted Order of the Crescent and issued a *firman* confirming his authority as naval minister. But Smith's triumph was short-lived. The collapse of the treaty, then rout of the Turkish army at Heliopolis, left Egypt still firmly in French hands. With the conflict in Europe entering a new and critical phase, the British cabinet was split over the issue, but eventually the threat to India overrode their reluctance to commit huge resources to this far-off theatre of the war. Preparations began for a large-scale British invasion under the joint command of two battle-hardened Scots: Admiral Lord Keith, Nelson's commander-in-chief in the Mediterranean, and General Sir Ralph Abercromby. They planned an amphibious assault near Alexandria, with a

Turkish force landing further up the coast. Meantime, a combined British and Indian force led by General Baird (in place of General Wellesley, future Duke of Wellington, who was suffering from ringworm) would land at Kosseir on the Red Sea. The first British redcoats started arriving in the eastern Mediterranean just as Nelson and the Hamiltons prepared to journey home in July 1800. General Sir John Moore, commanding the 51st Regiment, encountered them at Leghorn, where he found Nelson, 'more like the Prince of the Opera than the Conqueror of the Nile. It is really melancholy to see a brave and good man, who has deserved well of his country, cutting so pitiful a figure.'[2]

The British troopships converged at Marmaris in Turkey, and by February 1801 were ready to sail under escort to Egypt. Sidney Smith, licking his wounds after his humiliation at El Arish, proved essential in planning the campaign. Stripped of diplomatic power and of his controversial role commanding naval forces in the Levant, Smith was once again simply a captain in charge of his ship. But 'Smit Bey', as he was dubbed, had unrivalled experience of the region and enjoyed excellent relations with the Turks, unlike the fastidious Keith, who complained that, 'I do not much like their company.'[3] Smith attended high-level meetings with Keith and Abercromby, liaised with the Turks at Marmaris and was placed in command of a division of landing craft ahead of the invasion on 7 March.

The French were prepared for the assault, but its impact overwhelmed them and the town and fort of Aboukir, overlooking the scene of Nelson's great triumph, were quickly secured by the British. Scrawling a note to Keith from the beachhead, Smith admired, 'the determined courage of this gallant army, in the close contest they had to maintain with the enemy on the beach.'[4] Under covering fire from the gunboats off shore, the soaking British troops drove forward over the sand dunes, led by Sir John Moore waving his hat. 'The French were astounded, dismayed and disheartened,' recalled George Parsons, watching from a boat, 'and their want of that steady, persevering, and indomitable spirit, that nerves the brave man to encounter misfortune to the last, was now observable in their retreat.'[5] Only a lack of cavalry prevented an immediate dash for Alexandria; instead General Abercromby moved cautiously westward along the coastline, using Smith's local knowledge to source supplies among the Arab tribes.

On 21 March, the British were engaged by a large French force which had marched out of Cairo under General Menou. Smith, his blue naval coat almost causing him to be shot as a Frenchman, was in the thick of the action from the start as French cavalry repeatedly charged the British lines. When Smith's own sword was broken, Abercromby handed him a sabre taken from the lifeless hand of a French dragoon, shot dead after nearly running the general down. Soon afterwards, Abercromby was hit in the thigh by a musket ball which lodged in his hip, soaking his saddle with blood. Smith, too, was hurt when a musket ball glanced off his shoulder, knocking him from his horse. Both men remained dazed and bleeding on the battlefield until the brutal contest ground to a halt with the British claiming victory: their first of the war over Bonaparte's much-vaunted army. Abercromby was evacuated to *Foudroyant*, formerly Nelson's, now Keith's flagship. Parsons recalled:

> I saw this gallant and good old warrior extended on a grating, coming alongside the flagship, his silver hair streaming in the breeze which rippled the waters, his venerable features convulsed with agony, while the sun darted fiercely on him its intense rays, combining with his wound to occasion the perspiration to pour down his forehead like drops of rain.[6]

While Abercromby languished in terrible pain afloat, Smith, whose wounds was less serious, volunteered to go under a flag of truce into Alexandria to offer terms to Menou. Stopped at the French lines, he handed over a letter from Keith and Abercromby promising to repatriate the French army if it abandoned its weapons, treasure and shipping. The offer was refused point blank by Menou, who remained defiant even when the Capitan Pasha, High Admiral of the Ottoman navy, appeared in Aboukir Bay with three warships and transports carrying 3,600 fresh troops, including some 1,500 battle-hardened Albanian irregulars. In a short ceremony in *Foudroyant*, the Capitan Pasha was introduced to the British naval officers. He then presented Chelengks to Admiral Keith and to the ailing Abercromby, 'who just lived long enough to receive the compliment; the next minute that gallant Chief expired of the wound he received in the action of the 21st'.[7] Keith's Chelengk was magnificent, equal to Nelson's jewel in size and sparkling brilliance.[8]

Abercromby was succeeded as commander-in-chief of the land forces by the uncompromising General John Hely-Hutchinson. He was unimpressed by Sidney Smith's heroics and disapproved of such a junior naval officer meddling in the campaign. He pointedly failed to mention Smith in his dispatches, and asked Keith to recall him to his ship and away from land operations. This snub encouraged the many other enemies and rivals whom Smith had accumulated whilst wielding the sweeping powers of the sultan. They included the Capitan Pasha and Grand Vizir, both for so long subordinate to this infidel upstart, and Lord Elgin in Constantinople, who was whipping up bad feeling against Smith in London. Smith, who had taken to wearing Arab dress, still enjoyed the respect of the local sheikhs, who fed him vital intelligence, but his authority was fast draining away. On 1 May, he returned to *Tigre*, from where he naively sought Lord Elgin's help in removing the 'implied censure' he felt he was suffering from.[9] Embarrassed and unwilling to become involved, Elgin referred him vaguely to the 'proper authority'.[10]

Smith still had one powerful friend. After the landings in Egypt, Selim sent him a luxurious gold and diamond scimitar. Fearing a plot, the Capitan Pasha, his hostility to the sultan's favourite well known, handed over the sword with extreme trepidation during a short ceremony in his flagship *Sultan Selim*. 'When finally he buckled on the rich sword,' recalled Smith in his memoirs, 'he fully expected to see the glittering blade flash in the light, and that, in the next twinkling of his eye, his head would fly from his shoulders.' The rictus smile of the 'Old Turk' was so forced that everyone, Smith included, burst out laughing. This comforted the terrified capitan, 'for he took it for granted that such a man as Sir Sidney Smith could not look upon depriving of a poor Turk like himself of his head, to be the most fitting subject in the world for merriment'.[11]

Cooped up in *Tigre*, Smith impotently followed reports of the British advance up the Nile. When French resistance in Cairo collapsed, he watched as Hutchinson negotiated a treaty almost identical to the one he had concluded at El Arish, but at a much heavier cost in lives. The liberation of Egypt was assured, but it was not yet quite complete. General Menou still held out at Alexandria with the remnants of his defeated army, waiting in vain for reinforcements from Bonaparte. He finally capitulated on 31 August, surrendering the country entirely to the British, who – exhausted, riddled with disease and short of supplies – wasted no time handing it back to the sultan.

Seizing the chance for further fame, Smith pressed Lord Keith to be allowed to carry his dispatches home to England. Keith, uneasy at Smith's treatment at the hands of Hutchinson, agreed, on the condition he took Colonel Abercromby, son of the late commander, with him to share the acclaim. Duplicate dispatches would go by sloop in case of accidents. Before sailing for home, Smith fired off a final stinging letter to Hutchinson, accusing the general of colluding with the Capitan Pasha in a 'miserable intrigue' against him.[12] Unable to spare *Tigre*, a 74-gun ship of the line, Keith gave Smith the frigate *El Carmen*, a Spanish prize, to sail home. On his last day in his old ship, lying at anchor in Aboukir Bay, Smith was given a dinner in the ward room by his officers. Despite urgent prompting by the flagship to get under way, Smith was in no hurry to leave the company of men with whom he had shared such dangers for the last four years. 'Sir, I understand what the signal means,' he told the officer of the watch hovering at his shoulder, before reluctantly ordering his barge for the short transfer to *El Carmen.* The entire company of some 600 men climbed *Tigre*'s rigging to cheer their captain off, moving Smith, an emotional man, to tears.

With blatant nepotism, Hutchinson sent his younger brother Christopher to Constantinople with news of the victory. A lawyer by training but with a passion for the military, 'Kit' Hutchinson had taken no part in the action, having volunteered to accompany the expedition to Egypt as an honorary colonel, 'without having the least idea of being employed'. It should have come as no surprise, however, that his rank and red uniform would confuse the Porte. Believing he was dealing with the liberator of Egypt himself, Selim, in Mary Elgin's memorable words, 'chilinqued' Kit, awarding him a Chelengk and 'a most remarkable handsome pelisse'. He was still ostentatiously wearing these honours when he made a dramatic entry at an embassy dinner later the same evening, pleading 'that he had been charged to do so at the Porte'. 'How perfectly absurd of his brother sending him with such news as this,' exclaimed Mary, 'instead of sending an officer.' When Kit then 'flung off all the trappings [he] appeared a young goodish looking whack', noted Mary, but she dreaded to imagine what Selim might do if he discovered he had 'paid such uncommon attention to a person who was not engaged in the expedition'.[13]

Mary also saw that Kit was wearing an unusual and large gold medal around his neck. Selim's private secretary Ahmed Efendi had also recorded in his diary how Hutchinson:

> was made to wear a sable fur and a bejewelled *çelenk* was placed on his hat. And one of the gold plaques with the Imperial cipher which were newly created and struck at the Imperial Mint in order to be given to those officers from among the English officials who were present at the campaign of Egypt, was suspended to his neck.[14]

The new gold medal was designed to extend the highly exclusive Order of the Crescent to all officers in Egypt, and was being minted in three sizes for the different rank of recipient. A first-class version of the new award was also dispatched to Nelson in England.

The liberation of Egypt was greeted with jubilation at Constantinople. There were firework displays, gun salutes, battle re-enactments and a general amnesty for the many Maltese slaves held in chains in the city. Selim ordered a palatial new British embassy to be built to replace the one destroyed by fire in Spencer Smith's day. 'All the Turks were as merry as Christians,' Mary Elgin wrote. 'I think they might have conquered Egypt over and over again had they but fired half the number of cannon in earnest they are now firing in joke.'[15] A frigate was dispatched to Egypt laden with jewels, diamond boxes, pelisses, medals and swords. The medals were distributed by the Capitan Pasha, attended by the restored Pasha of Egypt, over two days of investitures in early October on the battlefields near Alexandria where the war had been decided. The British officers were summoned in turn to a richly decorated tent erected in the desert between lines of Turkish troops, their flags flying and bands playing. Under the awning, the capitan sat on a sofa:

> dressed in a white robe of beautiful Persian satin, over which was the robe of state … of the finest red cloth, and on it was placed, below the breast, two *Aigrettes* of large diamonds; and in a sash of rich satin round his waist was fixed a dagger, the handle of which was so thickly covered with diamonds, as to render it impossible to discover [of] what other materials it was made. On his head he wore a superb turban, with rows of pearls placed on the different folds.

He stroked his long black beard meditatively throughout proceedings.

As Lord Keith had already taken the fleet away, his second in command, Admiral Sir Richard Bickerton, went to the ceremony for naval officers. Like General Hutchinson the day before, to the sound of gun salutes 'and other demonstrations of satisfaction, agreeable to the Turkish custom', Bickerton was knighted in the Order of the Crescent, receiving the diamond star, peach-coloured sash, gold medal of the order and a fur pelisse valued at £300. In total, thirteen British officers would be given the sultan's star, with those not already titled in their own country soon badgering the College of Arms in London to style themselves knight. As precedent, they cited the foreign knighthood granted to Sidney Smith by the King of Sweden, forgetting how scathing they had been at the time of that award.[16] Captains were then presented in order of seniority, each receiving a second-class gold medal but no star, sash or pelisse. Proceedings closed with refreshments of sherbet, coffee and sweetmeats. Hundreds of smaller gold medals then followed from Constantinople for distribution among the lower ranks in the expedition.[17]

Eager to break news of the victory in London, Sidney Smith had raced down the Mediterranean with Keith's dispatch. However, a decision to follow Earl St Vincent's advice and sail as close as possible to Africa cost him valuable time against adverse winds. By now, his behaviour was increasingly eccentric. He dressed like Robinson Crusoe and served roasted rats to his appalled officers, saying they 'fed cleaner and were better eating than pigs or ducks'. His only concession to English manners was to trim his luxuriant Turkish-style whiskers a little each day as they sailed west, a symbolic shedding of his life in the Levant. He landed at Portsmouth on 9 November, and despite the chilly autumn weather, appeared at the Admiralty the next morning theatrically 'attired in the Turkish dress, turban, robe, shawl and girdle round his waist with a brace of pistols'.[18] It is likely that Smith's diamond Chelengk glittered on his turban in a performance to equal Nelson's dramatic arrival exactly a year before. But it fell flat when Smith heard that the sloop which had followed him with duplicate dispatches from Egypt had beaten him to England by two weeks. Smith was denied the customary knighthood for delivering the news, and even his outlandish costume paled a little in a city already gone crazy for

Turkish fashions. Still only a captain in the navy, Smith could not be promoted except by seniority, nor receive the titles that had fallen on Nelson. But he was politely received by Prime Minister William Pitt, given a safe seat in parliament and a sword by the City of London, which he pressed 'with fervour to his lips'.[19] The Turkey Company, which had most to thank Smith for, awarded him a silver vase like Nelson's, whilst the East India Company voted a welcome £3,000. Smith had won public acclaim but little prize money, and was already struggling with rising debts which would eventually lead him to a spell in the King's Bench prison.

Unlike Nelson, however, Smith was warmly embraced by both people and high society. No embarrassment or sexual scandal was attached to him: only the glow of patriotism and glamour of adventure. At the Lord Mayor's Show, his carriage was pulled through the streets by a cheering mob. He was also warmly welcomed at Court and dined with the Prince of Wales at Brighton. Unable by convention to raise him to the peerage, the king gave Smith special permission to add supporters to his family coat of arms, normally a right restricted to nobility. Smith chose a tiger and a lamb, representing war and peace. He took '*Coeur de lion*' as his motto – a tribute to his idol King Richard the Lionheart – and depicted his Chelengk on a turban as his heraldic crest. This is the only reproduction of Smith's Chelengk, as, unlike Nelson, he was never portrayed wearing it. An original drawing of the crest, completed under Smith's supervision at the College of Arms, shows a similar jewel to his rival's, with radiating rays and a central star within a wreath and bow.

Having circled each other for years, it seems Nelson and Smith did not meet until May 1802, when they both attended a fancy-dress ball in Bond Street to celebrate the Peace of Amiens. Nelson went as a Spaniard – 'not the first time he dressed the Spaniard well', quipped the *Morning Post*, recalling the Battle of Cape St Vincent – and Smith in his robes as an 'Egyptian'.[20] A month later, more soberly dressed, they met again at the London Tavern for a fundraising dinner in aid of the Naval Asylum, an orphanage for children whose fathers had lost their lives in the navy. As guest of honour, Nelson spoke first, but it was Smith who was the star turn, giving an emotional address recalling his many friends killed in action, including Captain Miller, a Nile captain, who had died when his ship *Theseus* blew up off Acre. When he then broke down in tears, 'a solemn silence prevailed for several minutes and soft sympathy filled many a manly bosom, until Sir Sidney was roused by the thunder of applause which followed.'[21] Nelson's reaction to the lachrymose speech can be imagined. However, like Smith he willingly contributed to a monument, arranged by Alexander Davison and crafted by sculptor John Flaxman, to be erected in Miller's memory in St Paul's Cathedral.

Despite being upstaged at the dinner, Nelson was warming to Smith, in whom he saw so much of himself. Just days later, they both went to a garden party in Wimbledon hosted in the admiral's honour by his neighbour, the banker Benjamin Goldsmid. Wandering the lawns together, they enjoyed duets performed by Emma and the celebrated Jewish tenor John Braham.[22] When the Hamiltons then took Nelson away for the tour to Wales, the astute Goldsmid erected a Turkish-style tent and held a similar event for Smith. The two heroes dined again in public at the Mansion House in September, in a further display of patriotic unity and personal reconciliation. In a letter to Smith's father, Sir William Hamilton called them, 'the two greatest heroes of the age and one of the glories of my life is the having so united them, that it will not be an easy matter for the evil-disposed to part them asunder again'.[23]

Smith had many admirers, but found love harder to find than fame, or scandal. Like the similar-looking Lord Byron and the disfigured Nelson, he enjoyed rock-star status with his outlandish costumes, jewels, unconventional lifestyle and eye-catching exploits. After the Nile, George Matcham had warned Nelson that:

> every description of persons especially the young women have the serious intention to eat you up *alive* and God knows (the Barbarians) your physical, corporal substance will not go much

further than a sprat but I suppose they mean to intoxicate themselves with the spirit.[24]

Emma also knew about Nelson's sexual reputation and his attraction to women before they embarked on their affair. 'Pray do not let your fascinating Neapolitan Dames approach too near him,' Earl St Vincent had written to her before Nelson reached Naples, 'for he is made of flesh & blood & cannot resist their temptation.'[25] She had since become obsessively jealous of other women, despite Nelson assuring her that, 'I might be trusted with fifty virgins naked in a dark room'.[26] Likewise, Nelson feared the predatory Prince of Wales as a rival, growing agitated at the thought of the lascivious George dining with Emma when he was away at sea.

It was ironic then that Sidney Smith's most fanatical devotee was Caroline, Princess of Wales, who, after separating acrimoniously from her philandering husband, had retreated to Montague House at Blackheath to enjoy a succession of lovers herself. The famously filthy princess met Smith early in 1802, introduced by her neighbour Sir John Douglas, a colonel of marines and veteran of the siege of Acre, who had carried news of the Convention of El Arish to Nelson in Palermo. With indifferent health, Smith used Sir John's house as a refuge from his creditors and the bustle of town. Caroline was further drawn to Smith as his elderly father, General Smith, now languishing in Dover with a coterie of women, was rumoured to have saved her father, the Duke of Brunswick, from capture by the French in 1759. Soon Smith was frequently visiting her house, often clandestinely wrapped in a cloak and using a private entrance leading to Greenwich Park. Rumours started to spread. A pageboy found them 'sitting close together in so *familiar* a posture as to *alarm* him very much'.[27] Worse, a maid claimed she discovered the princess and Smith in a bedroom, 'in such an indecent situation that she immediately left the room and was so shocked that she fainted away at the door'.[28] There was talk of a child, never proved as the princess was in the habit of fostering children, muddling natural with adopted children being a common ruse also employed by Emma and Nelson.

Caroline blamed Lady Douglas for all the gossip, which she knew might be used by the Prince of Wales to divorce her. She retaliated by sending Sir John obscene drawings, apparently in her own hand, of 'Sir Sidney Smith doing Lady Douglas your amiable wife'. When challenged by Sir John, Smith flatly denied any impropriety, adding, 'and had I been so base as to attempt anything of the kind under your roof, I should deserve you to shoot me like a mad dog'.[29] Word of the escalating scandal soon reached the palace, which instigated a 'Delicate Investigation' into the conduct of the princess. The enquiry heard allegations of her other love affairs with politician George Canning, artist Thomas Lawrence and another naval officer called Captain Manby. Testimony was taken concerning the state of the royal bedlinen, with further evidence suggesting that breast milk had been seen staining the princess's gown before a baby appeared in her household. Lady Douglas even accused the princess of propositioning her, as well as revealing her pregnancy and many affairs over their private conversations. In her vigorous defence, Caroline admitted that, 'Sir Sidney's Smiths conversation, his account of his various and extraordinary events, and heroic achievements in which he had been concerned, amused and interested me.' She also could not deny that he had visited her often, but claimed he had done so to advise her on the decoration of one of her rooms 'after the fashion of a Turkish tent'. Smith had produced a drawing of the tent belonging to Murad Bey, the Mameluke ruler of Egypt defeated by the French, used for the signing of the treaty at El Arish, which now resided in the Shropshire garden of Colonel Hill of the 90th Regiment. Royal upholsterer Nicolas Morel had been engaged to drape the Turkish room in rich silks and satins, with Smith teaching the princess how to draw pretty 'Arabesques' on the ceiling.[30]

Despite evidence from servants that these cosy interior decorating meetings had lasted late into the evening, sometimes in darkness, nothing was proved. When the Duke of Kent then intervened to prevent the bitter dispute spiralling out of control and affecting his fragile-minded father the king, the matter was quietly dropped. The princess escaped with a royal reprimand and a warning about her future conduct. 'Whether the attractions of Sir Sidney Smith were only incitements to, or actually the cause of criminality with the Princess, he now only knows,' wrote Smith's biographer in 1839, when everyone else involved in the *cause célèbre* was dead.[31] Inevitability, given the vehemence of Lady Douglas's accusations, the case damaged Smith's reputation, further dividing opinion about him. Close friends rallied to his defence, but for others it seemed that, like Nelson, Smith was becoming:

> immersed in the vapours of his intolerable vanity; that all that ever was sterling in the man is totally evaporated, and that nothing remains of him but a gaudy shell, tricked out with ribbons and stars, and all the blazonry of which beggarly monarchs are so lavish, and fools so greedy.[32]

12

THE FAREWELL

Nelson had hoped and expected more from the Battle of Copenhagen in 1801. But the toppling then murder of Tsar Paul, whose sudden conversion from friend to foe had triggered the British attack, made the victory inconvenient for a government now courting the new tsar, Alexander. As a sop to Nelson, the king made him viscount, but there was no issuing of medals, grants or official awards this time. To Nelson's fury, even the usually generous City of London failed to offer its customary vote of thanks. The admiral was notoriously sensitive to criticism, and such insults were not easily forgotten, especially when they also affected his close-knit 'band of brothers', one of whom, Captain Riou, had died at Copenhagen. Nelson sulkily refused all future invitations to the Guildhall, and to the end of his life never again wore the king's medals for the battles of Cape St Vincent and the Nile. Lloyd's Coffee House gave Nelson another £500 for the purchase of more silverware, but only the Sultan of Turkey sent a decoration: his new gold Medal of Egypt, first class, to be worn with the diamond star of the Crescent. 'This mark of regard from the Sultan made a strong impression on my mind,' Nelson told Prime Minister Henry Addington, pointedly suggesting that perhaps the English king would like to bestow it on him? The Ottoman award simply highlighted his sadness over the lack of recognition from his own country, as Selim's medal would 'have its alloy' without one from his own monarch shining beside it.[1]

Nevertheless, Nelson's elevation in the English peerage, together with his accumulation of various foreign orders of chivalry since the Nile, necessitated a further change to his coat of arms. Viscount and ducal coronets were now added together with representations of the orders of St. Ferdinand and of the Crescent. Opportunity was also taken to correct the Chelengk heraldic crest which was still portrayed as the jewel seen by Spencer Smith in Constantinople and not the jewel with its thirteen diamond plumes presented to Nelson at Naples. The revised design shows the jewel painted by Beechey with flowerhead clusters and openwork design but it also revealed, for the first time, that the jewel's star was highlighted in red enamel not blue as on the original Chelengk, probably in tribute to the red ensign of the sultan's navy.

Titles and status needed money. Nelson returned to London from the Baltic with nowhere to live, having separated from Fanny. He still entertained unrealistic dreams of retiring with Emma to Bronte, but in the meantime he asked her to find them a suitably secluded property near London on a budget of £3,000. She found Merton Place, a neat but neglected property with some fifty acres in Surrey, costing three times as much. George Matcham and Alexander Davison offered loans of £3,000 each and Nelson took out a mortgage to cover the rest, but these further debts forced him to consider selling his diamond presents because, as he had once said, 'jewels give not money or drink'.[2] Emma had already sold most of her own jewels for £2,900 to Cripps & Francillon, jewellers in the Strand, afterwards complaining she had suffered 'a heavy loss' despite Cripps' proud boast that he gave 'the utmost value' for diamonds, pearls and gems.[3] Sir William was so touched by the sacrifice of Emma's diamonds that he had spent £169 on various small items to replace them, such as simple silver earrings and a Maltese cross set with blood-red garnets in honour of Emma's decoration from the tsar.[4] From sea, Nelson also sent his lover gold bracelets and Venetian long chains. 'I allow no one to make my own Emma presents,' he declared stubbornly, 'but her Nelson.'[5]

Bereft of precious stones, Emma pinned her hopes on winning the lottery for the Pigot diamond, a 48-carat glimmering Leviathan valued at £30,000. She was not alone. The *Morning Post* reported:

> At the return of the Naval Hero of the Nile, the fashionable fair, in compliment to his bravery have adopted the Turkish Aigrette as an elegant appendage of dress, and as they are composed of different materials, wishing to possess what others cannot have to 'grace their plume' they crowd the places of sale, in hope of purchasing the fortunate number that entitles them to that unparalleled stone, the PIGOT diamond.[6]

Nelson was rightly sceptical: 'buy the right number,' he told her, 'or it will be money thrown away.'[7] But the gambler in Emma would not be dissuaded, and she wasted two guineas on one of the 11,000 other losing tickets. The winner put the stone up for auction at Christie's, where it sold, this being wartime, for a cut-price £9,500 to an agent acting for royal jewellers Rundell & Bridge.

Nelson had criticised 'the distress, which Sir William must every day feel, in knowing his excellent wife sold her jewels to get a house for him'.[8] But he was now forced to do the same, discretely asking Davison to sell some of his treasures. The 'List of Diamonds' he had entrusted to Davison back in February was marked with those items he wished to cash in. They included the diamond boxes given by the tsar, the King of Sardinia and the Valida Sultan, and the 'picture' presented by King Ferdinand. The '*Aigrette from G Sr*' and his diamond star were not tagged for sale.[9]

The highlighted items on Nelson's list tallies exactly with a schedule of 'pictures boxes etc' prepared by his wife Fanny, found in Davison's papers. This confirms her knowledge of the sales and suggests the schedule was either the original instruction to sell, which Davison then used to annotate Nelson's list, or a query seeking recompense for herself. Like the disappointing sale of the much-hyped Pigot diamond, the offers Nelson received for these baubles were considered 'shameful'.[10] He hesitated to accept, but by December 1801 was writing disconsolately to his bankers to confirm the sale of 'Diamonds' to pay £3,000 back to Davison for his loan for the purchase of Merton.[11] Nelson felt aggrieved because the three boxes alone had been valued for £4,700 in the *Naval Chronicle*, but times were hard and he did not appreciate the difference between buying and selling.

After Emma's own unhappy experience with the wily old jeweller Cripps, the sale of Nelson's diamonds was probably arranged either through Rundell & Bridge, makers of the Egyptian Club sword and the Nile silver, or John Salter, who promoted himself on his trade label as a buyer of 'Diamonds Pearls, Old Gold & Silver'.[12] In his twenties, Salter was an ambitious young swordsmith who had recently taken over the business of a retiring jeweller and silversmith. Situated at 35 the Strand, beneath the sign of the 'Golden Star' near the fashionable Adelphi, Salter's shop was perfectly positioned to benefit from the passing trade of naval officers shuttling between the Admiralty in Whitehall and Navy Office at Somerset House. Growing up in Portsmouth, Salter was familiar with naval officers, having been apprenticed to William Read, one of just a handful of sword cutlers in the bustling sea port. Both Salter and Read were certainly known to Nelson. Using these skills and connections, it was natural that Salter should extend his new business in the Strand to making swords, as well as '*Epaulets, Sashes, Sword Knotts & Accoutrements*'.[13] Soon he was 'well known to all Naval Officers', building a thriving business supplying weapons to celebrated fighting captains such as Sir Edward Pellew.[14]

Nelson developed a warm regard for Salter. On his return from the Battle of Copenhagen, in a similar gesture to that enjoyed by artist William Beechey, he gifted Salter his hat worn at the action. This was a powerful endorsement of Salter's business, one he prominently displayed in his shop window, pinned with a cardboard replica of the Chelengk. Over his few remaining years, Nelson purchased many small gifts for family and friends from Salter, collecting the latest pattern naval sword from the shop just weeks before Trafalgar.[15] Salter knew the high value of Nelson's patronage. 'At any time [I] shall feel myself honoured with the commands of your Lordship,' he promised, 'and will execute them, with the greatest attention and punctuality.'[16] In May 1802, he visited Merton to prepare an inventory of Nelson's growing collection of silver and plate for use at home and at sea. Among the many domestic items he found there, many now decorated with Nelson's Chelengk crest, Salter noted down the 'Turkey Company' silver cup and 'Large Pedestal Ornamental & Emblematical figures', a present from Davison (now lost).[17] In 1804, following a spate of local burglaries, much of Nelson's silver was sent to town to join his diamonds in safe storage: first in the vaults of Alexander Davison's private bank in Pall Mall, then, when Davison was disgraced and imprisoned for electoral fraud, with Salter in the Strand.[18] John Lee, a midshipman in *Swiftsure* at the Battle of the Nile, saw them there with Nelson in September 1805 after encountering the admiral at Somerset House. As the two men headed down the street together, they were hustled on all sides by people craning to see the hero. With a smile, Nelson told the starstruck Lee how the excited crowd reminded him of his reception at Naples. Writing thirty years later, Lee could still clearly recall Nelson in civilian clothes, wearing green breeches, black gaiters, a yellow waistcoat, blue coat and cocked hat 'quite square'. He was also carrying a gold-headed cane, probably the one gifted to him by the merchants of Zante. An American tourist who also saw Nelson in the Strand recalled that his face was 'very much burnt from his having been long at sea' and how he walked with the familiar rolling gait of a sailor ashore. He pitied the admiral for the throng of excited people he attracted everywhere he went, which, 'if it be a gratification, while it is new, it must soon become extremely troublesome'.[19]

When they finally reached the sanctuary of Salter's shop, Nelson closed the door behind them, and with the faces of excited bystanders still eagerly pressed against the windows outside, he 'inspected all his swords which had been presented at different periods, with the diamond aigrette, numerous snuff boxes etc'. Lee had been in *Swiftsure* off Egypt when Kelim Efendi came looking for Nelson, so he was fascinated to finally see the sultan's famous jewel. It was probably also the last time the admiral handled his jewel before his death just weeks later.

By 1805, Merton had been transformed by Emma, at great expense, into a comfortable and handsome residence set in well-maintained grounds with sweeping lawns and a meandering stream. The purchase of neighbouring land had extended Nelson's domestic realm to over 160 acres, and there were plans to extend the house, which filled quickly with friends and family. Inside, the rooms were furnished with an eclectic collection of furniture, objects and artworks, some purchased, some inherited from Sir William, others recovered by Nelson from store in Soho. To English eyes, there was a distinctly foreign and garish feel to the decoration, the result of Emma's taste having been shaped in Naples. Gilded mirrors topped by his coat of arms reflected the fame of their owner through the house. The walls were lined with battle paintings, prints and portraits of Nelson. Trophies, captured weapons and his many luxurious presents lined the staircase and cluttered the rooms, the pale light glinting off silver and brightly coloured porcelain. A bill for £32 from upholsterer and interior decorator William Peddison reveals that at least six 'Ottoman stools' covered in Turkey carpet and scarlet cloth added an Eastern feel to the already vibrant interior.[20] Lord Minto thought it all in 'bad taste', carping that Nelson's house was 'a mere looking glass to view himself all day'.[21] But criticism of Merton was criticism of Emma, and Nelson would not listen. 'I will admit no display of taste at Merton but hers,' he told Davison. 'She bought it and I hope will continue to improve and beautify it to the day, at least, of my death.'[22] Yet all these improvements and the expensive furnishings came at a high price, forcing Nelson to sell still more jewels 'and other valuable presents' to (since 1804) Rundell, Bridge & Rundell, the royal goldsmiths on Ludgate Hill.[23]

Merton was a home and a refuge, with the bustle of servants and the hubbub of guests and family joined, in August 1805, by Nelson's daughter Horatia, fetched from care in London. When the admiral himself appeared after almost two years at sea, Emma rhapsodised that she was living in 'a paradise'.[24] These were busy days, with a queue of callers to the house and daily trips to town for news. After sharing so many dangers for so long, Nelson's officers gave him a beautiful gold watch to mark the end of their tour which played tunes and charted the lunar date.[25] But the happiness hid anxiety, and several times Emma took to her bed with growing dread of the call which eventually came with a report that the combined enemy fleet was preparing to leave port. At the Admiralty, Nelson pressed to return to sea and face the enemy for his grasp at immortality. His appeal was irresistible, and after just two weeks ashore, his bags were repacked and forwarded to *Victory* at Portsmouth ahead of the admiral's arrival. Time beat faster now. On 8 September, Sidney Smith was summoned to Merton, where he dined with Abraham Goldsmid and impressed young George Matcham when he 'talked of Acre' (recounting his exploits at length gained Smith the nickname 'Long Acre', after the famous London street).[26] Since his last meeting with Nelson, Smith had been elected to parliament on his family interest, endured a chilly posting to the North Sea, become embroiled in his affair with the Princess of Wales and been imprisoned for debt. Despite these setbacks, he remained irrepressible. Released from prison, he had been busily developing rockets and torpedoes for madcap operations against the French in the Channel, demonstrating them in person to William Pitt. Flush with government money, he ordered a new carriage, painted black and yellow.[27] Such an impetuosity with money blighted Smith's life.

As newly appointed commander-in-chief of the Mediterranean, Nelson had a more important task for his former rival than playing around with novelty weapons. 'With the map before us', he explained to Smith how he wanted him to take a squadron and defend the Kingdom of the Two Sicilies, which was again threatened by the French.[28] It was a concern close to his, and to Emma's heart. By posting Smith to such a sensitive region, Nelson was paying him a high compliment, and acknowledging his earlier misjudgement. They would return to the Mediterranean and fight side by side. The two men met again just days later in Downing Street. Nelson was there to collect his sailing orders from Foreign

Secretary Lord Castlereagh, although it was his awkward encounter with General Wellesley, later Duke of Wellington, which is now better remembered. Wellesley had recently returned from a triumphant campaign in India laden with luxurious trophies and carrying a magnificent diamond-hilted sword gifted by the residents of Bombay which rivalled anything of Nelson's. The admiral failed to recognise the suntanned general and at first spoke to him, so the duke liked to recount, 'in, really, a style so vain and silly as to surprise, and almost disgust me'. With dawning realisation, Nelson adjusted his tone, and Wellington his opinion, eventually conceding that the admiral was, after all, 'a very superior man'.[29]

In the throng of other officers impatiently awaiting orders at the Foreign Office, Nelson spotted the unmistakable figure of Sidney Smith. He invited him to dine again at Merton the next day, his last at home before departing for his ship. It was a strained and difficult meal, with Emma subdued and tearful, drinking and eating little. Most of Nelson's family had gone home, 'that they might escape the dreaded agonies of so painful a separation', leaving only the Matchams and Goldsmids as guests.[30] It is likely Smith tried to buoy everyone's spirits, but there was no escaping the dread hour when the carriage would arrive to take Nelson to Portsmouth. The visitors slipped away, leaving Nelson to whisper a prayer beside his sleeping daughter and to kiss Emma goodbye. Then he was gone.

The next morning, Nelson was glimpsed for a final time ashore by Benjamin Silliman, the American who had seen the admiral in London. By chance, Silliman was also in Portsmouth that day and caught sight of Nelson as he pushed through the crowds to reach *Victory*'s waiting barge. Perched on a gun battery, he noted how 'elegantly' Nelson was dressed for what would be his last public performance. Quoting Alexander Pope, Silliman jotted in his journal:

> coat blue and elegantly illuminated with stars and ribbons, of which his Lordship is said to be immoderately fond:
> *Or sigh for ribbons if thou art so silly*
> *Mark how they grave Lord Umbra or Sir Billy*
> Yes the hero of the Nile is pleased with stars and ribbons.[31]

13

THE DEATH

It was at Bath that Fanny heard that her husband had been killed. Susannah Bolton's daughter had glimpsed her there earlier that summer, telling Emma with stunning insensitivity, 'She looks shockingly really and very old. Mrs Matcham often wishes she was in heaven, we join, and make no doubt we have your good wishes on the occasion.'[1] Now the cruel jibes turned to sympathy. Lord Braham, First Lord of the Admiralty, wrote as soon as the dispatch arrived that:

> it is with the utmost concern that in the midst of victory I have to inform your ladyship of the death of your illustrious partner Lord Viscount Nelson. After leading the British fleet into close action with the enemy and seeing their defeat he fell by a musket ball entering his chest.[2]

The courier sent to Merton to tell Emma found her in bed wondering at the bells ringing in the village. 'I believe I gave a scream and fell back,' she recalled, 'and for ten hours after I could neither speak nor shed a tear.'[3] Sidney Smith heard at Dover, where he was waiting to attack Boulogne with his rockets and torpedoes. 'Alas, poor Nelson!' he exclaimed, 'I grieve on every account.'[4] Yet the heavy casualties at Trafalgar also lifted him up the Navy List to flag rank.

For selfish reasons, William Nelson had always followed his brother's campaigns closely. After Nelson sailed to meet the enemy in September, he had gone each morning to the public library in Canterbury to read the newspapers. He did the same as usual on 6 November 1805, but to spare him the pain of hearing the news in public, he was intercepted in the cathedral precincts by the mayor of Canterbury. 'They met on the Church pavement,' remembered a witness. 'I was present. Mr Bristow gave the news. The Doctor seemed much affected and shed tears, and turned back to his house, applying his white handkerchief to his eyes. In a few hours came the news directly from Government.'[5] A thousand thoughts and emotions must have surged through William's head. Now second Baron Nelson of the Nile, he knew he had to act quickly to secure his legacy, so together with a dazed Sarah he hurried to London that same day to rent rooms in a fashionable part of town.

As he hoped, the government was swift in propelling William to still dizzier heights of the peerage. Just four days after news of the battle reached England, he was dining with his lawyer William Haslewood when a note arrived from ailing Prime Minister William Pitt, 'communicating', as Haslewood put it:

> His Majesty's intentions to advance Lord Nelson to an earldom under the title of Earl Nelson of Trefalgar (or, as Mr Pitt spells it, Tresalgar) with the same remainders as in the present barony. His Majesty means, likewise, to apply to Parliament for an adequate provision to accompany the title.[6]

In his letter, Pitt had hoped the award 'will contribute some degree to sooth the feelings of those who have to struggle with the weight of domestic affliction, added to the sense of national loss, which pervades the whole country'.[7]

The new earl was fulsome in his thanks, and unusually humble. He replied that same evening:

> I am at a loss to express the complicated feeling of a heart borne down at once with the deepest affliction for the loss of my good and gallant brother, and with gratitude for the magnificent

> intention of our gracious Sovereign towards the family of his departed servant.[8]

To a friend he explained, a little defensively, that, 'No titles, no distinctions which all the potentates of the earth can bestow, can make amends for the loss of such a man. But it was the will of god and to his will we must submit.'[9] It was Cuthbert Collingwood, second in command at Trafalgar, who expressed the opinion of many when he heard about William Nelson's elevation. 'Nature never intended him for anything superior to a village curate,' he exclaimed, 'and here has Fortune, in one of her frisks, raised him, without his body and mind having anything to do with it, to the highest dignity.'[10]

Of immediate concern to William was his brother's will. Nelson's final testament, dated 10 May 1803, had been officially registered, with no less than seven codicils, by his solicitor William Haslewood as soon as news of Trafalgar reached London. As joint executor of the document with Haslewood, William was the first to know its contents, although he was probably already familiar with them. Yet, knowing his brother's habit of changing his mind, he may have feared other undiscovered codicils. In the will he was left Nelson's 'Egyptian Club' sword, its gold hilt shaped like a crocodile, and a gold Freedom box from the City of London. Other recipients of personal bequests included Nelson's sisters, and close friends like Captain Thomas Hardy, who was bequeathed the admiral's telescopes, and Alexander Davison, who was passed 'my Turkish Gun, Scimitar and Canteen'.[11] These were the trophies gifted by Albanian warlord Ali Pasha of Ioannina after the Battle of the Nile, which Nelson knew his ambitious agent would cherish.

Nelson had always wanted Emma to have the diamond star of the Order of the Crescent 'to wear for my sake', and this desire was repeated in his last will. Just months later, Emma sent her 'dymond star' to the jeweller John Salter, 'as he is to do something to it'.[12] It then disappeared, possibly converted to a diamond anchor decorated with Nelson's initials to better broadcast Emma's former association with the hero. She would spend a further £2 6*s* with Salter for repairs to this 'brilliant anchor' in 1812 before it was then sold or pawned to Davison.[13] Emma was also bequeathed Merton and seventy of its rolling Surrey acres. The rest of the land was to be sold to pay legacies and help enable the executors to purchase an annuity paying £1,000 a year to Nelson's widow Fanny.

Reading his will, it was obvious that Nelson had laboured over the future of his duchy at Bronte in Sicily. As Ferdinand had given him permission to nominate his successor, he placed the duchy in trust, naming William as heir. Nelson instructed that the duchy should follow the same route allowed to his English titles by remainder. This meant that failing William's male heirs, Bronte would go in turn to the sons of his sisters Susannah Bolton and Catherine Matcham. This way all his titles could be kept together. He also gave permission for the trustees to sell the duchy if they wanted, so long as the proceeds were used to purchase an estate in Britain. The Bronte trust also included those most precious jewels which Nelson deemed family heirlooms, 'the diamond hilted Sword given to me by His said Sicilian Majesty, the diamond Aigrette presented to me by the Grand Signior, my Collar of the Order of the Bath, Medals of the Order of Saint Ferdinand and Insignia of other Orders.' In this way, the sultan's jewel was to be held in future by the person then 'entitled to the possession of my real estates in the Kingdom of Farther Sicily'.[14]

With his private life veering in a new direction with Emma, and facing an uncertain future, Nelson had fiddled endlessly with his will, adding several codicils before his death. The second, dated 6 September 1803, detailed a legacy of £4,000 to 'my adopted daughter Horatia' and the desire that she would one day make 'a fit wife for my dear nephew Horatio Nelson'.[15] But it was his final written instruction which would have the lasting and most profound impact. This was sensationally revealed when *Victory* returned to England in December 1805 carrying Nelson's decomposing body. Described by his flag captain Thomas Masterman Hardy as 'a kind of codicil',[16] the note had been written by Nelson in his pocket book on the morning of 21 October with the enemy on his horizon. Witnessed by Hardy and Captain Blackwood of *Euryalus*, it detailed the admiral's desire that Emma should be rewarded by government for her vital role in securing the victualling of the British fleet before and then after the Battle of the Nile. In highly unorthodox and theatrical manner, Nelson left Emma as 'a legacy to my King and Country, that they will give her ample provision to maintain her rank in life'.[17] The controversial plea was composed after months of agitation by Emma and Nelson that she should be awarded with her own government pension for her work in Naples. As widow of a former ambassador, there was precedent for such a grant. But low-born, lacking interest and with a scandalous reputation, Emma's claims had been ignored. Written on the verge of battle, Nelson was seeking now to hold the government to ransom in the event of his death.

Just hours later, as he lay in agony below decks in *Victory,* battle raging overhead, Nelson had gasped to 'let my dear Lady Hamilton have my hair, and all other things belonging to me'.[18] It was a death bed entreaty which acquired a sacred urgency to his shocked and grieving captain, Thomas Masterman Hardy. As soon as *Victory* anchored off Portsmouth, Hardy wrote to Emma and assured her that, 'I have his hair, lockets, rings, breast-pin and all your Ladyship's pictures in a box by themselves, and they shall be delivered to no one but yourself.'[19] Mention of Nelson's 'breast-pin' suggests that the admiral had the diamond star of Order of the Crescent with him at Trafalgar, and that Hardy knew it was destined for Emma. Together with the soon infamous pocket book and a copy of Nelson's will, these personal belongings were delivered to Emma in London on 16 December by Blackwood, who also carried remnants of Nelson's bloodstained uniform. As executor, William insisted he was present at this highly charged meeting, departing afterwards with the will, pocket book and the uniform coat his brother had being wearing when fatally wounded, together with other items he considered family heirlooms. Still numb with shock, Emma had weakly complied, but learning that, almost with his last breath, Nelson had instructed Hardy to give her 'all other things belonging to me', she soon agitated to have the coat returned.[20] The Trafalgar coat had quickly acquired a near sacred status for her.

Eventually, under pressure from his embarrassed wife, the earl agreed to the coat's loan. Sarah Nelson had struggled to cope with the seismic shift in her family fortunes since the admiral's death and the ill-blood it was already creating. Within a month of the devastating news, she had written 'from my heart' to Emma wishing, 'you and all of us to live as dear friends and to make our short lives as comfortable to each other as we can, and any little foibles each may have to overlook them for we are none of us perfection'.[21] Now she wrote again, firmly but kindly informing Emma that:

> there can be no doubt to whom this precious relic belongs [but] My lord is willing, tho' done with a bleeding heart, to part with it to you, for your life provided, my dear friend, you give us assurances it shall at some future time be restored to the Heir of the Title, to be by him preserved.[22]

She suggested Emma display the coat in a glass case, 'Hermetically sealed'. Instead, Emma took to draping the coat melodramatically across her bed in the months which followed. One of the Goldsmid children who saw it like that was thrilled to see 'the hole where the bullet passed through stiffened with congealed blood'.[23] Emma had no intention of ever returning the coat to the Nelsons.

The pocket book codicil was irritating for William, causing him more work. Its contents did not affect him directly, and although he may have failed to promote its contents, he certainly did not stand in its way. His friendship with Emma was fast cooling, but he diligently fulfilled his duty as executor, bringing this unorthodox document which carried moral but little legal weight to the attention of ministers. He also allowed Horatia's surname to be changed from the pseudonymous 'Thompson' – used to disguise her parentage – to the glorious (and true) one of Nelson. The earl could not be blamed for a failure of government to fulfil Nelson's last wishes, yet he was now condemned to years of accusation and demands for money from Emma.

On 22 February 1806, the sultan's jewel changed hands again when, having given Emma ample time to fetch Nelson's diamonds from Salter's shop, William hurried to Piccadilly to collect his heirlooms. He scrawled a receipt for:

> The diamond aigrette presented to his Lordship by the Grand Signior, the sword presented to him by the Captains who fought at the battle of the Nile, the diamond sword presented to him by the King of the Two Sicilies and the Collar of the Order of the Bath.[24]

Had she been pressed for the sultan's pelisse too, Emma might have remembered that Nelson had previously willed it to her. But a gold City of London freedom box awarded after the Battle of Cape St Vincent was not forthcoming, and William was still chasing it a month later. When he was told that Fanny had the gold box, he urged Haslewood to recover it '*without delay*', sending a grudging apology when it was then discovered at Merton after all.[25]

As was custom, William returned his brother's sash for the Order of the Bath to the king, who took it back ungraciously, fumbling with the red silk before walking away without a word. Undeterred, William launched into an unctuous speech of how his brother had died in 'the true religion that teaches to sacrifice one's life for one's King and country'. To which the king turned and bluntly replied, 'He died the death he wished.'[26] The diamonds and boxes were deposited for safekeeping at Rundell's, with John Salter now seen perhaps as too close to Emma and no longer a safe custodian. The earl was given a receipt by Rundell's employee George Jeffreys for 'a brillt Sword, a Rose Diad aigrette, a Gold snuff box to lay in our Store Room to be returned to him or his Order without Gratuity; Casualties by Fire, Thieves or other Accidents excepted'.[27] In 1815, this same Jeffreys would steal £1,500 from his firm and flee to America.[28]

Alexander Davison, Nelson's friend and agent, found it still more difficult taking delivery of his promised 'Turkish Gun, Scimitar and

Canteen' from Emma. She sent the gun –a distinctive Balkan type of long firearm beautifully decorated in silver, ivory and mother of pearl – and the water canteen, a luxurious flask similarly embellished, in July 1806, but in September Davison was still pressing her for the sword. Emma appears to have been confused about which sword Nelson was referring to in his will (he had many). She may not have been present when Nelson took possession of these trophies from Ali Pasha in January 1800, and had clearly not given them much thought since, unlike the diamond boxes and jewels, they were not especially precious to her. The 'Turkish sabre' sword she eventually sent Davison was a French cavalry sabre decorated in fashionable *faux Damascus* style with pseudo-Islamic script. This was more likely the weapon drunkenly presented by the Turkish captain in Palermo when he delivered the tsar's box and which Emma had theatrically kissed, than the sword given to Nelson by Ali Pasha.[29] Nevertheless, Davison accepted it in good faith, then perpetuated a lasting myth by having it engraved, 'This Scymeter together with a Gun and Canteen were presented by the Grand Signior to Horatio, Viscount Nelson and by will bequeathed to his friend Alexander Davison, 10th May 1803'. Nelson had never mentioned any connection between the Sultan of Turkey and these trophies, but nor had he publicised their gift from Ali Pasha (a feared and controversial figure). It seems Davison simply assumed they were presents from the sultan, and was happy to display them as such. With the delivery of the City of London presentation sword and gold Zante cane to Catherine Matcham, the collection of the silver Turkey Company cup by Susannah Bolton and the division of the service of Nile silver among the family, Emma had now been stripped of all the trophies won by Nelson. Only the flagstaff of *L'Orient* remained at Merton, and this she gifted to a church being built at Milford.

The earl also had to deal with his sister-in-law Fanny, whom he had not seen or heard from for months. A draft of his letter of condolence shows him agonising over its tone as he sought to be conciliatory. He wrote carefully:

> If I could feel pleasure amidst so many mournful reflections as press upon my mind, it would be in the opportunity afforded me of renewing with your Ladyship that intercourse of affectionate and kind offices which I once hoped would have always marked our lives which untoward circumstances deeply to be lamented have occasioned some interruption of.[30]

The letter reached Fanny at Bath, with her short reply, newly discovered, offering her only surviving and heartfelt comment on her husband's death. 'This truly melancholy event,' she wrote, 'has affected me most sincerely notwithstanding his long estrangement from me as a husband and protector.' Her words suggest that being abandoned caused Fanny more anguish than her husband's sexual betrayal, which she had offered to forgive, as no doubt she had done in the past. They reflected the vulnerability of a deserted wife in an era when women had few legal or property rights. It made the behaviour of her family, to whom she had turned for support but received only abuse, still more inexcusable. Understandably, she was reluctant to accept the earl's awkward attempt at reconciliation now. She was too hurt and rightly sceptical of his motivation. 'The latter part of your lordships letter,' she responded stiffly, 'is I think meant in extenuation of your conduct towards me which has its due weight with your lordships very humble servant Frances H. Bronte & Nelson.'[31] But it would take another five years before she agreed to see the Nelsons, a difficult meeting arranged in Bath by their daughter Charlotte. 'I think they have received some satisfaction from a shake of my hand,' Fanny reported to her banker after the awkward meeting.[32]

When Fanny returned to town in December 1805, she spent £48 on clothes to mourn the man who had deserted her.[33] She also consulted her lawyers about her husband's will, learning she would receive an annuity of £1,000 to replace the £2,000-a-year alimony agreed at the time of their separation. In accepting the annuity, Fanny was asked to drop all future claims on Nelson's estate. For the first time, too, she read openly about Horatia, telling a friend wearily, 'that she does *not know who the girl* is that was so particularly mentioned in Lord Nelson's will, and left to the care of Lady Hamilton *who knows who she is*'.[34] The child was awarded £4,000, with Nelson's further desire that she might one day marry his nephew, William's son Horace Nelson, now Viscount Merton, 'if he proves worthy, in Lady Hamilton's estimation, of such a treasure as I am sure she will be'.[35]

Like the new earl, Fanny was given a £500 silver gilt commemorative vase from the Patriotic Fund, but she had little else to show for eighteen years of marriage to England's greatest naval hero: no house, no trophies and few relics. When the marriage broke down in 1801, the Nelsons' belongings had been put into store in a Soho warehouse, with Nelson ordering its manager 'not permit the smallest article to be removed or taken away by any person without an order from *myself*'.[36] Fanny had asked for some linen, glass and porcelain, 'no great quantity but of great consequence to me. I look upon these things as mine although nothing passed on the subject.'[37] This included silver from her first marriage, a porcelain wine cooler decorated with Nelson's coat of arms sent her by Davison after the Battle of the Nile (which, inadvertently, showed the undelivered Chelengk) and a pair of porcelain vases decorated with scenes from Nelson's battles given to her by Earl and Lady Spencer.[38] With all eyes on Emma, Fanny maintained a quiet dignity, signing herself, as she was entitled, 'Nelson & Bronte': a reminder that she remained Duchess of Bronte. Now when she walked past the print shops in St James's Street, she saw not a biting satire of her husband by Gillray but a depiction of his death framed like the Passion of Christ.

A £2,000 a year government pension was awarded to Fanny, triggering a dispute with her husband's executors who had instructions to cancel her £1,000 annuity if she received an equal or greater sum from the government following his death in battle. She might have let the matter drop if it had not been for the torrent of money poured on the earl by parliament. 'Here I am,' he had grumbled ungratefully, 'an Earl of the United Kingdom, without a single inch of landed property & without a shilling in my pocket.'[39]

Now he was given an annuity of £5,000 and a huge grant of £120,000 (maybe £8 million today), comprising £90,000 to purchase a mansion and estate, £10,000 to furnish it and £10,000 for each of his surviving sisters (William's request for a further £2,000 a year for his wife was refused point-blank). Even in the heady and charged days following Trafalgar, there was opposition in parliament to such extravagance. Colonel Mark Wood MP queried whether a country with a national debt of £500 million could afford it, and Sir Philip Francis MP questioned the justification of using the gift of Blenheim Palace to the Duke of Marlborough as precedent for presenting the Nelsons with a mansion. Sir Philip pointed out:

> What makes the essential difference, in the two cases, is that the duke of Marlborough was alive and had children living. He, who received the reward, had earned it by acts of his own. Lord Nelson's collateral relations personally, are unknown to the public, and can have no claim but what they derive from the accidental honour of bearing his name, and from services, in which they had no share. The gratitude, due to his memory, would, in my opinion, be better expressed with less profusion.[40]

However, critics of the award were rowing against the powerful tide of popular feeling lifting William and Sarah Nelson into their fortune. According to Emma, the Nelsons were dining with her when news of the vote in parliament confirming the grant came through. Triumphant, the earl had taken his brother's pocket book, containing the admiral's desperate last plea to government on Emma's behalf, then 'threw it to me, and said with a very coarse expression, "that I might now do as I pleas'd with it"'.[41] William was summoned to the palace to receive the grant of money from the king in person. His son and heir Horace went too, dazzling onlookers by wearing the diamond-hilted sword presented to his uncle by the King of Sicily: 'the most brilliant ever exhibited at this court', thought one observer.[42]

Hearing that the earl was planning an 'official' life of his brother, penned by John McArthur and the Prince of Wales's personal chaplain James Stanier Clarke (to add 'rank' to the enterprise),[43] Emma paid a down-at-heel hack writer called James Harrison to rush her own side of the story into print. Harrison, who lived at Merton whilst he hurriedly worked on the book, was unashamedly biased towards Emma as he tried to strengthen her claim on government. Among his many aims was to portray her relationship with Nelson as 'a pure and virtuous attachment' and to vilify and slander Fanny. As a flavour, Harrison noted:

> The present Earl and Countess will long remember the mortifying *hauteur* which they so often experienced from her ladyship, even at their brother's table, as well as other occasions, where they were then deemed of insufficient consequence to appear in company with so lofty a personage as their elevated sister-in-law, over whom they now triumph in rank: such are the fluctuations of fortune: such, not unfrequently, the salutary checks to the career of vain ambition.[44]

The book sought to dispel the impression that Nelson had died rich, revealing to its shocked readers how the admiral had sold 'many jewels and other valuable presents' to pay off his large debts. 'His income,' wrote Harrison, under Emma's direction, 'had been rendered considerable, it is true: but the grandeur of his character had rendered him too great for his income; it ought therefore, to have been sufficiently enlarged. The nation will never be ruined by rewarding such men!'[45] When it appeared, Fanny thought Harrison's *Life of Nelson* 'the basest production that ever was offered to the public … replete with untruths'.[46] Criticism of her son Josiah in the book was especially hurtful to her. Fanny had her revenge within weeks of Emma's death in 1815 when a bestselling account of her rival's life, entitled *Memoirs of Lady Hamilton*, was published anonymously. 'Written for the Viscountess', according to a shocked family member, the book castigated Emma and the 'inexcusable failings' of Nelson.[47]

Like the earl himself, Clarke and McArthur's three-volume *Life and Services of Horatio Viscount Nelson* sought to rise majestically above its racier rivals. Like many 'authorised' lives, this made it a dull and uninspired read, enlivened only by lavish illustrations commissioned at ruinous expense on the urging of the Prince of Wales and the earl. The frontispiece was ordered from the American-born artist Benjamin West, who portrayed the apotheosis of Nelson as the hero is offered up to Britannia by Neptune, god of the sea. Among a crowd of cherubs, one is seen removing the sultan's jewel from the hero's lifeless body, its sparkling diamonds turned away and dimmed in death. The book's vivid battle scenes were provided by master of the genre Nicholas Pocock, whose son Isaac, also an artist, re-imagined Nelson's childhood home in Norfolk from a sketch in the earl's possession. Trained by George Romney, whose portraits of Emma had propelled her to international stardom back in the 1780s, Isaac Pocock was also engaged to paint full-length portraits of Charlotte and Horace Nelson for the family's private collection. Styled by Emma, in her portrait Charlotte is shown in an Arcadian setting, wearing a long silk fringed shawl, looking poised and self-assured. For his portrait, Horace was dressed in the pastel pink clothes of an esquire to a Knight of the Bath, as he had been for the inauguration ceremony of his uncle's award at Westminster Abbey in 1801. Both paintings have since been cut down, but photographs of the originals show Charlotte beside a classical column with a stream beyond, possibly the so-called 'Nile' which burbled through the gardens at Merton. Horace was depicted in the abbey, cap and sword in hand, standing in front of the tomb for a fallen knight beneath a funeral hatchment for his dead uncle.

The publication of Nelson's will in the newspapers at Christmas 1805 seemed to confirm Emma's growing suspicion that the earl was 'leaky'.[48] The public was gripped and anxious to read all the juicy details. They had watched as Nelson earned his jewels, medals and orders; applauded when he wore them; and now thrilled to know where they would all go next. Most of all, they wanted to see his decaying remains back in London.

14

THE EARL

For three days after Christmas, Nelson's body lay in state in the Painted Hall of the Royal Naval Hospital at Greenwich, beneath sumptuous scenes of maritime glory. The body rested in the simple coffin crafted by Hallowell from the timbers of *L'Orient* within an outer lead-lined casket covered in black felt and gilt emblems by the upholsterer William Peddison. The earl had fretted about moving his brother's corpse from his ship, 'not knowing whether it would be corrupted and produce any disagreeable smell by being kept out of spirits so many days before the internment'.[1] In the Painted Hall, the coffin was displayed beneath a soaring black velvet canopy embroidered in silk with coronets and silver Chelengks. At its foot were arranged the heraldic trophies of a fallen knight: a sword, gauntlet, shield and a helmet crested by a naval crown, 'ornamented with the *cheleek* on triumphal plume, with models richly gilt'.[2] This large gilded wood Chelengk, glittering in the light of 200 candles, sat at the very heart of the moving spectacle. Borne by Somerset Herald, an officer of the College of Arms, the helmet with its Chelengk crest would follow the body to its internment in St Paul's, followed by Captain Laforey, a Trafalgar veteran, carrying a standard similarly emblazoned.

It was said that 30,000 people came to see the lying in state. There was a stampede on the first day, with many injuries and the cavalry called out to control the crowd. Earl Nelson went to

Greenwich with his son before the spectacle opened to approve the arrangements and see Reverend Dr Alexander Scott, the chaplain in *Victory* who had been with Nelson when he died. Scott would remain with the body day and night until its internment, 'and so emaciated and afflicted was his appearance at the funeral, that many persons, who saw him there, said, "he looked like the chief mourner"'.[3] Young Horace Nelson 'was very much affected, and wept a great deal' as he listened to Scott's moving account of his uncle's last moments.[4] Having already spoken with Hardy, the earl was interested to hear Scott's version of his brother's death and what exactly he had said about Emma. There was another sensitive issue between the two men. Before Trafalgar, Nelson had fully expected his brother to be promoted in the church in the event of his victory – probably to Dean of Canterbury – promising to then secure William's vacant prebendal stall for his chaplain. 'I must not ask for both now,' he had confided to Scott, 'for the stall is a good thing to give up to get the deanery; but if I meet the French fleet I'll ask for both, and have them too.'[5] Although William had not been advanced in the Church after the battle – being made earl and receiving vast sums of money was considered reward enough - it was widely thought he should still honour his brother's promise and resign the valuable stall in favour of Scott. But the earl was immovable, despite personal appeals from the Prince of Wales 'and others whom it seemed hardly possible he could refuse'.[6] William clung onto his stall – with its comfortable house in the Cathedral Close – for the rest of his life, leaving the popular Scott to eke out a living as a country vicar. It was another promise of his brother which William found impossible to honour.

On 8 January 1806, the body was conveyed up the Thames to Westminster to rest overnight at the Admiralty before the funeral the next day. As the pageant barge left the hospital mooring, it was forced around the stern of *Antelope*, the 14-gun sloop occupied by Sir Sidney Smith during his recent operations in the Channel.[7] Smith may have visited the Painted Hall to view the coffin, possibly with the Princess of Wales, who walked down from Blackheath for a private viewing with a 'few personages of high respectability and distinction'. On the day the funeral barge left Greenwich, however, he travelled to Plymouth to join his new flagship *Pompée*, which would take him on Nelson's mission to protect Sicily. Fanny Nelson would also miss her husband's funeral. As a woman, convention denied her, and Emma, any role in proceedings, so she returned to Bath ahead of the lying in state, anxious to avoid the public's prurient curiosity and refusing to accept callers, 'even my female friends'.[8]

As heir to the deceased, William should have been the chief and most visible mourner at the funeral. But in return for footing the estimated £30,000 bill, the government, rocked by recent scandals and setbacks in the war, took over the event to curry popular favour. William was forced to surrender the role of Chief Mourner to Admiral of the Fleet Sir Peter Parker. Being supplanted by an 84-year-old political appointee infuriated the touchy earl. 'It does not appear,' he complained ahead of the funeral, 'that I am to have anything to do with it, as a mourner or in any capacity whatever.'[9] In a further snub, he was not given spare tickets for the procession or granted the six coaches he requested for his family.[10] Instead, he was reduced to vetting the bloodlines of the guests and ordering the College of Arms to reduce the importance of Fanny in his brother's family tree, as 'it is enough to say he married the widow of Dr. Nisbet, a physician on the Island of Nevis, without mentioning whose daughter she was'. Josiah's name was to be erased altogether. 'Captain Nisbet's name can have no business in the Nelson pedigree,' he thundered. 'My family has no consanguinity nor even *affinity* with him now. I must absolutely forbid it.'[11]

Gold memorial rings decorated in enamels with Nelson's motto, monogram and coronets were ordered from John Salter for distribution among family and friends, fifty-eight in all.[12] Salter, who promoted his mourning jewellery business, worked rapidly, as George Matcham received his 'very handsome' ring in Wiltshire as early as 25 November.[13] Before the funeral, George visited Salter's to collect his mourning sword, a short ceremonial weapon with black japanned blade and hilt. A month later, Salter submitted his bill for the rings of £139 10*s*, complaining politely when the earl short-changed him by ten shillings.[14] He might be excused this oversight as, apart from arranging the legacies to Emma and Fanny, the earl had had to deal with the mountain of debt at Merton. His brother had owed over £17,000 in unpaid tradesmen bills and loans from friends at the time of his death, around £1.2 million today.[15] Even with prize money due from Trafalgar (some £7,000), this was a challenging task and Haslewood was given strict instructions not to pay any further debts incurred by Emma, although some still slipped through. By February 1806, the most pressing bills had been settled, except Emma's grocery bill, which the earl, relieved the worst was over, agreed to pay. 'After so many hundreds we have already paid it would be folly to boggle at a few quarts of Turtle soup,' he told his lawyer, 'though by the dates my poor brother evidently was not in England.'[16]

When the day of the funeral finally arrived, the earl wrapped himself in 'deep sables' against the bitter chill and played a low-key role in the rituals, travelling in a mourning coach with his son at the rear of the snail-like procession to St Paul's Cathedral. *The Morning Chronicle*, an opposition newspaper edited by Nelson's Merton neighbour James Perry, noticed these slights. The paper reported that the earl:

> received from the people the most marked tokens of respect. We are sorry to say, that those who had the ordering of the spectacle were not equally attentive to him. While he and his son, Lord Viscount Merton sat in their mourning coach at the Admiralty, the undertaker's people took out of the traces a pair of horses, because they said they had not enough for the other carriages![17]

After Nelson was safely interred in the cathedral crypt, a large monument in marble was ordered from John Flaxman to join those of the many other heroes clustering the aisles of the cathedral above. They already included memorials to Captain Westcott, killed at the Nile; Captain Miller, who perished at Acre; and General Abercromby, frozen in stone at the moment he was fatally wounded in Egypt. Framed by traditional images of British valour such as the figure of Britannia and a lion, Flaxman chose to portray Nelson full length in modern uniform, not classical garb, with the Turkish pelisse draped over his right shoulder masking his amputation. With the exception of Gillray's biting satire, it is the only contemporary representation of the admiral wearing his fur robe, which the artist sculpted plushly luxurious out of the white marble. Flaxman used the pelisse as a device to mask the admiral's amputation, which may have appeared a jarring disability in a pantheon of idealised heroes.

There was a further rebuff to the earl when he asked for his brother's former agent and banker, Alexander Davison, to be made a trustee of his parliamentary grant, 'so that he may have a confidential friend to communicate with from time to time'.[18] As a government contractor, Davison had excellent political connections, but his reputation had been badly tarnished by a recent spell in prison for electoral fraud and rumours of his peculation. Ignoring the earl, parliament instead appointed high-profile politicians to manage the money, including future Prime Minister Lord Liverpool, Chancellor of the Exchequer Nicholas Vansittart, First Lord of the Admiralty Viscount Melville and George Rose, Treasurer of the Navy. News that the order had been sent to the exchequer to pay the grant was greeted with jubilation by the earl. 'This will put us in velvet,' he rejoiced.[19] On the first anniversary of the battle, the newly formed Trafalgar Trust received £90,555 18*s* 5*d* by cheque from the Treasury (about £6,500,000 in today's terms[20]). The sum included a year's interest, which the earl queried, telling Davison, whom he had retained as his personal banker, that it should have been backdated to the very day of the battle, 'if the 21st is included it will be day's more interest & pensions making more than £20 difference I think.'[21]

The payment was designed to pay for the mansion for the Nelson family, as Blenheim Palace had been gifted to the first

Duke of Marlborough after his triumph over the French a century before. In the debate to approve the grant, William Wilberforce MP had proposed that the property:

> should be placed in such a situation as to be conspicuous to our seamen on their approach to England, or on their setting sail, perhaps, in quest of an enemy. When they beheld such a testimony of the gratitude of the country, it could not fail to inspire them with an ardent desire to imitate his glorious example.[22]

Others also suggested building a monument on the coastline. The earl, however, was fixed on Norfolk as it was:

> the native country of the hero and his family, or the adjoining county of Suffolk and I make no doubt I shall be able in due time to meet with one along that great extent of sea coast from Cromer to Harwich which will be approved by government and my trustees, and where an obelisk may be erected according to Lord H. Petty's idea. That whole coast is very bold and is in the direct track of all the trade from the river Thames to the north, and all Men of War from the Downs and Portsmouth and other places in the Channel.[23]

The earl wanted his new estate to 'be called *Trăfălgar*' (pronounced Trefagur), an affectation he may have picked up from the dying William Pitt. Obsessed by his family's connection with the powerful Walpole dynasty – Prime Minister Sir Robert Walpole having been his mother's uncle – he hungrily eyed Houghton Hall, the Walpoles' magnificent seat in Norfolk, 'as it will be cheaper than building a new one although it is a large house'.[24] This bold suggestion flabbergasted Houghton's owner, the Earl of Cholmondeley, who 'knew nothing about it, nor had he any intention to part with it'.[25]

Even the tactless earl did not deserve the crushing blow to come. Since his brother's death, all William's ambitions had been channelled into his likeable son Horace. After Eton, Horace had followed his father to Christ's College, Cambridge, where he had lived the high life: hunting, going to balls and racing around town in his single-seater grey Landaulet. Even at school he had often been in debt. His famous uncle, who paid his school fees, indulged Horace and bailed him out of trouble several times, making his father fear for his future. In August 1806, after a tour of Scotland with his tutor, Horace was taken by his parents on a cruise in the North Sea on board *Majestic*, a 74-gun veteran of the Battle of the Nile (the earl, recalling his own unhappy experience at sea, nervously drafted his will before sailing). Given his exalted destiny, there was little prospect of a naval career for Horace but no escaping his illustrious name either. The officers in *Majestic* were naturally curious to meet their hero's nephew and namesake. A small, slender boy with a pale complexion, it was noted that Horace bore a strong resemblance to his uncle, 'which was more peculiarly striking if at any time he had on the hat of a naval officer'.[26]

Horace loved animals, keeping a dog at Merton whilst at school and bringing an eagle back from Scotland as a pet.[27] Despite his obvious zest, it was said that Horace always 'looked like one of those who are destined to be taken away early in life'. He may have sensed it too, celebrating the birth of a Matcham cousin in 1806 by wryly observing that there would be no shortage of heirs now.[28] So when Horace fell ill with a fever in December 1807, his father grew quickly alarmed, moving him from Canterbury to a London hotel to be near the best doctors. Davison sent over chicken broth for the patient and two bottles of Madeira for the worried parents. All was in vain. Horace, heir apparent to the Nelson titles and treasures, died at 10 o'clock in the evening on 17 January 1808, aged just 19. The cause of death was given as typhus fever, although others thought Horace had simply 'taken more exercise hunting etc than his constitution would bear'.[29] A week later, his body followed his uncle's into the crypt of St Paul's Cathedral. There were no crowds and none of the pomp of two years before. Just a man on horseback carrying a viscount's coronet on a crimson cushion, followed by the hearse and three coaches carrying the distraught earl, Davison, Haslewood and Thomas Bolton. Poor Sarah Nelson was 'blinded with my tears' at losing her only son. Charlotte, for so long a distant second in the affections of her parents, was Sarah's only comfort, as the tragedy caused a breach in her marriage. 'My lord and I make each other worse,' she confided miserably to a friend. 'He looks I think very ill.'[30] Sarah's inability or reluctance to give him more children was now painfully evident to her grieving husband.

The earl was crushed by the death of his son and heir. The whole edifice of his life collapsed now that it seemed that his own flesh and blood would no longer inherit his titles and the family heirlooms. A churchman, he may have feared Horace's death was divine retribution for all those years of self-seeking. He was now paying the price for gaining titles and money at the cost of his brother's life. His misery deepened still further at the end of the year when his closest friend Captain Bowen – George Bowen, who had commanded *Trusty* in the Egyptian campaign – died unexpectedly. The death of this 'constant companion' left the earl still further isolated and adrift. 'God knows,' his sister Catherine Matcham told Emma, 'we see the fallacy of titles and riches, for he was much more respected as a country parson and a happier man than he is at present.'[31] With unseemly haste, the earl's brothers-in-law Thomas Bolton and George Matcham started pressing to have Bolton's eldest son Tom, now heir presumptive to the earldom, change his name to Nelson. This had been a long-held desire of the dead admiral, but stricken with grief it was far too soon for the earl to contemplate such as move. Knowing the application needed his approval, he ordered the College of Arms 'to signify to the proper offices that it is my most particular wish that no such petition shall be complied with'.[32]

During this sad year, reports filtered through the English press of a coup in Constantinople. Since the liberation of Egypt, the Sultan of Turkey's love affair with England had cooled beneath the blandishments of self-anointed emperor Napoleon I. He had played on Selim's deep-rooted admiration for France and French culture, restoring through treaties many of the trading rights and Ottoman privileges enjoyed by the French before the invasion of Egypt back in 1798. Relations with Britain deteriorated so rapidly that in 1807, a squadron of warships had even been sent to the Bosphorus, not to defend but to threaten the Porte. Nevertheless, the Turks still held the English in high regard, reported a tourist, and 'ever since the affair of Egypt they talk of Nelson and Sir Sidney ... with delight and enthusiasm'.[33] Despite the perils, Selim also pressed on with his reforms of the Turkish army, triggering a revolt by the Janissaries, his reactionary bodyguard. In May 1807, they overthrew the sultan, placing his cousin Mustafa on the throne instead. Unusually, Selim survived the coup and was incarcerated within the gilded splendour of the Seraglio with his music, books, poetry and many wives. He might have survived for years in this way, hidden away in his luxurious prison, but during the summer of 1808 rumours reached Constantinople of a plot to restore him to the throne. On the night of 28 July, with the counter-revolutionaries at the gates of the palace demanding Selim's restoration, Sultan Mustafa sent 'two black eunuchs and eight trusty Moors' into the harem armed with daggers and garrotting wire.[34] Screaming, the women threw themselves between Selim and his assassins, but they were dragged off and he was quickly cut down by the knife thrusts, his delicate perfumed form crumpling beneath the raining blows. When it was over, his torn body was dragged outside for display to his horrified supporters. They had arrived too late to save Selim, but they did then topple his usurper, placing his rightful heir on the throne as Sultan Mahmud II. He destroyed the Janissaries who had deposed his cousin and slashed the power of the over-mighty governors who ruled in his name across the Ottoman Empire. Ali Pasha of Ioannina was defeated and his head sent to the gleeful new sultan as a trophy.

Public interest shifting to Tom Bolton emphasised Earl Nelson's strange isolation, especially in London's aristocratic circles, which were knitted together by titles, money and family. Even by the fluid standards of his day, his escalation to the highest reaches of the peerage had been abrupt and remarkable. Propelled from a Norfolk rectory to the House of Lords, he was ill-equipped to cope with the jibes aimed at his exalted position and the widespread criticism of his behaviour, especially towards Nelson's widow. Lady Catherine Walpole, a Nelson cousin, reacted like many when she failed to 'acknowledge Lord and Lady Nelson being much disgusted with their behaviour to Lady Nelson'.[35] Fanny, meanwhile, remained a more than welcome guest at Wolterton, the Walpoles' seat in Norfolk.

The Nelsons were no longer even invited to Merton, which Emma was still desperately clinging to, and with the death of Bowen it appears the earl's few acquaintances in London were limited to his professional advisers, who had their own commercial reasons to stay close. Emma bitterly rebuked Davison that before Trafalgar he 'had always detested the present Earl Nelson nor would you let him come within your house'.[36] When Davison was then sent to Newgate prison for fraud, the earl's life in London diminished still further, with no prospect yet of his long-promised country mansion. By 1814, a 95ft-high obelisk to his brother's memory had been erected above Portsmouth to inspire passing sailors, and an even taller pillar would soon be erected on the coast of Norfolk at Yarmouth, but the earl was still, in Davison's words, 'on the sharp look out for a situation of Trafalgar House'.[37]

Since the rebuff over Houghton, the earl's sights had lowered but remained fixed on East Anglia. Haslewood placed adverts in the local press for 'NORFOLK or SUFFOLK AN ESTATE and MANSION Wanted to be purchased in either of the above counties, of the value of about ONE HUNDRED THOUSAND POUNDS'.[38] These yielded viewings of Benhall Manor, empty since 1807 following the death of Admiral Sir Hyde Parker, and Branches Park, a mansion with 1,000 acres near Newmarket which the earl's trustees came close to buying. Searching for houses further afield scarcely made their task any easier. 'A few which appeared at first view to be eligible,' they reported, 'have been minutely investigated, and after being surveyed and their value ascertained, a price has been offered for the purchase, either at public auction or by private treaty, but without success.'[39] One property that Henry Lichfield, the property agent acting for the trust, looked at closely was Newstead Abbey, the rambling mansion in Nottinghamshire belonging to Lord Byron. The crippled Romantic poet was an ardent fan of the maimed admiral, whom he titled 'Britannia's God of War'. By comparison with Nelson, Byron considered Wellington to be a mere 'corporal'.[40] In 1812, a cash-strapped and deeply indebted Byron had put the abbey and its 3,000 acres up for auction. Young George Matcham remembered the earl discussing buying Newstead with his parents.[41] When Newstead failed to reach its reserve at auction, it was sold by private treaty for a substantial £140,000, still too much for the Trafalgar House trustees who may have considered a lower offer. In fact, just two years later the buyer defaulted and Newstead went back on the market, selling again for a more affordable £94,500. But by then the earl's trustees were focused on another property in Wiltshire called Standlynch, which had become available following the recent death of its owner.

Built in 1733 on the site of a medieval manor house, Standlynch was an elegant country retreat in a commanding position above Salisbury, modelled in soft red brick with stone facings. In 1765, the house was purchased from a Sir William Young – to whom Sarah Countess Nelson, née Yonge, was said to be related[42] – by Henry Dawkins, whose family had made a fortune in the Jamaican sugar trade. Dawkins, a member of the Society of Dilittanti, had expensive collecting habits, enlarging Standlynch with pavilions to house his many artworks. The house was centred on a theatrical two-storey hall with rococo plasterwork and fresco paintings, the perfect setting for Dawkins' collections. All these embellishments came at a high price, however, and with other estates to manage, Dawkins instructed his executors to sell Standlych after his death to settle his debts. In addition to the mansion, the estate comprised a hamlet of cottages, a chapel, a water mill and 2,500 acres of prime farmland. Valued at £120,000, after negotiation – helped perhaps by citing the difficult sale of Newstead – the earl's trustees agreed to pay £93,450. As the price was over their statutory budget of £90,000, the trustees were forced back to parliament for more money. Ten years after the high emotion of Trafalgar, there were plenty of MPs now willing to speak out against extending the already lavish grant, and sixty-six of them voted to oppose it. Passed with a small majority, the purchase of Standlynch was completed in 1815 just weeks before the end of the war which had immortalised Nelson.

The generosity of government towards Nelson's brother contrasted sharply, however, with its steadfast indifference towards his mistress Emma Hamilton. She had died in January that same year in pitiful lodgings at Calais, exiled from her creditors and with her bewildered daughter by her side. Dogged by debt and health problems, her final years in England had been very difficult. Pryse Lockhart Gordon, the old acquaintance from Naples who had befriended Kelim Efendi, was shocked at her decline when he encountered Emma by chance in 1811. She was on an excursion to Greenwich with 10-year-old Horatia and a noisy party of children travelling in a dilapidated hired carriage. Gordon was a critic of Emma, having witnessed her intrigues close at hand in Italy, but he was moved by her pathetic condition. Her embarrassment at seeing him was painfully obvious, and his mention of Naples brought tears to her 'still beautiful' eyes. 'Age and circumstance had made sad ravages and changes in her formerly splendid countenance,' he noted sadly. Her once luxurious hair was grey and tucked into a large cap and her dress, 'once so gay and gaudy, was now sombre and shabby'. Yet Gordon was astonished to recognise the tatty cashmere shawl she clung to:

> I knew it to be one I had seen her formerly wear; it was a remarkable one, and had been presented to Lord Nelson by the Grand Signior, along with the *pelisse* and *aigrette*. The admiral had given her this shawl, and often have I seen her kiss it, and hear her boast 'that she had wrapped the queen's feet in it on their passage from Naples'.[43]

The publication in 1814 of Emma's private letters to Nelson destroyed any last hope of her salvation. Emma blamed a thief for hacking her papers, but everyone believed she had sold the letters herself, for a reputed £1,000. The bestselling *Letters of Lord Nelson to Lady Hamilton* stained the admiral's fame, fatally damaged Emma's cause and was deeply hurtful to the earl, many of whose own letters were leaked. In the book, he read how his brother had mocked him for being 'as big as if he was a bishop' with a love of food and wine, and how Emma had made the admiral laugh 'when you imitate the doctor'.[44] The letters made difficult reading for Fanny too, who, among many jibes, saw herself described by William Nelson in a flirty letter to Emma as '*Tom Tit* (that bad bird)'.[45] The leaks continued beyond Emma's death, forcing the earl to take legal action in 1816 to prevent still further damage to his tattered reputation.[46]

Nevertheless, the earl did not entirely abandon Emma, and there was even a reconciliation of sorts before she died. Perhaps the death of his only son had softened him, made him more sympathetic to her plight, even made him look favourably on Horatia compared to the pushy Boltons. In his will, Nelson had left instructions that Emma should receive a £500 annuity, paid twice yearly, from the rents of his duchy at Bronte.[47] The earl had pressed his agents in Sicily to ensure it was paid promptly, as 'it might be inconvenient to Her Ladyship not to receive it'.[48] But managing the vast Bronte estate from England in the middle of a war was an onerous task, and the rental payments soon became irregular, then dried up altogether. By October 1814, the earl had 'not had a word or a farthing for nine months' from Sicily. Far from being a rich seam of income, the duchy was becoming a time-consuming and stressful drain on his capital. For years, he considered renting the estate out, breaking it up or even selling it altogether, as he was entitled to do under the terms of his brother's will. Before his downfall, Emma had suggested to Alexander Davison that he might buy it. 'Believe me,' she wrote, 'the speculation is worth thinking on. He that has it does not value it and would rather have half the value in money you would be the noble possessor of what belonged to your heroic friend.'[49] The earl was only stopped from selling by his sisters, whose sons now stood to inherit the duchy. Instead, he struggled with a series of incompetent, indolent and often corrupt agents. In 1816, the British banker charged with managing the earl's finances in Sicily, an old friend of Nelson's, shot himself to avoid bankruptcy. Trained in the Church, the Reverend Earl was wholly unsuited to the role of absentee landlord of his complex and turbulent far-off estate, and woefully prone to the tricks and deceits of the people charged with running it.

Despite all these difficulties, it appears the earl continued to pay Emma her £500 annuity from his Bronte income or out of his own pocket. Worth perhaps £30,000 today, this should have allowed her to live a reduced but comfortable life (the popular belief Emma lived out her days in 'abject poverty' was strongly resented by the earl's descendants).[50] So more begging letters were unwelcome. 'It cannot be more disagreeable to you to receive a letter from me than it is for me to write to you,' she wrote from debtor's prison in 1814. 'I ask not alms I ask not anything but right and to know whether I am to receive my due or not.'[51] The earl sent £250, freeing Emma and allowing her to escape, deeply embittered, to France. He then loaned her a further £10 to help pay her rent in Calais (the kindly Matchams forbade Horatia from settling this debt after her mother's death).[52] When news came that Emma had died, the earl hurried to France to recover her few possessions, anxious to see what she had kept and perhaps recover his brother's Trafalgar coat. All he discovered was a pile of scruffy pawnbroker tickets, which he refused to redeem, returning to England empty-handed. Among the pledged items were several cashmere shawls, those cherished souvenirs of the Levant and props for her famous Attitudes, now dirty, threadbare and worn, which Emma had kept to the very end.[53]

Standlynch, grandly renamed Trafalgar Park, was purchased at the very top of the property market. Just a month later, the Battle of Waterloo brought an end to the long wars with France, pitching the country into an economic depression. The house was far from Norfolk but close to the earl's daughter Charlotte, now married and living in Somerset, and came with a beautiful view over water meadows to Salisbury Cathedral. It was unfurnished, but the many post-war bankruptcies gave the earl ample opportunity to furnish his house at bargain prices, using the £10,000 granted by parliament for the purpose. One sale which attracted him was the dispersal in April 1817, on the premises in St James's Square, of the magnificent collections of Nelson's former agent and banker Alexander Davison, who since his release from prison was labouring under heavy financial penalties. His private bank had collapsed amid acrimony and bitter recriminations. The depositors, including the earl, were bailed out by banker Thomas Coutts, who now also took charge of the sultan's jewel, storing it in his firm's newly built strong rooms beneath the Strand with their 6ft-thick walls, iron gates and grilles. Safeguarding Admiral Lord Nelson's greatest treasure became a proud boast for a bank keen to recover its £10,000 investment in this impregnable vault.[54]

Davison's two-week auction contained many items of family interest, including relics sold or pawned by Emma *in extremis*. Among the highlights was an enamel portrait of Emma as a bacchante after the oil painting by Elizabeth Vigée le Brun, which had hung over Nelson's bed at Naples. The enamel had been given to Nelson by Sir William Hamilton, then sold to Davison by Emma in 1812 for £200. At the auction it fetched £153 8*s*. Another miniature portrait of Emma mounted with her hair and initials, offered as Lot 830, was said to have been worn by Nelson at the time of his death, but this only reached £25 4*s*. Of tantalising interest was Lot 828, 'A highly finished miniature of the Emperor Paul, from the hilt of a sword given to Lord Nelson'. No such sword is recorded and the miniature may have been a remnant of the box with the tsar's portrait presented to Nelson in Palermo, which had been broken up for its diamonds on his return to London. Among a large quantity of printed portraits of his dead friend and client,

Davison had also preserved 'a drawing of the Egrette', a memento of his former custodianship of this precious jewel.[55]

Despite enjoying a shopping spree at the government's expense, the earl appeared to derive little pleasure from his new country seat. The life of a great landowner fell short of the long-held dream. He found his £5,000 annuity (£300,000 today) barely enough to keep up Trafalgar House as well as a large London property in Portman Square. A visitor to the house's once-famed gardens remarked that, 'the place was in tolerable keeping, considering the little assistance that was allowed to the gardener; but the present proprietor, I believe, is not distinguished for any great love of horticulture.'[56] Sporting activity on an estate once thriving with game declined: in two days of shooting, young George Matcham only had five shots.[57] Rattling around its cavernous rooms with an elderly wife - Sarah was approaching 70 – and with the knowledge that everything would one day go to his nephew was dispiriting for the earl. It was perhaps no surprise then that the couple retreated to live in just one wing of the mansion. One consolation was Trafalgar Chapel, a small private church in the grounds which reminded the earl of his earlier calling. When George Matcham married Harriet Eyre, the daughter of the owner of his neighbouring estate, in February 1817, the earl willingly surrendered his house to the newly-weds for a year. William had been instrumental in making the match, which tied the estates together, performing the marriage ceremony for the young couple. He did the same when his heir Tom Bolton, more resistant to his uncle's dynastic scheming and wary of his motives, married Harriet's cousin, Frances Eyre, four years later. Ahead of his wedding, Tom had complained that, 'my uncle so pesters me and all around him with matrimonial schemes and speculations that I am determined to avoid it.'[58] Tom was entitled to feel bitter, as a previous engagement to Lucretia Folkes, an heiress worth £6,000 a year, had been broken off when his tactless uncle admitted to Lucretia's shocked father that, 'should Lady Nelson die, he should marry again with the hope of having a son to inherit the title.'[59] As Frances Eyre's family also owned land bordering Trafalgar, Tom's marriage completed a trio of adjoining estates to stretch for thousands of acres across the rich Wiltshire landscape.

With the future of his estate secure, and growing old, it seemed the earl was reconciled to Tom inheriting his titles. He attended the House of Lords to speak against the Catholic Relief Bill, then sat in the chamber during the 1820 'trial' of the Princess of Wales, whose husband, now King George IV, was seeking a divorce. The case against her collapsed, and a year later the earl was in the procession of peers which followed the king to his coronation at Westminster Abbey, during which Caroline, barred from proceedings, hysterically hammered on the abbey doors demanding entry. Countless feathered plumes waved in the summer breeze that day, but none outshone that of Prince Nikolaus Esterházy II, who 'glimmered like a galazy' in an outlandish hussar's uniform embroidered with pearls and diamonds, wearing a vast aigrette on his hat, said to be the largest diamond jewel in the world, 16in high and set with 5,000 stones. Now in his mid-50s, the playboy prince had entertained Nelson and the Hamiltons at his Hungarian palace during their journey home in 1800. Somehow such flamboyance now jarred in the post-war age of austerity.

15

THE BRIDE

Earl Nelson's unguarded remark in 1817 that he still hoped to remarry one day and produce a male heir was vividly recalled when his wife Sarah died on 15 April 1828, aged 78. A week later, her body was interred in the vaults of St Paul's Cathedral beside her son and between the tombs of her famous brother-in-law and his Trafalgar commander, Lord Collingwood. Before committal, the coffin was covered with a crimson cloth emblazoned with the family's armorial devices and topped by the countess's coronet on a red plush cushion. The cathedral was an extraordinary final earthly destination for Sarah Yonge, daughter of a Devon vicar; and yet her husband still disputed the £92 funeral bill.

The death of his 'jewell' presented the 70-year-old earl with his longed-for second chance to sire another son. Within months of Sarah's death, he was laying siege to a widow called Hilare Barlow, the daughter of Admiral Sir Robert Barlow, a relative of the late countess, veteran of the Battle of the First of June 1795 and now elderly resident of Canterbury. Hilare's first husband had been her cousin George Barlow, an officer in the 4th Dragoons who had died of fever in India in 1824. The earl's intentions were coarsely blatant, and at first Hilare (pronounced Hilary) recoiled from his clumsy advances. The gossip columns related with relish how 'the earl's proposals were made several times before they were accepted'.[1] But Hilare needed money. Her elderly father had a large family to support on a modest income, and she was surviving on an army pension of just £150 a year. When William offered her £4,000 a year plus his house in Portman Square, she accepted his proposal. The earl's relatives were horrified, as the union threatened the future settlement of the family's titles, estates and money. All the ancient rancour between him, the Boltons and the Matchams rose boiling to the surface. Even the usually loyal Charlotte Nelson was appalled at her father's behaviour and by the prospect of having a stepmother thirteen years her junior. She wrote a very 'unkind' letter to the earl, forcing him to angrily defend the 'amiable qualities of the Countess Elect'.[2] 'She is admired and beloved by everyone who knows her, both high and middle ranking as well as the poor,' he raged at Charlotte's husband. 'For my part I despise them all and care not what observations the newspapers may make.'[3]

The support of the Yonge family to the earl's remarriage 'softened' Charlotte's opposition. Another reason for objecting to her father's marriage was less easy to admit. This was the possibility of a half-brother, as Charlotte was currently heir to the dukedom of Bronte through a quirk in Sicilian law that her father had stumbled upon back in 1810 a few days after Charlotte's own wedding. In sending his congratulations, the Neapolitan minister in London, Fabrizio Ruffo, Prince of Castelcicala, had let slip that:

> [He] had carefully read that part of Lord Nelson's will relating to the disposal of the Bronte estate and was clearly of the opinion he had no power to give it as he had done, that it was contrary to the Sicilian law, it was contrary to the laws of the Franks as specified in the grant or patent.[4]

By the terms of its original grant, King Ferdinand had allowed Nelson to nominate his successor to the duchy. Nelson, anxious to keep his titles together, had accordingly entailed his duchy to follow the same route as the special remainder attached to his English barony. This meant that if male descent failed in his brother's family, Bronte would pass in succession to the sons of his sisters Susannah

Bolton or Catherine Matcham. This contravened Sicilian law, as a jubilant earl now told his lawyer, which decreed that property:

> must descend to heirs *female* failure of heirs *male* that as long as I had any children whether male or female it must descend to them and their houses and could not go to collatarel branches so long as my own line existed, that females stood in the place of males, and daughters in the stead of sons.

However, the minister had urged the earl to be cautious, 'for if my sisters knew it they might apply to his Sicilian Majesty and possibly get the grant altered as his was an arbitrary monarchy.' Glimpsing a means of at least preserving his dukedom and duchy for Charlotte, the earl had made discrete legal enquiries in Sicily. The issue hinged on which law took precedence. When King Ferdinand then abolished entails altogether, making the earl absolute owner of Bronte, it appeared to release him from his brother's last wishes. Keeping this discovery a secret from the Boltons and Matchams, the earl wrote out a new will naming 'my dear daughter' Charlotte as 'absolute heiress' to 'all my said hereditary estates in the said Kingdom of Sicily'. Preparing his daughter for her future role, the earl also pressed Prime Minister Earl Grey to convert her husband's Irish barony to an English one, using his vote for Grey's cherished Reform Bill as leverage to achieve his aim.[5] His Sicilian will was witnessed in London, then proved in Italy under Sicilian law.[6] It was now a ticking time bomb under the family.

The earl and Hilare married quietly by special licence at St George's, Hanover Square, on 26 March 1829, before returning to Trafalgar House for a party attended by the earl's tenants. The new Countess Nelson, Duchess of Bronte threw herself into her role. Within weeks, she was presented at Court by Lady Sidmouth wearing a white tulle robe trimmed with silver and garlands of lilies and pink roses. The lovestruck old earl obviously wanted his bride to make an impact to silence his critics, as the fashion press noticed that Hilare was also wearing, 'the superb diamond Chelengk, or plume of triumph presented to the late Viscount Nelson by the Grand Signor!'.[7] Her hair was again dressed with a plume of feathers and 'brilliants' when she returned to court in May 1833.[8] A month later, she dragged her elderly and increasingly deaf husband to a ball at the Admiralty, making him dance quadrilles until four in the morning. She wore her Court gown again for a portrait ordered by the earl from artist George Sanders for 250 guineas. Sanders' studio neighboured the Nelsons' house in London, although it appears he travelled to Wiltshire for the sitting as Hilare was portrayed standing before an open window in the saloon of Trafalgar House. The arresting image received a mixed reception when it was exhibited at the Royal Academy in 1834. As one critic caustically observed, with her startled look and open mouth, Hilare 'seems to us to be just on the point of sneezing'.[9] Unnoticed by the reviewers, in her portrait Hilare has an arm through the sleeve of a luxurious fur pelisse falling across her back and over the gilt wood chair beside her. Forty years and softer English light may have muted its colour since it was painted by Leonardo Guzzardi in Sicily, but this may be the ceremonial robe presented to Nelson by Selim in 1798.

In contrast, the fur-lined robe visible in a portrait of Fanny Nelson completed around this same time is clearly that of a viscountess. The miniature was painted in the last year of Fanny's life and shows her wearing a jewelled anchor on her bonnet, mourning rings for her two dead husbands and a cameo of Nelson on a bangle on her wrist. Since Trafalgar, Fanny had lived quietly out of the public eye, moving between London, Bath and Exmouth in Devon, where she purchased a clifftop villa in 1815, the year of Waterloo and Emma's death. She had lived comfortably on the £1,000 annuity left her by her husband and the £2,000 pension from the government, travelling occasionally to the Continent, where it was said she met Lord Byron in 1822.[10] Nelson's former flag captain, now Admiral Sir Thomas Hardy, and the Hood family, old acquaintances from her early life in the West Indies, remained close friends, but she distanced herself from her husband's family, for good reason. In 1808, Susannah Bolton dismissed rumours that Fanny was going to marry a rich merchant in Lynn. 'She would never lower her dignity to marry a tradesman,' she told Emma.[11] Susannah suspected that Fanny was really attempting to engage Josiah to the merchant's daughter to secure her son a large dowry. Like many, she failed to see how Fanny could still love and admire the husband who had so publicly abandoned her. Admiral William Hotham, who had served with Nelson as a young officer, recalled how, 'she continually talked of him and always attempted to palliate the injuries she had received – was warm and enthusiastic in her praises of his public conduct and bowed down with submission to the errors of his domestic life.'[12]

For long periods, Fanny resided with Josiah in France. He had remained on the Navy List after the death of his stepfather but never went back to sea, pursuing instead a successful business career on the Paris Bourse (stock exchange). The loss of three of his six children in infancy may have hastened Josiah's own early death, probably from heart failure, in 1830 aged 50. Apart from his family, the only named beneficiary of Josiah's will was his old companion Thomas Capel, bearer of the Nile dispatch and now also an admiral. Fanny was with Josiah when he died, and as Paris was again on the verge of revolution, she hurried his body, together with the exhumed corpses of her grandchildren, back to England for burial. The strain of her son's death and the escape from Paris took a heavy toll on a woman in her 70s who had already endured so much. When Fanny met Hotham again in London, she spoke of her loss, appearing 'the very picture of illness and despondency'.[13] She died a few days later on 6 May 1831 at her rented house in Harley Street, only a fortnight after the death of the equally long-suffering wife of the Duke of Wellington.

In her simple will, Fanny left an annuity to Josiah's widow, naming Lord Bridport as her executor. She also intended her few possessions to pass to her grieving daughter-in-law, but as soon as Fanny died, Charlotte Nelson swooped on her house at Exmouth and 'carried away' the battle vases given to the Nelsons by Earl Spencer after the Nile. Lady Louisa Hardy, wife of Nelson's former flag captain, was forced to intervene and see the precious vases returned to their rightful owner. Louisa, who thought Nelson had been 'completely humbugged' by Emma Hamilton, admired how Fanny 'retained to the last the most extraordinary devotion to his memory and excused even his partiality to her rival'.[14]

Convention prevented Louisa attending her friend's funeral, but her husband Admiral Hardy went, together with Earl Nelson, who travelled down from London to be there. Whilst he was away in Devon, the earl's house in Portman Square was burgled and Hilare's jewel case and bureau broken open and ransacked. It was the second time in recent months that the house had been targeted by thieves, possibly attracted by the frequent mentions of Hilare's gems in the press. Among the jewels taken were several emerald, diamond and ruby rings, a garnet necklace and brooch, a topaz cross, gold long chains and bracelets, and some silver-topped dressing table bottles engraved 'HN'. The loss was estimated at £1,000, although the thieves were said to have missed an improbable £80,000 worth of other diamond jewels scattered by Hilare around her dressing room, including a 'most valuable' diamond necklace lying on a shelf.[15] The theft happened early in the evening of Friday, 13 May, although it took another day before it was reported to the local magistrate. At first it was believed that the thieves had clambered over a neighbouring rooftop to reach the house, a theory supported by the discovery of an empty jewel box near the back wall. But the timing of the burglary, with the occupants at dinner, and the thieves' apparent familiarity with the layout of the house, strongly suggested an inside job. Suspicion quickly fell on the under-butler, who had recovered the empty jewel box. He had been seen by Hilare's sister, Maria Barlow, earlier that day, talking confidentially to a strange woman, 'the singularity of whose dress attracted her attention'. Officers from the 'new police establishment' – the Metropolitan Police, founded in 1829 – were sent to investigate, but 'had done nothing the whole day but sat in the kitchen with the servants eating, and drinking, and laughing'.[16]

The sultan's jewel had a narrow escape. The thieves, *The Times* reported, 'might readily have laid their hands upon it, as it was loosely wrapped in a piece of brown paper; and carelessly thrown into the bureau'. As the *Morning Chronicle* revealed, Hilare had worn the famous jewel to the palace the day before the burglary, when she had presented her sister Maria to the new King William IV and Queen Adelaide, a report of which might have caught the thieves' attention.[17] On her exhausted return to Portman Square, Hilare had taken off her jewels, dropping them around her dressing room to sort out later. Her relief at finding the sultan's jewel undisturbed was surely mixed with dread at telling her husband about the break-in. Her delay in reporting the crime was certainly commented upon. It was said that she had feared the thieves would return and that, with her husband away, she did not know what to do. The 'fashionably dressed gentleman' who did eventually go to the police on her behalf said she 'had a very limited intimate acquaintance with gentlemen' and 'had not seen any gentleman but himself to call her assistance'. This failed to explain why she did not simply send a servant instead, or her sister. This unknown man apologised for the delay, saying that Hilare had been unable to reach him all day as he had left town early on the Saturday morning to go to a military review at Hounslow. The *Morning Chronicle* 'understood' the gentleman 'to be a relation of Lord Nelson's'. But the delays, the behaviour of the police, the laughter in the servants' room, the timing of the theft and her panic all suggest that Hilare, whose first husband had also been in the army, might have been enjoying a liaison with a lover whilst her husband was away at Fanny's funeral.[18]

The earl was unusually silent on the whole matter. On his return to London, he offered a modest £50 reward for the recovery of the stolen jewels, dismissing reports that some had been found in a house in Essex. No action was taken against the under-butler, or anyone else, but he did ensure that the sultan's jewel returned to the safety of Coutts, whilst Hilare, terrified of another break-in, offered to surrender her key to the safe at Portman Square. In its coverage of the burglary, *The Times* suggested that the earl had once refused an offer of £20,000 for the jewel (some £1.5 million today).[19] The report followed rumours that Nelson's old rival Sir Sidney Smith had recently sold his own Chelengk for £13,000.

Smith was still living in Paris, having left England back in 1815 with his wife and stepchildren to escape his many creditors. He had dedicated himself to the campaign to abolish the slavery of Christians in North Africa, living on the £1,000 pension granted by the government after the Egyptian campaign. There is no evidence, however, that he sold his Chelengk, an act which would have been out of his proud character. Its more likely fate was revealed in an article written for the *Naval & Military Gazette* after Smith's death in 1840. Its author claimed:

> The writer knows that Sir Sidney Smith gave away every jewel of it, at various times, to different brothers-in-arms, who had derived more laurels than gold for their service. At last its setting was all that remained; but its image stands as the second crest in his armorial bearings.[20]

Such a gesture was more in keeping with a man known to have driven around the streets of Paris at night, distributing food to 'the poor and unfortunate inhabitants of garrets and hovels, many of whom had seen better days, and were too proud to beg'.[21]

Laden by debt for many years, there was no mention in Smith's 1833 will of his Chelengk, diamond star of the Order of the Crescent or the sultan's scimitar presented by the terrified Capitan Pasha. Smith did give instructions, however, that after his death his body should be examined for 'incipient putrefaction, that the vital spark is actually extinguished': as if he could hardly contemplate his own extinction.[22] After Waterloo, which he witnessed as a spectator, Smith had sought to pawn his City of London presentation sword rather than see it 'melted down for its nominal value'.[23] Such a tragedy may also have befallen the sultan's scimitar, although the discovery in the Thames near Windsor in the 1960s of fragments of a beautiful gold and diamond-set sword decorated with the Order of the Crescent suggests another possible fate. Of the handful of men awarded the Order of the Crescent, only Smith is known to have also received a sword from the sultan. Broken and lost in the mud of the river bed, the sword fragment strangely symbolises Smith's posthumous reputation.

When Smith died in Paris, the French gave him a funeral in ways more touching and spontaneous than the state-controlled cavalcade awarded to Nelson in London. A hundred carriages followed the hearse to the cemetery of Père Lachaise, where Smith's body, his coffin emblazoned with his heraldic achievements, was interred beside his wife's tomb. Among the pallbearers were French admirals and generals, and seventy years later, Smith's step-grandson could still recall 'the impression made upon me by the sombre pageant of the funeral, the brilliant uniforms, the velvet trappings of the hearse, the crowd that thronged our otherwise quiet street'.[24] In the days after the funeral, he paraded around the house in Smith's medals and decorations before they were unceremoniously sold at auction. 'I cannot understand our being allowed to make playthings of these mementoes of a splendid career,' he wrote in 1902, 'which, for their historical value alone, should have been treasured in the family.'[25] The principal beneficiary of Smith's estate was his nephew William, Spencer Smith's son, a captain in the Royal Navy. The decision to sell the medals, swords and other precious relics of a remarkable career to pay debts may have been forced upon him. Only one treasure escaped the *salle des ventes* (sales room). As Smith lay on his deathbed, the gold cross of the Knights Templars, given him after he used his Chelengk to prevent a massacre by Turkish troops of Christians in Cyprus, was found under his waistcoat close to his heart, where it had resided for some forty years. His dying wish was to see the cross returned to the Templars in Jerusalem to be worn by 'the grandmaster and his successors in perpetuity'.[26] His desire was fulfilled, although the jewel cannot be traced today.

Earl Nelson's final years were overshadowed by renewed dispute with his family when the Boltons discovered he had been secretly corresponding with lawyers in Sicily about the inheritance of the Bronte duchy and its title. They issued a writ pressing the earl to produce his legal opinion. They also accused the earl of trying to cash-in the diamond-hilted sword presented by the King of Naples and 'other valuable property given by the Grand Seignor to the late Admiral Viscount Nelson'.[27] They suspected the earl was trying to sell these treasures to deprive the Boltons of their inheritance in case he failed to secure the duchy for Charlotte. After a hearing in Chancery, the judge rejected the Boltons' charge, declaring that the earl had as much right to summon legal opinion from Sicily as he had to buy himself a book in Italian. However, in his ruling, the judge left open as 'speculation' the 'effect of Sicilian law with respect to Lord Nelson's will', as it was outside the scope of the case.[28] By doing so, he was paving the way for future litigation.

There was rancour at the end of Earl Nelson's long and eventful life, but happiness too. In Hilare he found a warm and loving wife who soon became 'familiarised to manners which strangers found unpleasant'. Childless from her first marriage, and 38 at the time of her second, the earl misjudged Hilare's potential as a mother and his own prowess, but, recalled a friend, he was always 'very kind and indulgent' towards her. Yet no child appeared and time was running short. By 1834, the earl was 'exceedingly and impatiently deaf' and relying on a hearing trumpet.[29] In October that year, he was knocked down by a carriage whilst crossing the street in Salisbury, and Sir William Hotham thought he looked 'in a bad way' when he next saw him in town.[30] He died in London a few weeks later, on 28 February 1835, 'about one o'clock on Saturday morning without much apparent suffering': a peaceful death in contrast to the violence of his brother's demise thirty years earlier.[31] Back in 1806, William Nelson had expressed a wish to be buried at Burnham Thorpe beside his father, 'unless Trafalgar House had been bought and a proper Tomb made there'.[32] But the deaths of his son then first wife propelled the earl to join them in the vault of St Paul's Cathedral. Even in death he caused problems when his body was impossible to shift some twelve years later to allow the recently deceased Duke of Wellington to be entombed beside Nelson, so that 'our two greatest naval and military heroes might rest side by side under the dome of the metropolitan cathedral'.[33] But the not inconsiderable mortal remains of William were in the

Presentation of the French ambassador Count de Vergennes to the Sultan of Turkey in the throne room of the Topkapi Palace in 1755, showing the nervous-looking count being thrust forward wearing a sable pelisse. His retinue bear gifts for the sultan. Note the cubicle for the display of the sultan's turban jewels. Black chalk and opaque pigments heightened with gold after an engraving by Antoine de Favray, France or Istanbul, eighteenth century. (©2017 Christie's Images Limited)

Lambros Katsonis (1752-1804), a Greek officer who joined the Russian Imperial Navy becoming a hero in the struggle for Greek independence against Ottoman rule. He is wearing a simple metal Çelenc pinned to his Fez. (Oil miniature by unknown artist, National Historical Museum, Athens. Author's Collection)

Newly discovered Turkish drawing of the Çelenc selected by Selim III to be presented to Nelson. Josiah Nisbet titled it 'drawing of the Chelingh which was given to his Gallant Father Lord Nelson of the Nile by the Grand Seignior 1798'. (Author's Collection).

Newly discovered drawing of the jewel actually sent to Nelson by the sultan revealing its full exoticism before it was altered by Charlotte Bridport. (© College of Arms, MS Coll. Jernemnentia, Vol.5, p.3)

Nelson's coat of arms as they appeared on the porcelain ordered by his agent Alexander Davison after the Battle of the Nile. The Chelengk crest is based on the drawings of the original jewel selected by Selim III. Note the blue detail. (Author's Collection)

Nelson's coat of arms as corrected by the College of Arms after Nelson returned to England with his new aigrette jewel. (© College of Arms, MS Coll. Jernemnentia, Vol.5 pt 3, p.4)

Nelson's rival Captain Sir Sidney Smith wearing the sultan's medal for Egypt and the cross of Richard the Lionheart. The Greek Orthodox Church presented the cross to Smith after he prevented a massacre of Christians on Cyprus by wearing his Chelengk to quell the bloodlust of the Turkish troops. By Louis-Marie Autissier, *c.* 1800, miniature watercolour on ivory. (Royal Collection Trust / © HM Queen Elizabeth II 2017)

The only known image of Sir Sidney Smith's Chelengk drawn by the College of Arms for his heraldic crest. (© College of Arms, MS Coll. I. 36 p.294)

Nelson's silver 'Turkey' cup presented by the Levant Company and the gun and canteen sent by Balkan warlord Ali Pasha of Ioannina. (© National Maritime Museum, Greenwich D4424)

The 'Chelengk' portrait of Nelson, painted with the approval of Fanny Nelson for John McArthur's Naval Chronicle by Lemuel Francis Abbott (1758–1805). (© National Maritime Museum, Greenwich, Greenwich Hospital Collection BHC2889)

Left: Nelson's hat with an imitation Chelengk in silver wire and spangles sewn on its cockade. Nelson bought embroidered replicas of all his Orders for his undress uniform. (© Dean and Chapter of Westminster)

Right: Exact life-size replica of Nelson's lost jewel in rose diamonds, decorated in enamel and set in silver and gold with a clockwork mechanism, by Philip Denyer for Symbolic & Chase, London 2017. (Author's Collection)

Full length portrait of Nelson painted in 1800 by William Beechey for the City of Norwich with an accurate representation of the sultan's jewel and pelisse. Nelson gave the artist the hat in the painting. Oil on canvas. (© Norfolk Museums Service, Norwich Castle Museum & Art Gallery)

Frances, Viscountess Nelson painted in the last year of her life wearing memorial jewels for her husband and son. Watercolour on ivory by J.B. Beech, 1831. (Private Collection)

William, first Earl Nelson, who inherited his brother's titles and reaped the rewards of his fame but none of his admiration. Oil on canvas, attributed to Isaac Pocock (1782–1835), *c.* 1806. (Private Collection)

Nelson's nephew Horace Nelson dressed as an Esquire as he was for Nelson's installation as Knight of the Order of the Bath. Painted shortly before Horace's untimely death which destroyed his father's hopes of a Nelson dynasty. Oil on canvas, by Isaac Pocock (1782–1835), *c.* 1806. (Private Collection)

Nelson's niece Charlotte Nelson, later Lady Bridport and Duchess of Bronte who would inherit the Chelengk. Charlotte is wearing a fashionable eastern shawl like those used by Emma Hamilton in her 'Attitudes'. Oil on canvas, attributed to Isaac Pocock (1782–1835), *c.* 1806. (Private Collection)

Earl Nelson's second wife Hilare painted in the saloon at Trafalgar House possibly wearing Nelson's fur pelisse. She almost lost the sultan's jewel in a burglary and failed to provide her husband with his longed-for heir. Oil on canvas by George Sanders (1774–1846), 1834. (Private Collection)

This rare head and shoulders version by Leonardo Guzzardi of his portrait of Nelson wearing the jewel belonged to the famous collector Alfred Morrison and has been recently rediscovered having been lost for over a century. Analysis has shown that the Order of the Crescent was added after the portrait was completed, probably when the decoration arrived in Palermo in the autumn of 1799. The artist has shown the star on the left-hand side of Nelson's coat to make it more visible. Found rolled-up in Italy in the 1880s, this portrait may have been intended for the Egyptian Club. Oil on canvas, 1799. (Private Collection)

way. Eventually the old duke's coffin was perched awkwardly on top of the Nelsons' sarcophagus, whilst his own tomb was built 20 yards to the east.

The earl died a rich man, with a personal fortune estimated at £71,480 (about £6 million today),[34] so he could well afford to leave a substantial £1,500 for a self-aggrandising marble monument to be erected to his memory in St Paul's, with a further £100 for the placing of a commemorative tablet in the chapel at Trafalgar House. The tablet was completed, but the church authorities baulked at allowing a monument to the Reverend Earl on the scale of the statues of the many heroes crowding the cathedral aisles. Only a modest plaque was granted, placed close to his brother's sarcophagus, which, overlooked by tourists today, commemorates the earl, his wife and son. The money earmarked for the earl's statue was spent instead by Charlotte on a bizarre monument in her local church of Cricket St Thomas showing her father reclining with a book, watching as an angel wafts two of his dead infant grandchildren to heaven.

Only Hilare and Charlotte were named as beneficiaries in the earl's will. Hilare, who had relinquished all property rights on her marriage, was left £7,000 and 'all her paraphernalia': her personal jewels, clothes, ornaments, watches and trinkets. In addition, she was given her portrait, the earl's carriage with its four horses and all the furniture and linen in Trafalgar House. The mansion itself was entailed with the earldom. Hilare could also enjoy the use of all the family silver – many pieces once belonging to the admiral - until her death or remarriage, when everything would revert to Charlotte. This happened just two years later, when Hilare wed George Knight, a nephew of novelist Jane Austen. She died in Paris on 28 December 1858; she never did have children.

In his will, the earl carried into effect his long-held desire to name Charlotte as heir to Bronte, in accordance with Sicilian law but at variance with his brother's wishes. Without his own son, he could do nothing to stop Tom Bolton from succeeding to the English earldom and the Trafalgar estate. But as Duchess of Bronte, Charlotte would inherit all the heirlooms attached to the Sicilian title by his brother before Trafalgar: the busts, medals, collar of the Order of the Bath, swords, watches, portraits, the City of London gold box and 'the diamond aigrette presented to my said brother by the Grand Signor'. The earl also passed down full-length portraits of himself and of his brother, together with a painting of Sir Robert Walpole 'in his hunting dress', presumably an heirloom which had descended through his mother's family and may have once been in the prime minister's own collection.[35] However, as the earl was desperately clinging to the hope of an heir when he wrote the will in 1832, Charlotte would have to relinquish all these treasures if Hilare still produced a son – or share them if she had a daughter. The earl had already given away the star for the Order of the Bath to prevent it falling into the hands of the Boltons, sending it, following Horace's tragic early death, to Admiral Sir Richard Keats, a friend of Nelson's who had served with him in the Mediterranean. Disguising the reason for his unexpected gift, he told Keats that the star was sent 'in testimony of your esteem for, & the mutual friendship which subsisted between yourself & my lamented & beloved brother'.[36]

Back in 1808, George Matcham had railed against his brother-in-law's selfishness. He had told Emma:

> I could never have conceived he could have so betrayed Tom Bolton, but it is evident that he is as great an enemy to us as our dear lost friend was our patron. The extinction of the whole family would be a matter of the greatest exultation to him, with the exception of his own dear self and Lady Charlotte. God only knows what his shocking rancour will lead to, but while this man exists I can safely say there is one person with whom I would not exchange situation moral or wordly. God mend him and preserve his wife, a wish comprising his punishment and restoration.[37]

By 1835, these worst fears were realised and soon the family were back in court arguing over titles and money. This time the outcome would decide the unhappy fate of the sultan's jewel.

16

THE DUCHESS

Charlotte was 11 when she realised that her family was famous. She had been at home in Norfolk when news of the Battle of the Nile reached England. Not fully understanding the scale of the event, she was taken with her brother Horace to watch the local militia fire salutes, then to nearby Swaffham for the celebration ball. There she met the Hostes, who had letters from their son William in Naples telling how he had carried Nelson's dispatch to the jubilant city. 'It was as full as could be expected' Charlotte wrote excitedly to her aunt. 'Mrs Hoste's ribbands which she had from London were half Navy Blue and half red to signify the Knights of the Bath, and of the Navy. She gave me a medallion of my uncle which I wore around my neck.' Charlotte then danced with Mrs Hoste, admiring Mrs Micklethwaite's 'very handsome cap from London inscribed in gold spangles: "The Hero of the Nile"'.[1]

Despite the festivities, she hardly knew her now-famous uncle. Her only faint memory of him was of 'building toy houses with bricks on the floor' before war broke out in 1793.[2] He was so often at sea and so rarely in Norfolk that when she sent him her congratulations, she shyly admitted that, 'I am afraid I have quite forgot you, but as I see your picture every day and hear so much about you it is impossible not to long to be acquainted with one who is so nearly related to me.'[3] Charlotte could not know that her life would never be the same again. Unable to afford school fees, her father was educating her at home in his draughty parsonage. But victory had brought titles and money to her Uncle Horatio, and now he offered to pay for her schooling, to support his family's new status. Aunt Fanny approved a school for educating young ladies in Chelsea, and soon Charlotte was spending more time in London than Hilborough or Canterbury. Her aunt doted on her, buying her cakes to take to school and lending her jewels to wear at a ball in January 1800. There, her head spinning with excitement, Charlotte stayed up until two in the morning dancing with Captain Hardy, who had just returned from Naples. A hero of the Nile, the unmarried Hardy cut an impossibly romantic and dashing figure to her impressionable eyes. But her father already had other ideas. He was planning to marry his daughter to Thomas Berney, a scion of solid Norfolk gentry with 'an estate between 3 and 4 thousand a year I should think, but I don't know exactly'.[4]

Charlotte's name brought her celebrity at school. When news of the Battle of Copenhagen came, the other girls put on a musical performance in her uncle's honour to celebrate this new triumph. She also quickly attracted the attention of Emma Hamilton, who saw in Charlotte a means of binding her lover's family still more closely to herself. When Merton was purchased, Charlotte was invited for holidays and was soon living there as a companion for Emma. William and Sarah Nelson were thrilled to see their daughter in the care of the celebrated and, in their eyes, sophisticated Lady Hamilton, who could better train her in the essential skills of dancing and music than her staid Aunt Fanny. And without such 'accomplishments', Sarah Nelson told Charlotte sternly, 'you would be nothing'.[5] She encouraged Emma to groom her daughter into 'a girl of fashion' and one fit for a good husband. 'Perseverance shall do it,' she declared.[6]

Emma loved the role of preceptress, spoiling her 'Carlotta' with expensive gowns, trips to the seaside and the best dancing and music teachers. Fanny had been saving up to buy a second-hand piano for Charlotte, but Emma now found her 'one of the best that Broadwood ever made'.[7] Unaware of her currency in the growing feud within her family, Charlotte warmly returned the affection shown to her at Merton. Life there was much more fun than being with her aunt or parents. Canterbury 'is *so dull*', she would complain ('so it is', agreed Emma, egging her on).[8] She willingly practiced walking through doors in a hooped gown, an essential skill for Court, or sitting down and getting up in a lady-like fashion. 'Beauty will not do without Grace and Elegance' was Emma's mantra.[9] She was even given dumb-bells to use to keep her trim. All this training paid off when Charlotte was noticed by the Duchess of Devonshire and started to receive invitations to the best balls and parties in town. Everyone was curious to meet Admiral Lord Nelson's beautiful young niece. As Charlotte's chaperone, Emma gained entry to houses otherwise barred to her, delighted to have outwitted Fanny's threat to 'shut me out' of high society. 'Tom tit is in town, bursting with rage and envy,' she gloated.[10] Such close attention inevitably brought risks, however, with Charlotte becoming conceited and prone to tantrums, showing flashes of that violent temper common to the Nelsons.[11]

Charlotte was living at Merton when Nelson returned from the Baltic after the Battle of Copenhagen. In excited letters to her parents, she described the noisy salutes of the local volunteers, watching as fireworks lit up the sky. Nelson found his niece had 'very much improved' under Emma's supervision, bringing tears to Charlotte's eyes when he told her that her mother Sarah 'was a fortune of £100,000 to my brother and I am prouder to have her for my sister than any woman in the Kingdom'.[12] He took her fishing and gave her a small diamond ring. He even persuaded Charlotte's headmistress to give all the girls a holiday on his return. Charlotte excitedly reported:

> Miss Veitch gave us apple pies, also custard and then negus to drink my uncle's health. Miss Veitch gave us the toast, it was 'Lord Nelson – may his future years be as happy as his past have been glorious.' How proud I am to have the approbation of my most glorious, victorious, virtuous uncle.[13]

At Merton, there was no avoiding how Nelson had earned such praise. The house was richly decorated with his portraits, trophies and naval paraphernalia. When Nelson was at home, the house was often crowded with fascinating and famous people: from dashing young officers to newspaper magnates, politicians, even royalty. When Horatia, retrieved from foster care in London, was cautiously introduced to the household as Emma's ward, Charlotte took her under her wing, earning her uncle's eternal gratitude. Emma presided happily over it all: a large and noisy presence swathed in colourful Kashmir shawls who filled the house with laughter and young people. Starry-eyed girls from Charlotte's school came to dine with the handsome progeny of Nelson's officers like Samuel Hood, grandson of the much-revered old admiral Viscount Hood. 'Sam Hood is quite delighted with Charlotte,' Emma mischievously told Sarah Nelson. 'He seemed to devour her with his eyes. *That* would be a good *match*.'[14] Sam, scion of a naval dynasty, was also cousin of the Nile captain Samuel Hood, who had entertained Kelim Efendi at Alexandria before directing the Turkish envoy with his precious cargo to Nelson at Naples.

In November 1801, Nelson was invited to ride in the Lord Mayor's coach for the annual parade which marked the end of the mayor's term in office. The ceremony was the highlight of the City of London's year, with crowds lining the route to see the beautiful coaches of the Livery Companies and glimpse the many celebrities they carried. Estranged from his wife, propriety prevented Nelson taking Emma as his guest, so he asked Charlotte to sit beside him as their coach, its horses taken from the traces, was pulled by the crowd through the streets of London. Behind them in the procession, the carriage of Sir Sidney Smith, fresh back from the Egyptian campaign, was similarly conveyed by excited bystanders. 'I wish you could have seen all the people jumping up at the carriage to see my uncle,' Charlotte breathlessly told her mother. 'All the ladies had their handkerchiefs out of the windows when my uncle passed, they and the people calling out, "Nelson for ever".'[15] The Guildhall was so crowded that many women fainted even before hero of the hour Smith (no longer Nelson) had made a speech and the dancing started. The room shimmered with diamond aigrettes. Lady Mary Price, wife of the new mayor, wore a 'superb' example with a towering plume of ostrich feathers.[16] In full uniform, it is likely Nelson wore his too to satisfy the crowd.

Christmas that year was especially boisterous: possibly the happiest of Nelson's life. Merton was full of friends and family, with Emma organising the fun and games to keep them entertained. Always highly theatrical, she designed her own production of 'The Favourite Sultana', a popular music hall routine. Children, servants, Nelson's secretary, a visiting artist and probably Nelson himself were all roped into the performance. Charlotte and her over-excited cousins Kitty and Lizzy Matcham were made up as Turkish ladies, whilst the gentlemen were all given 'negro' masks, robes and false moustaches to act the 'Moors of Quality'. Naturally, Emma took the leading role of the Sultana, wearing a floaty silk kaftan and satin jacket with colourful pantaloons, Turkish slippers and gold anklets. She smothered herself in jewels, wearing bunches of jangling bangles, rings on every finger and a necklace with a bottle holding scent which she wafted around the room. Her hair was loose and decorated with strings of pearls and a diamond circlet, which glittered on her glistening forehead. The performance brought the zest of the Levant to a chilly corner of Surrey and reduced the awe and splendour of the Sultan of Turkey to a pantomime figure.[17]

On 29 October 1805, Sarah Nelson wrote listlessly to her daughter at Merton complaining of the weather and the lack of news from 'your dear uncle'.[18] A week later, Charlotte heard the distant boom of guns announcing a victory, then watched as a carriage arrived with a scared looking officer from the Admiralty. There was a pause, then an awful atavistic scream tore through the house, freezing the servants in their routines and filling Charlotte with terrible dread. Her family descended on Merton. Bewildered, Charlotte helped with the letters of condolence which flooded in. Within days her life changed utterly. She became Lady Charlotte

Nelson, and by January her father had withdrawn her from Merton and away from Emma. The next month, she was presented at Court, not by Emma as so longed for, but by Mrs Fisher, wife of the Bishop of Exeter (and a future Bishop of Salisbury).[19] Emma was left reeling from grief and a burning sense of betrayal. Susanna Bolton's daughter Kitty offered sympathy, telling her that:

> Lady Charlotte is certainly good-tempered, but she has got no heart or she could not behave unkind to you, who have been so very kind to her, but she is one of those characters that are always governed by the opinions of those they are with.[20]

Faced with Emma's tears and her bitter recriminations, Charlotte awkwardly apologised. 'I am truly grieved that you should be so displeased with me,' she wrote. 'It is never my intention to offend you in anything.'[21] Emma had to maintain an uneasy relationship with the earl as he paid her income, but Charlotte was spared none of her bile and bitter accusations. She now claimed to have spent over £2,000 coaching Charlotte in manners, music and dancing, scrawling, 'Is it true that Lady Charlotte Nelson can be ungrateful to her benefactress Lady Hamilton?' on a printed copy of Nelson's will before sending it to Canterbury.

With his family now titled and wealthy, William Nelson raised his sights from Charlotte becoming simply Mrs Berney as so long planned. It was a near-run thing. Thomas Berney, her intended fiancé, had turned 21 in July 1805, and in August William had been to stay with the Berneys to hammer out the financial details of an engagement. After Trafalgar, the proposal was quietly dropped as the earl's ambitions for his daughter now extended beyond Norfolk gentry. They reached still higher after the death of his son in 1808. Charlotte was stunned by this fresh tragedy. Ignored by her hysterical mother and speechless father, she had been found by Bishop Fisher hours after her brother died, 'sitting in a state seemingly absorbed in sorrow'.[22] She was now the heartbroken earl's sole hope. When she returned to Court in 1809, the newspapers noticed her wearing the jewel 'presented by the Grand Seignior to her illustrious uncle'.[23] It was a powerful statement of her new role as heir to Nelson and how the meaning of the sultan's jewel was already shifting from an Ottoman order of chivalry to Nelson family ornament.

Charlotte obeyed her parents and indulged their dynastic scheming, allowing her name to be linked in the press with millionaire landowner Sir Gregory Turner. But she had not forgotten young Sam Hood, nor he her. Since meeting Charlotte at Merton, Sam had been to Cambridge University and was planning a career in politics and the law. He was heir by special remainder to the Irish barony of Bridport awarded to his octogenarian great uncle Admiral Alexander Hood after the 1794 Battle of the First of June. Despite marrying a much younger second wife, the admiral remained childless, and on his death Sam would also inherit his uncle's estates at Cricket in Somerset, centred on a beautiful mansion house newly built by the celebrated architect John Soane. Earl Nelson gave swift approval to a match linking two such illustrious names, hosting a sumptuous ball and supper for 300 people at Portman Square to celebrate the couple's engagement in May 1810. Two months later, Charlotte and Sam were married at Marylebone church (where Emma and Sir William Hamilton had wed in 1791). From afar, Fanny Nelson, who was close to the Hood family, proudly called it 'a union of names that will not be easily forgotten'.[24]

It was around the time of Charlotte's marriage that Prince Castelcicala had first hinted to the earl that his daughter might inherit Bronte through a quirk in Sicilian law. Keeping this a well-guarded secret, he had started to involve Sam and Charlotte in the running of his distant and draining domain. Their visit to Bronte in 1828 was the first by any member of the Nelson family some thirty years after its royal gift. Appalled by the poverty she found there, Charlotte also vowed it would be her last stay, 'unless there was a revolution in England and even then she would probably go elsewhere'.[25] The duchy's only apparent benefit was her use of the sultan's beautiful jewel, which Charlotte seems to have worn often, and not always as intended. Attending Court in 1820, a journalist spotted her wearing it on her gown as 'a diamond stomacher composed of part of the aigrette given to her uncle, the late Lord Nelson by the Grand Seignior'.[26]

Sam entered parliament in a lacklustre way, losing interest when he inherited the family's barony and mansion at Cricket. Now Lady Bridport, Charlotte's move to Somerset probably motivated her father's purchase of Standlynch in neighbouring Wiltshire. Aware of the misery caused to her own parents by their lack of children, Charlotte had nine in quick succession, all girls, until Alexander, born in 1814.[27] Three further boys died in infancy, leaving Alexander her only and precious son. After the turmoil of her youth, she now lived a conventional upper-class life, oscillating between town and country. She enjoyed needlework, hated cats and, a legacy perhaps of her early life at Merton, loved to fill her rooms with strongly scented flowers. She also firmly believed that Horatia Nelson was not her uncle's daughter, 'for reasons known in the family'.[28] After a frosty start, she developed an affectionate relationship with her likeable stepmother Hilare, appearing at Court with her in 1833. The elderly earl was particularly pleased to see that his grandson Alexander, 'gets on amazingly well with his new grandmamma. He has written her a very nice letter since his return to Eton, which she has answered; they are become great correspondents.'[29]

The Boltons bided their time when, as they had feared, Charlotte assumed the title Duchess of Bronte on her father's death in 1835. Tom Bolton, now second Earl Nelson, had grown up with Charlotte and was reluctant to confront her. He was guarded in replying to his lawyer's puzzled enquiry as to why he did not use the ducal title himself. 'I can only say at present it is claimed by Lady Bridport,' he responded, 'how justly I must leave to the law or his Sicilian Majesty to decide.'[30] But when Tom died within just ten months of inheriting, the trustees of the third earl, Tom's 12-year-old son Horatio, launched an action against the Bridports to recover the duchy and honour Nelson's original desire to keep his titles together in the family. If they failed, the trustees threatened to force a sale of the duchy, provision for which had also been made by Nelson in his will. Ironically, the same law in Sicily used by the Bridports to claim the duchy also helped the Nelsons, as it ordered the sale of property to compensate any disinherited family members.

The case dragged on for years, ten in all, mired in claims and counter-claims which drained any remaining goodwill between the two branches of Nelson's family and soured their relationship for decades to come. The Bridports shipped lawyers from Italy to argue their cause, leaving the less well-heeled Nelsons at a disadvantage. In 1845, the arguments were heard in Chancery by Master of the Rolls Lord Langdale, who quickly became mired in obscure legal precedent. Sam Hood thought the judge's summing-up so 'adverse' that he left court before hearing the judgement, telling Charlotte, who was anxiously waiting at home, that, 'we have lost the day, but cheer up we have enough money to get on with.' However, their son Alexander had stayed behind in court to listen, and he soon returned, 'bringing the good news' that their claim to Bronte 'had been declared valid after all'.[31] Lord Langdale had dismissed the Nelson family's argument, although, his head spinning with Sicilian case law, he admitted the judgement hung in the balance. Apart from losing Bronte, the Nelsons were stripped of 'certain decorations and jewels' specified in the admiral's original will as heirlooms linked to his estate in Sicily, including the sultan's jewel and the heraldic crest on their coat of arms which featured it.[32] One observer wrote:

> One feeling only, that of deep regret, must be entertained, that such memorials, of no value in themselves, except in connection with the history of the glorious deeds for which they were bestowed, should be so separated from the bearers of that title.'[33]

The only heirloom attached to the diminished earldom was the silver gilt Trafalgar vase awarded to the family by the Patriotic Fund after Trafalgar. The death of the second earl, coming so soon after that of the elderly first, then the crippling cost of their failed court case against the Bridports, forced the Nelsons to sell the remaining contents of Trafalgar House. The youthful third earl then devoted the rest of his long life to rebuilding a family collection of relics around his 'paltry share'.[34] Besides the Trafalgar vase, he owned the silver Turkey Company cup inherited by his grandmother Susannah Bolton and a model of HMS *Victory*'s main mast sent by Hilare, dowager Countess Nelson, in sympathy.

With the accession of Queen Victoria in 1837, Charlotte, still barely 50, attended the Court of her fourth monarch. Raised on the seafaring stories of her favourite uncle, 'sailor' King William IV, the young queen was fascinated by Nelson, whose public reputation was slowly recovering after the scandalous exposure of his affair with Emma. Although perplexed by the 'very singular way' Charlotte had inherited her title as Duchess of Bronte, Victoria invited her to launch the 120-gun goliath HMS *Trafalgar* at Woolwich Dockyard in 1838.[35] Albert, Prince Consort, who accompanied Victoria, told his father in Germany that, '[it] was the most imposing sight which I can remember. There were about 500,000 people present and the Thames was covered for miles with ships, steamers, barges and boats.'[36] Watched by the aging veterans of her uncle's fateful last battle, Charlotte named the ship with a bottle of wine preserved by her family from Nelson's private supply in *Victory*.

With his brother George IV, William had begun a royal tradition of collecting relics, portraits and artefacts connected to Nelson. In 1828, he gifted the coat worn by Nelson at the Nile to the Royal Hospital Greenwich after receiving it by will of the sculptor Anne Seymour Damer. There was already a Naval Gallery of art and relics at Greenwich, which William, a former messmate of Nelson, was keen to encourage. After he succeeded to the throne, he ordered a bust of his friend for Windsor Castle, to be displayed on a section of *Victory*'s shot-damaged main mast given him after Trafalgar.[37] Struck by the size of the crowds at the launch of *Trafalgar* and their adoration of Nelson, the politically astute Prince Consort, anxious to overcome public prejudice of his foreign birth, was then instrumental in securing for the nation the bloodstained coat worn by Nelson when he was fatally wounded.

This sacred relic had been returned to Emma Hamilton after Trafalgar following a tussle with the Nelsons, on condition that she preserve it for the 'Heir to the Title'.[38] However, in 1813, facing debtors prison, Emma had pawned the coat together with other relics and artworks for £400 to a friendly benefactor called Joshua Smith, a former Lord Mayor of London. Many of these items had been recovered for Horatia by the Nelson family after Emma died, but others remained hidden in crates until 1831, when they were examined at a London warehouse. Various things were then disposed of, others put back into store and some, including the contents of 'Prickel No.3', were collected by Joshua Smith and taken home. Listed in this crate was, 'Sword, one old coat, one pair of old breeches, three cocked hats, one tin case containing two feathers'.[39] After Smith's death in 1834, these items remained with his widow for a further ten years until they were brought to the attention of Thomas Evans, a dealer in historic autographs and curios in London's West End. His informer was a former servant of Smith's called John Kinsey, who told the dumbstruck dealer, in awed expression, that the 'old coat' on the list was 'THE COAT'. Kinsey offered an introduction to Mrs Smith, and a few weeks later Evans found himself with mounting excitement examining the coat, with accompanying bloodstained waistcoat, in suburban Twickenham.[40]

He 'was astonished to find it so well preserved. I folded the fronts of the coat together, to enable me to see the number of decorations upon it. There were four orders, or stars, of silver embroidery, sewn on the left breast, also epaulettes.'[41] He then put his finger through the hole in the coat left by the ball which killed Nelson, although he was sceptical that the heavy black staining on the coat's white silk lining was blood. Among other relics, Mrs Smith still possessed full-length portraits of Nelson and Emma Hamilton, a bust, a large quantity of letters and a sword which Evans afterwards claimed had been displayed on Nelson's coffin at his funeral. Unfortunately, Mrs Smith no longer had the cocked hats mentioned in her husband's old inventory, as they 'had got so eaten up by the moths, that I was obliged to have them thrown away'.[42] The 'two feathers' in the tin case were probably embroidered replicas of the sultan's jewel ordered for Nelson to wear on his undress uniform hat.

Anxious to buy the coat, Evans fell into competition with Sir Nicholas Harris Nicolas, then busily editing Nelson's letters for publication. Nicolas, a dogged antiquarian with a naval background, was being helped in his task by Charlotte, who had inherited many of Nelson's papers and his family correspondence. Her involvement in the project inevitably led to suggestions that she suppressed some documents to show her father and uncle in the best possible light. Nicolas's other collaborator was Horatia Nelson, long since married to a curate and living quietly in Kent. She had recently met Nicolas at John Salter's old shop in the Strand, now managed by his nephew George Widdowson. Horatia had fond memories of Salter, who had stood godfather to one of her children, as he had remained supportive of Emma long after her other friends deserted her, hopeful perhaps that her fortune might one day be restored. Between May 1810 and February 1812, he had even allowed Emma to spend £166 8*s* 9*d* (£10,000 today) on jewels – many commemorating Nelson – silverware and repairs at his shop, with little prospect of ever being paid.[43] He had then loaned Emma £150, taking much of her silver back as security, including dishes from Nelson's famous Nile service.[44] When Horatia retrieved a number of family miniatures from Joshua Smith after her mother's death – 'of little value', she assured him[45] – it was to Salter's shop that she sent them for safekeeping, as her father had once done with his own jewels. Salter also acted for Horatia to prevent the sale of various heirlooms seized by Emma's creditors after her death. He had done similar for Emma in 1813, going to an auction of her belongings to buy back, for a hefty £25, a luxurious four-poster bed.[46] This was probably the same bed 'fill'd with best goose feathers' supplied by Peddison in 1805 in which she and Nelson had passed their last night together before Trafalgar.[47]

Salter had died in 1834, but Widdowson still owned the hat gifted to his uncle by Nelson after the Battle of Copenhagen. Despite receiving a 'large' offer, 'nothing would tempt me to part with it', he declared.[48] Horatia also remained in touch with Salter's widow Ann, introducing her to Nicolas, as the old lady possessed private testimony from Emma that Horatia was 'the true and beloved daughter of Viscount Nelson'. The Hoods contested this claim, although Nicolas agreed to publish it, alongside Emma's denial in her lifetime that she was Horatia's mother. That person was 'TOO GREAT to be mentioned', she had told Mrs Salter, probably to protect her sensitive appeal to government for a pension.[49]

Horatia knew Mrs Smith and was happy to help Nicolas secure the worn relics and deprive the dealer Evans of his prize. Nicolas was especially anxious to see the coat to investigate suggestions that Nelson had somehow courted death by wearing his sparkling jewels during the battle. Reports that Captain Hardy had urged the admiral to cover up his decorations during the action had circulated almost immediately after Trafalgar. It was commonly believed, even by his own family, that 'the brilliancy of his dress' had attracted the sharpshooter who killed Nelson.[50] It helped to make sense of his inexplicable loss. Confirmation that Nelson was wearing his barely less brilliant embroidered copies of his orders on his coat during the action failed to scotch talk of his wilful self-destruction.

As neither Nicolas nor Horatia could afford Mrs Smith's asking price of £150 for the Trafalgar coat and waistcoat, an appeal was made to the palace to support a public campaign to buy them. By return came Albert's offer to purchase the bloodstained relics outright, as 'it will be a pride and a pleasure to present them to Greenwich Hospital'.[51] As the *Illustrated London News* remarked, and the prince had no doubt hoped, 'nothing could so help identify the Queen's husband with the British people as such little tributes to their maritime pride.'[52] Nicolas delivered the coat to Albert in person. He then faced furious accusations from Thomas Evans that he had colluded with Horatia – 'an artful, cunning woman'[53] – to prevent the dealer buying such highly charged relics. As the Nelsons and Bridports had already discovered, fighting over the admiral's earthly remains was an expensive and emotive business.

17

THE GENERAL

Despite his illustrious name, Charlotte's son Alexander Nelson Hood did not follow his ancestors to sea. The Royal Navy lost its glamour, rewards and ships in peacetime. As Lord Byron mournfully put it:

> Nelson was once Britannia's god of war,
> And still should be so, but the tide is turn'd;
> There's no more to be said of Trafalgar,
> 'Tis with our hero quietly inurn'd:
> Because the army's grown more popular,
> At which the naval people are concern'd,
> Besides, the prince is all for the land service,
> Forgetting Duncan, Nelson, Howe and Jervis.[1]

So instead of joining the navy, after schooling at Eton, Alexander purchased a commission in the Royal Scots Fusilier Guards, a line regiment which had formed a guard of honour at his great-uncle's state funeral in 1806. Joining the army was a break with family tradition, but it offered more secure employment and aristocratic company than the Victorian Royal Navy. After two years guarding convicts in Western Australia, Hood returned with his regiment to England to marry Lady Mary Hill, daughter of the Marquess of Downshire. Mary was related to several famous military commanders of the recent wars, including the Duke of Wellington. Her family was reputed to be the largest landowner in Ireland, with estates centred on Hillsborough Castle in the north. An upbringing at the heart of the so-called Ascendency in Ireland had made Mary an 'ardent conservative and protestant' with a stereotypical love of horses and hunting.[2] In his wedding speech, Hood's father, Lord Bridport, extolled 'the happy connection of the naval and military glories of this country in the names of Nelson, Hood and Bridport, now allied with those of the illustrious Duke and his gallant companions in arms, Lords Hill and Combermere'.[3] As children started arriving to the newly-weds, a financially crippling ten in all, the romantically minded Benjamin Disraeli noted that, 'in them alone, the blood of Nelson and Wellington is blended!'[4]

In 1841, just weeks after his mother launched HMS *Trafalgar*, Alexander was lifted out of the army and appointed a Groom-in-Waiting to Queen Victoria, with Mary becoming one of her Ladies-in-Waiting.[5] These positions in the Royal Household required daily attendance on the monarch to support her constitutional and social functions. Seemingly mundane, such appointments were extremely sensitive, as the queen discovered when she became embroiled in the damaging 'Bedchamber Crisis' when Victoria had refused demands by the ruling Tory party to dismiss Ladies in her household married to opposition Whig politicians. Victoria was known to be strongly partisan towards the Whigs and their charismatic leader Lord Melbourne, and her obstinacy over the appointments was seen as dangerously unconstitutional. Tory Prime Minister Sir Robert Peel had even refused to take office over the issue, restoring Melbourne to power but damaging the young Victoria at the outset of her reign. Melbourne's government had fallen after just two years, forcing elections in June 1841 around the time of *Trafalgar*'s launch. The result was a Tory landslide, with the queen conceding defeat and dismissing three of her most contentious Ladies. It was in this fraught atmosphere, with every appointment under close scrutiny, that Alexander Hood joined the household. He was a shrewd and populist choice. After a thirty-year lull, there was renewed interest in Nelson now that veterans of the war were growing old and the impact of scandalous revelations about the admiral's private life were receding. A stone column commemorating the hero was rising in London's new Trafalgar Square, and a wave of complimentary biographies were planned alongside the eagerly anticipated publication of the admiral's letters by Sir Nicholas Harris Nicolas.

Hood was temperamentally well-suited to a life at Court, with its stultifying routine and protocol. Tall, like his father, he was said to be reserved, even a little austere. 'His manners were those of a courtier,' his son remembered, and 'the beau ideal of an English gentleman'.[6] No doubt Hood learned such conduct from his mother, herself so rigorously trained by Emma Hamilton. Despite moving to Windsor, Hood remained on the Army List, rising inexorably through the ranks without ever seeing action and effortlessly accumulating honours hard-won in the past by his ancestors. Near in age, he grew especially close to the Prince Consort, sharing many of Albert's interests. When his regiment went to war in the Crimea, Hood stayed behind at Windsor to manage the prince's farm with its prize herd of cattle and to hunt the royal hounds. Undoubtedly a favourite retainer, he was given grace and favour apartments for his growing family at Cumberland Lodge in the Great Park. The fastidious Disraeli, who stayed with the Hoods in 1860, thought the house was 'a large uncouth red-brick pile in the worst style of the Georgian age, situate in the most exquisite sylvan scenery in the world'.[7] Nevertheless, it was still devastating when the property was gutted by fire a few years later. The queen had hurried over from the castle to offer help in her galoshes, complaining in her journal how she was 'pumped upon and got very wet' as she and Hood stepped disconsolately through the charred ruins.[8]

With the death of his father in 1868, Hood, who had risen to major-general in the army, inherited his family's barony, becoming Lord Bridport. As a mark of special favour to her loyal courtier, the queen also revived an English title dormant in the Hood family since 1814, naming him Viscount Bridport on strict condition that he would not dabble in politics. It was said Hood declined an earldom on grounds of cost, the same reason given when his great-uncle rejected a baronetcy back in 1797.[9] Five years later, with the death of his mother Charlotte, aged 85, he succeeded to the Dukedom of Bronte too. Like her father, to avoid further litigation from her Nelson cousins, Charlotte had lodged a will in Italy under Sicilian law stating her only son's succession to the duchy and its title.[10] Her will also confirmed his inheritance of 'the diamond aigrette presented to my said late uncle by the Grand Signior, my diamond necklace consisting of fifteen pieces, my large diamond brooch and the collar of the Bath'.

In fact, Charlotte passed the sultan's jewel to her daughter-in-law Mary Hood for her use long before her death. Mary wore it regularly at Court, on one occasion causing confusion to a visiting Turkish dignitary. According to family tradition, the envoy had ignored Victoria, throwing himself instead at the feet of Mary, 'as she was wearing this emblem which in the Mohammedian world corresponded to the highest order of chivalry in the Christian'.[11] This was the same reaction Nelson generated when the Turkish naval officer delivered the Tsar of Russia's box in Palermo. The brief friendship between Constantinople and London after the Battle of the Nile had been revived by the recent war in the Crimea, when once again Turkish and British soldiers fought and died alongside each other on campaign in the east. The rapprochement culminated in a state visit to England by Sultan Abdul Aziz in 1867 during the first trip to Western Europe by an Ottoman emperor.

The 37-year-old potent was son of Mahmud II, the sultan placed on the throne after the assassination of Selim III back in 1808. Like his ill-fated forebear, Abdul Aziz was a highly cultivated man, a talented composer with a love of art and literature. He also shared Selim's fascination with his navy – still the third largest in the world after the British and French – spending a fortune on new warships. But the cracks evident in the Ottoman Empire of Selim's day were now gaping, with Turkey on the verge of bankruptcy and facing decades of conflict which would lead inexorably to the total collapse of the empire after the First World War. For now, the splendour, majesty and awe of the sultan still fascinated the West, with people curious to see this much-mythologised figure. So there was some disappointment at the short, portly and bearded figure who stepped off a French royal yacht at Dover. The sultan was dressed in a blue coat richly embroidered in gold over trousers and topped, not by a turban, but by the simple red fez introduced as a modernising measure by his father. He also wore the red and green sash of the Order of the Medjidie, instituted in 1851 to replace the long-neglected Order of the Crescent and widely awarded in its different classes to British officers during the Crimean War.

The sultan was welcomed to England by the Prince of Wales, attended by General Hood, who, in a nod no doubt to his family's former ties with Turkey, was appointed equerry to Abdul Aziz during his stay in England. He joined the prince and the sultan for the journey by railway to London, the train festooned with flowers and decorated with the arms of England and Turkey.[12] On 13 July, Abdul Aziz lunched with the queen at Windsor. Six years after his untimely death, Victoria was still mourning her husband, complaining to her journal that, 'It is so dreadful to me to have to do this all alone!' Yet she was keenly interested in her exotic guest, who despite being 'broad & stout' had 'a fine, dignified, pleasing countenance, with a pleasant smile'. Unused to cutlery, the sultan had his food cut up for him during lunch; nevertheless, the queen, a hearty eater herself, was impressed by his appetite. She also noticed with approval that he 'never touched' his wine.[13]

The highlight of the week-long visit was a review of the British fleet off Portsmouth, when some fifty Royal Navy warships gathered in terrible weather to salute the queen and her imperial guest. Gales of rain dampened the celebrations, whilst the heavy swell drove the queasy sultan down to his cabin in the royal yacht. However, he emerged unsteadily on deck to receive the Order of the Garter from the hand of the queen herself, 'which he had set his heart upon', she confided, 'though I should have preferred the Star of India, which is more suited for those who are not Christians'.[14] In return, the sultan decorated the two youngest royal princes, Arthur and Leopold, with diamond stars of the Order of Osmanieh. Recently introduced by Abdul Aziz himself, this Ottoman order of chivalry was more prestigious than the Medjidie and the highest honour afforded a Western recipient. Before he departed, the sultan would bestow this same high honour on Alexander Hood, handing him also precious snuff boxes.

Like Selim before him, Abdul Aziz's gentle manner and love of culture could not save him from the bloody fate of so many of his predecessors. Ten year after his visit to England, in May 1876, the sultan was deposed in a palace coup and thrown into prison, where he was found dead a few days later with his wrists slashed open by a pair of scissors, improbably by suicide. News of Abdul Aziz's downfall and death was greeted with dismay by Queen Victoria at Windsor, who had grown fond of him during his short stay. 'How dreadful!' she exclaimed. 'What an end, when one thinks of his triumphant visit to England!'[15] When the sultan's successor supposedly went mad within days, Abdul Hamid II came to the throne. He had travelled with his uncle Abdul Aziz to Europe, and although drawn towards Germany as his own empire collapsed around him, memory of that trip with its choppy afternoon in the royal yacht resulted in an unexpected gift to Britain. Responding to a request from a wealthy tourist to purchase the version of Nelson's portrait by Leonardo Guzzardi sent to Constantinople by the admiral back in 1799, and at that time hanging in the Imperial Treasury, Abdul Hamid arranged for a copy to be made instead by Italian artist Luigi Acquarone. Before it was shipped to London, the painting was mounted in an elaborately carved gilt wood frame decorated with trophies, flags and the sultan's coat of arms. It was unveiled in 1888 at the new National Portrait Gallery in Trafalgar Square, beneath the watchful eye of Nelson's statue high up on its towering column and just a few hundred yards from the original painting in the Admiralty boardroom on Whitehall, long since recovered from the former Packet, now titled Lord Nelson Hotel in Milford.

Memories of the past like this kept breaking into the present. A constant worry for General Hood was Bronte, his family's distant and troublesome domain. Passing through it in the late 1820s, Charlotte Bridport had vowed never to return. When she inherited, she had handed the running of the duchy entirely over to her agent William Thovez, who had long struggled against local insurrection and corruption. In 1848, together with the rest of Sicily (and much of Europe), the duchy openly rebelled against royal rule. An army sent from Naples subdued the revolt and pacified the island, but when the insurgent Giuseppe Garibaldi and his thousand-strong army landed at Marsala in May 1860, all the simmering discontent flared up into bloody violence. The liberation of Sicily from Bourbon rule raised local hopes in Bronte that the duchy might be dissolved and the land shared out. Years of feuding and bitter local rivalries fed into the dispute, leading to mob rule as scores were bloodily settled. Over several days in August, in scenes reminiscent of the horrors in Naples back in 1799, Bronte descended into an orgy of violence, with executions, lynchings and murders. Only the arrival of troops sent by Garibaldi ended the bloodletting, leaving the town in smoking ruins and strewn with charred and mutilated corpses.

The terrible events of 1860 highlighted the neglect of the duchy and, together with the early death of the Prince Consort the following year, which lessened his workload, roused the general to visit Bronte with his family several times over the coming years. With no roads, the Bridports explored their land by mule, much as Charlotte had done thirty years earlier. With his interest in agriculture, Hood wanted to modernise and diversify the many small farms, with their staple crop of pistachios, and restore his dilapidated woodland and decaying vineyards. On acquiring Bronte in 1799, Nelson had immediately seen its potential for supplying his fleet with wine, which his officers drank in prodigious quantities at his cabin table. There was a long-established wine trade in Sicily, managed by British merchants who specialised in the island's distinctive Marsala wine. Some of this wine had been rebranded

Bronte Madeira to exploit Nelson's fame, although it was not produced in the duchy itself, which, badly managed and under-resourced, had struggled to cultivate its own vines. The general, however, encouraged by his enthusiastic younger son Alec, now invested heavily in the wine business, launching Duchy of Bronte wines on the London market in 1890 with mixed results. Alec had been struck by the wild beauty of the duchy on his very first visit as a teenager, developing a deep love of the region and its people. Alongside his own career at Court, he now dedicated himself to preserving and restoring the estate, making its sprawling castle at Maniace a home by filling it with English furniture, battle paintings and portraits of his naval ancestors. His delighted father recognised this passion by naming Alec his successor as duke ahead of two elder brothers.

With Alec engaged in running Bronte and life at Court growing less arduous as the queen grew old, the general retreated to Cricket House and the comfortable life of a country squire, surrounded by his many treasures. A visitor to Somerset commented:

> His Lordship is greatly respected by his tenantry and neighbours, and beloved by his labourers, to whom he is a true friend, as also the Viscountess and their numerous family. The hospitality of Cricket is proverbial in the neighbourhood, for the establishment is kept up in the good old English style so rapidly becoming a thing of the past.[16]

In September 1889, George Lathom Browne, author of a recent biography of the Duke of Wellington, stayed at the house to research the thirty-seven bulging volumes of Nelson's letters in the library for a new life of the admiral. Most of these documents had already been published by Sir Nicholas Harris Nicolas, but Browne returned to them with the aim of burnishing Nelson's reputation after its tarnishing by other biographers. His book, which was dedicated to Queen Victoria, exonerated Nelson's behaviour in Naples, denied he was Horatia's father and accused Emma of forging his love letters: all of which were Hood family preoccupations. If Browne's book was of little use to scholars, it did offer one gem. During his stay at Cricket, Browne was permitted to photograph the Nelson relics in the family collection. These were carefully assembled at the house by Alec and captured by a local photographer from Chard. The photographs show all Nelson's orders, medals and decorations, plus the admiral's Freedom boxes and other relics like the gold combination knife and fork made for a disabled man and Nelson's pocket watch, which had been mounted by Charlotte Bridport in a clock case. Framed by the sashes of Nelson's chivalric orders, the staging of the relics appears to deliberately imitate his elaborate coat of arms.

Easily overlooked in the photographs is the fur draped around the base of the displays, suggesting that the sultan's pelisse, possibly glimpsed in the portrait of Hilare Nelson, still survived. The photographs also revealed that Nelson's gold crocodile-hilted sword and the diamond sword presented to him by Ferdinand IV were missing their blades, an apparent wilful act of vandalism to better store them.[17] The only object absent from the photographs is the sultan's jewel, which, now seen more as an ornament than a chivalric order, was probably with other family gems in London or Windsor. Two years after the photographs were taken, most of these medals, decorations, sword hilts and relics were loaned by the general to the Royal Naval Exhibition, a vast enterprise which sprawled over the grounds of the Royal Hospital, Chelsea, for six months in 1891. Conceived as a celebration of Britain's maritime past and present, the show combined historic relics, artefacts and artworks with displays of modern weaponry and shipbuilding. Opened by the Prince of Wales, this blockbuster event attracted over two million visitors with its replica of HMS *Victory*, gory waxwork *tableau* of the death of Nelson by Madame Tussauds and pavilions packed with almost 6,000 exhibits valued in excess of £220,000 (over £20 million today). Given this number of objects, and the haste with which they were assembled, the organisers were unable to guarantee the authenticity of the cataloguing. *The Times* wryly pointed out that no less than three identical gold medals for the Nile (two lent by Viscount Bridport, one by Earl Nelson) all claimed to have been worn by Nelson. Touching as it did the highly sensitive issue of family inheritance, the comment drew a furious complaint from Alec Hood, who retorted that his family's medals were the real ones and the example loaned by the Nelsons was 'probably never in possession of the admiral'.[18]

The sultan's jewel was not exhibited at Chelsea either and remained hidden until 1895, when a series of bizarre events dragged it back to public view. That January, a hatter from Oxfordshire called James Hawtin sued his wife Annie for divorce on the grounds of her adultery with co-respondent Llewelyn Wynne, who he claimed had fathered her recent child. Wynne was senior partner in a highly respected firm of London solicitors with offices in Lincoln's Inn, a town house in Berkeley Square and a mansion near Banbury. Founded in 1773, his firm managed funds for many upper-class families, including the Bridports. A prospective Conservative Party candidate for parliament, Wynne angrily refuted the charge, hiring top lawyer Sir Edward Clarke QC as his barrister. As their neighbour in Oxfordshire, Wynne claimed to have helped the Hawtins with various legal issues relating to a property transaction. He denied any impropriety with Annie, despite evidence of hotel assignations, locked doors during clandestine meetings and unexplained gifts of flowers and jewels sent by Wynne from Monte Carlo. He accused the Hawtins of colluding in a conspiracy to blackmail him, telling the court he had withdrawn a previous action against them for slander.[19]

Despite Wynne's high standing and the best efforts of Sir Edward Clarke, the jury hearing the case was unable to reach a decision and a retrial was ordered. As Hawtin could not afford further legal fees, the case was dropped, freeing Sir Edward Clarke to act for Oscar Wilde in his disastrous libel prosecution of the Marquess of Queensberry just weeks later. However, the adverse publicity generated by the tawdry case, with its salacious detail and talk of visits to the gambling tables of Monte Carlo, rattled Wynne's clients. They began to withdraw funds, triggering a run on the firm which ended on 2 March 1895 when Wynne abruptly told his partner he was 'going away'. The partner, Wynne's put-upon younger brother, filed for bankruptcy when he then discovered the firm had debts of £250,000 (about £25 million today). Wynne had been running a so-called 'Ponzi' scheme for years, paying dividends to clients with funds invested by others. Meantime, he had been helping himself to upwards of £30,000 (£3 million today) a year of their money to support his own lavish lifestyle and political ambition. A warrant was issued for his arrest, but despite rumoured sightings in Vienna, Bucharest and Cape Town, and a letter from him to his distraught wife begging for money, he was never seen again. In consequence of his actions, hundreds of his well-heeled clients were 'reduced to beggary'.[20]

Now in his 80s, the fraud was a devastating blow to General Hood. His finances were in a dire state already, with Cricket heavily mortgaged to Wynne and Bronte jointly pledged to Wynne and an Italian bank. Only the intervention of a relative had prevented him going bust back in 1894. In addition to these mortgages totalling about £96,000 (£10 million today), he had about £9,000 cash invested with Wynne in various trusts, whilst his in-laws – Mary's family the Downshires – stood to lose a further £5,600.[21] A secluded life at Court had not made the general a rich man, nor a worldly one. For years he had been living on debt to support his title, falling into a trap Nelson had also tried to avoid. He had even invited Wynne to Bronte, getting himself tangled up in the solicitor's many other dodgy deals which left him mired in litigation for years to come. Thankfully, Wynne's scheme to put the duchy into a company with himself as director was forestalled by his own legal problems. As the Italian bank was its principal creditor, Bronte could still be saved, but Cricket was doomed. In May, Wynne's creditors called in all his mortgages, pushing the general to the very brink of bankruptcy and forcing him to take desperate measures. He was 'very anxious to save the family and what may be termed their hereditary place (since it was purchased by the prize monies won by Lords Nelson, Hood and Bridport)', but it was now obvious he had clung onto Cricket for far too long.[22]

His advisers Capel Cure & Ball reported that Lord Ashburton was willing to lend £100,000 to save the Bridport family from the 'disgrace of bankruptcy', but only on condition that all the general's properties in England were immediately sold. A member of the wealthy Barings banking family, Ashburton was married to the general's cousin, Mabel Hood. With this loan, Capel Cure hoped to save Bronte, with its valuable forestry, farms and vineyards. However, 'the only source from which the necessary funds can be obtained to pay the premium of £1,000 and the expenses incidental to the transfer of the Morgages', Capel Cure firmly instructed the general's lawyers, 'is by the sale of the Nelson portrait, plate, Orders &c which are heirlooms and of which Lord Bridport is trustee. We ask the family to approve of a breach of trust being committed.' 'The benefits which will accrue to the holder of the title,' they concluded, 'will we think be admitted to exceed the advantages of possessing even these valuable and interesting heirlooms.'[23]

Immediately Christie's started cataloguing the medals and relics, whilst Alec Hood sought agreement from the rest of the family to sell them. The Christie's expert admitted it was 'impossible to put any sum on them as their value was really dependant on the competition for them'. However, to secure the prestigious sale and meet their client's pressing need, Christie's advanced £1,000 against the auction. The general hoped the nation might buy the sixty bulging volumes containing hundreds of Nelson's letters in his library. If not, Christie's 'thought the volumes should be split up and the most valuable sold by themselves and the less valuable in small bundles'.[24] The general also had a 'strong desire' to save 'the actual orders and medals worn by Lord Nelson', telling his distraught son to send the sale catalogue to the queen 'to ascertain HM pleasure to become the purchaser of them for the Windsor Castle collection'.[25] The matter was urgent, as the sale was planned for 11 and 12 July, leaving little time for slow-moving bureaucracy. Christie's helpfully suggested listing the medals at the end of the auction so they could be withdrawn at the very last moment if government intervened or the earlier lots exceeded expectation. In the event, they were scheduled to open the second day's sale.

The queen responded quickly, as her husband had done fifty years before when Nelson's coat was in jeopardy. At her urging, £3,000 (about £300,000 today) was voted by parliament to purchase Nelson's letters for the British Museum. Then Alec Hood was summoned to see Victoria's private secretary Sir Arthur Bigge, 'with regard to some of the heirlooms being purchased by the nation'.[26] Just a day before the auction, Chancellor of the Exchequer Sir Michael Hicks-Beach approved an offer of £2,500 for Nelson's medals and orders, telling Christie's 'to inform the public who attend the sale that the nation has purchased them'.[27] This 'patriotic' and 'highly popular action' was unprecedented and warmly praised in the press, as there was still a conviction in the public's mind that these shining medals 'were almost certainly the indirect occasion of their wearer's death', despite the evidence of the coat at Greenwich with the stitched replicas worn by Nelson in the battle. *The Morning Post* declared:

> It is a matter of congratulation that they were not submitted to what under the circumstances would have amounted to the vulgar ignominy of a public auction. There would be something revolting in the idea of things so priceless in a national sense being exposed to the bidding of the speculative collector and perhaps falling into the hands of strangers.[28]

The decorations saved for the nation comprised Nelson's three gold medals for the battles of St Vincent, Copenhagen and posthumously for Trafalgar; his stars for the Orders of the Bath, St Joachim, Malta and St Ferdinand; and the gold medal for Egypt. The sultan's jewel, its status as an emblem of Ottoman gallantry having now sunk to little more than a family bauble, was excluded from the nation's purchase and condemned to the auction. The only jewel preserved by the family was the collar for the Order of the Bath, which, appointed to that Order himself in 1891, the general now wore himself. The sale catalogue also shed light on two other jewels he had inherited from his mother: her large diamond brooch and a diamond necklace. The brooch was identified by Christie's as 'the fastening to the "Cloak of Honour" presented to Lord Nelson by the Sultan of Turkey after the battle of the Nile', and the necklace as 'consisting of the stones removed from the Sword of Honour presented to Lord Nelson by the King of Naples'.[29]

Following the last-minute withdrawal of the medals, the Chelengk was the first lot offered on the second day of the auction. Catalogued as 'AN AIGRETTE OF ROSE DIAMONDS *Presented to Lord Nelson by the Sultan of Turkey after the Battle of the Nile*', it opened at an unpromising £100 before 'brisk competition' took it up to £710 (£75,000).[30] The buyer was court jeweller Fraser & Haws, acting for Mrs Constance Eyre-Matcham, who was related by marriage to the Nelsons and Bridports. No doubt she had used an agent in the saleroom to spare the family blushes. Fraser & Haws also bought the diamond necklace made from the stones taken from the sword for a hefty £1,250; this was the top price of the sale and a reflection that it was set with valuable brilliant not rose diamonds like the aigrette. The necklace eventually found its way to the Earl of Mexborough. Stripped of its precious stones by Charlotte Bridport, the sword's hilt was left unsold at £170 and had to wait until after the sale, when it was snapped up by Lady Llangottock for her famous collection of Nelson relics.[31] The brooch said to be the clasp from Nelson's pelisse, and 'formed partly of rose diamonds and partly of imitation pastes', fetched £260 from Sir William Fraser, a wealthy collector of literary and military relics who already owned one of Nelson's swords.[32] After deduction of Christie's fees, the sale of the Bridport heirlooms fetched £14,144 (about £1.5 million today).

Alec Hood called the auction the 'great grief of my father's life'.[33] Yet added to the £5,500 from government for the medals and papers, the proceeds only met the most pressing claims on the family from Wynne's creditors.[34] The contents of Cricket down to the door scrapers had to be auctioned too, and the house itself sold to Francis Fry of the famous chocolate-making family. The disconsolate general retreated to Royal Lodge at Windsor, its use donated by the sympathetic queen. Besieged by creditors to the end of his long life in 1904, he clung resolutely to Bronte and its title, passing them at his death to Alec. But like Nelson's earldom, they too were now devoid of the sparkling treasures which had once adorned them.

18

THE PEOPLE

After their purchase for the British nation, Nelson's medals went first to the British Museum, before being handed over to the Lords Commissioners of the Admiralty for display in the Painted Hall of the Royal Hospital, Greenwich. Once the site of the admiral's lying-in-state, the hall was a place of pilgrimage, with a gallery of maritime paintings and exhibition of naval relics. The highlight was Nelson's Trafalgar coat, which after its purchase by the Prince Consort in 1845 had been reverentially placed in a purpose-made mahogany cabinet on the dais at the far end of the hall where Nelson's body had once lain. Writer Virginia Woolf 'burst into tears' when she saw it there in 1926:

> There was too, his little fuzzy pigtail, of golden, greyish hair tied in black; and his long white stockings, one much stained, and his white breeches with the gold buckles, and his stock – all of which I suppose they must have undone and taken off as he lay dying. Kiss me Hardy &c., Anchor, anchor, – I read it all when I came in and I could swear I was on the Victory.[1]

The medals were arranged in a long display case, where they were photographed in 1898 for a series of fortnightly magazines called *Nelson and His Times*.[2] With interest in Nelson rising ahead of the centenary of Trafalgar, the magazines were a huge hit, but unfortunately, they may also have contributed to the disastrous events of Saturday, 8 December 1900. That evening, a thief, after concealing himself in the hall at closing time, escaped through a window then shinned down a drain pipe with many of Nelson's most precious treasures. It was not until the following afternoon that the display case was found smashed and its irreplaceable contents missing. Eighteen items were taken, including all of Nelson's naval gold medals, his gold medal for the Order of the Crescent and the Grand Cross of the Order of St Ferdinand and Merit.

Press attention turned inevitably to a suspicious-looking party of Frenchmen seen in the hall the preceding Friday, then again on the day of the burglary, 'apparently deeply interested in the priceless collection of treasures that Great Britain holds as her past prestige, and which have caused her sons, in upholding British supremacy, to take up arms against the Boers'. A 'dastardly' political motive was suspected by a foreign power, and 'that secret service money was employed in the cause'.[3] A flaw in this theory was the targeting of objects of the highest monetary not patriotic value, as the gold medals were stolen but the iconic uniform coat left untouched. Horatio third Earl Nelson, who had spent a lifetime rebuilding a collection of relics for Trafalgar House, called the robbery 'a disgrace to our country'.[4] At Windsor, General Viscount Bridport's old heart must have nearly broken at the news of a catastrophe ultimately caused by his own financial problems.

With the thief long gone and no leads to pursue, the police posted a £200 reward for information leading to a conviction or recovery of the stolen property. Far short of the £2,500 paid for them by government for the medals just five years earlier, but higher than their scrap value, the bounty was designed to encourage the safe return of the medals, as they were considered far too recognisable to sell on the open market. Four years later, this plan seemed to work when an itinerant young shoemaker called William Carter returned from Australia and asked after the reward. He offered up a missing gold watch, but his reasons for owning it were so implausible that he was committed for trial at the Old Bailey and found guilty of receiving stolen property and being involved in the theft. The judge described Carter's crime as 'an offence against the nation', and sent him to prison for seven years with hard labour. He was also 'sorry to say that a large quantity of relics were still no one knew where', as Carter had given the police no further information on the whereabouts of the other items.[5] To the end of his life, the police detective involved in the case believed the medals might have escaped the melting pot for 'the hands of some collector of antiques, who knows nothing of their value to the nation or of their true character'.[6] Carter, too, on his release from prison, suggested that the medals might have survived. In a written confession, he revealed that he had sold them for just £105 to a handler of stolen goods in North London called Alf Sutton before escaping to Australia. Blaming Sutton for encouraging his crime, he claimed he had been told they would be preserved rather than melted down. Despite Carter's apparent remorse, his story was not believed and Sutton escaped investigation. As the price he had paid equated to the medals' scrap value, they probably were destroyed, although hope remains that something may one day turn up.

Among the other treasures lost were some important items bought at the Bridport sale by the publicly spirited Mr Mullens, a railway executive from Sussex. He had purchased the Egyptian Club gold sword hilt and a gold and enamel freedom box from the City of London at the Christie's sale, but after gifting them to Greenwich Hospital had watched in horror as both were stolen with the medals. The theft seemed to highlight the unsuitability of Greenwich – criticised as a 'huge slum' by Admiral Fisher in 1905 – as a safe repository of the nation's maritime treasures.[7] Unnerved, Mullens donated other items, such as a gold combined knife and fork gifted to Nelson by Lady Spencer, to the rival Royal United Services Institution in Whitehall. 'In handing them over to the nation,' he declared, 'I have only done what any Englishman in my place would have been eager to do'.[8] Conceived by the Duke of Wellington as a national museum for the army and navy, the RUSI had been a prime mover behind the 1891 Naval Exhibition at Chelsea. With royal support, it had been granted use of the Banqueting House in Whitehall to display its growing and eclectic collection of sometimes dubious relics and weapons. At its peak, the collection comprised some 8,500 objects gifted or loaned by the families of the original recipients, among them George Eyre Matcham, whose great grandmother had been Nelson's sister Catherine. In 1901, Matcham loaned the RUSI Nelson's City of London presentation sword and the gold and diamond-set cane sent to the admiral by the people of Zante, both of which had descended through his family.[9] From a wealthy banking family, it was George's wife Constance who had bought the sultan's jewel at the Christie's sale, motivated by a sense of family and public duty. Ironically it was the decision not to secure the jewel for the nation in 1895 that had saved it from loss. Beyond her links through marriage, Constance had her own distant connection to Nelson, as her great grandfather Sir Richard Carr Glyn, a former Lord Mayor of London, had voted the City of London sword to the admiral after the Nile. Ahead of an exhibition of Nelson relics to celebrate the centenary of Trafalgar in 1905, Constance also deposited her jewel at the institution, where it was displayed as an 'Aigrette of Brazilian Diamonds, presented as the rarest distinction by the Sultan of Turkey to Lord Nelson after the battle of the Nile'.[10]

In a jingoistic age, the centenary exhibition at the Royal United Services Institution, under the patronage of King Edward VII, was a huge success, with its illustrated catalogue providing the first known photograph of the sultan's jewel. The curator of the show was at pains to avoid exciting 'the feelings of foreign visitors', particularly the French. But with Britain engaged in a naval arms race with Germany, the iconic figure of Nelson was seized upon as a symbol of the nation's indomitable fighting spirit. The exhibition was so popular that it was extended for a month, with many of its highlights, like the jewel, remaining on display long after it closed. However, a young American tourist, Marianne Moore, was disappointed not to see the fabled relic when she visited the museum in 1911, as Constance had taken the jewel out to wear. 'The warden showed us a peg from which an ornament (a diamond aigrette) was missing,' she wrote to her brother back in New Jersey:

> He looked very significant and said Mrs So and So (Lord Nelson's descendant who had lent it) had taken it out as she was attending court functions and so on. He said the Sultan of Turkey had presented it to Nelson; that it had a 'vibratin' plume and a revolvin' rosette of diamonds;' you could wind the rosette and it would revolve slowly for some time.

Constance probably borrowed the jewel to wear for the celebrations surrounding the coronation of King George V on 22 June, just a week after Moore's visit to the museum. Yet something about this strange, elusive object stuck in her imagination, as the Trafalgar coat would for Virginia Woolf. Some fifty years later, by then a celebrated Modernist poet and friend of Ezra Pound and T.S. Eliot, Moore evoked the aigrette in her poem 'Tell me, tell me':

> Why, oh why, one ventures to ask, set flatness on some cindery pinnacle
> as if on Lord Nelson's revolving diamond rosette?
> It appeared; gem, burnished rarity, and peak of delicacy – in contrast with
> grievance touched off on any ground – the absorbing geometry of a fantasy.

The sultan's jewel still astonished and amazed. In 1928 it 'created wonder' when Constance's daughter Valentine took it to the palace for her presentation to the king as a debutante.[11] Recalling the occasion in 1952, Valentine believed this was the last time the jewel was worn in public. Shortly afterwards, hit by the financial depression of the 1920s, her parents were 'compelled by financial exigencies to part with' their most precious Nelson treasures.[12] To attract interest from buyers, Constance lent the jewel – and her husband his City of London sword – to an exhibition organised by fine art dealer Captain Jack Spink to raise money for the 'Save the Victory Fund', a campaign to conserve Nelson's iconic flagship.[13] In its review of the exhibition at Spink's, *The Times* noted that the jewel had been 'much admired' by Queen Mary when she visited the exhibition, commenting that:

> some fears are entertained that the best of these relics may be lost to the country in the near future, for offers have already been made by American collectors, and the organisers of this exhibition would be glad if some means of saving them could be devised.[14]

The plea prompted an immediate response. Lord Wakefield, the millionaire founder of the Castrol motor oil company, came forward to purchase Nelson's City of London sword. A former Lord Mayor, Wakefield gave it back to the Corporation of London for display at the Guildhall.[15] However, it was more difficult finding a benefactor for the sultan's jewel. Perhaps it lacked the heroic status of the usual military relic. Public sale again seemed likely, raising fears that, 'if the Chelengk reaches the auction room there will be international contest for it and none can foretell the result'.[16] Anxious to do all they could to secure its future in Britain, in 1929 the Eyre-Matchams gave the Society of Nautical Research an option to buy the jewel for £1,500: a price in line, after inflation, with the cut-price of £710 they had paid at Christie's back in 1895. Founded in 1910 to preserve and promote Britain's naval heritage, the society had led the campaign to save *Victory*.It now sought to re-energise its cash-weary members before the November deadline with a stirring appeal by naval historian Geoffrey Callender, who conjured up the threat of a sale to America. Callender declared:

> That such a jewel, an outward symbol of the greatness of the Nile, should pass to a nation for which he made no sacrifice is unthinkable. The Chelengk should be secured for the Nation

> and reverently laid beside the clothes which Nelson wore at Trafalgar.[17]

With the deadline looming and the society struggling to reach its target, the National Art Collection Fund stepped in. It offered to lend the society the purchase money for the sultan's jewel to allow it more time for fundraising. In a typically impassioned letter to *The Times*, the fund's chairman, Robert Witt, played on the spectre of a foreign buyer of 'perhaps the most important of all the Nelson relics'. Evoking the admiral's famous last signal, Witt broadened the appeal to 'all who feel, as they do, that [it] is their duty to retain so personal a relic in Nelson's own land in order to lay it with the blood-stained uniform he wore at Trafalgar'.[18] Witt's intervention had an instant and electrifying impact on the stumbling campaign. Within a day of his letter being published, several donors contacted the society, among them Lady Barclay, whose husband, Sir Colville Barclay, the British ambassador to Portugal, had recently died. The daughter of famed African explorer-turned-sculptor Herbert Ward, Sarita Barclay, had inherited a fortune worth £40,000 a year from her American financier grandfather.[19] She offered to buy the jewel outright and present it to the British nation in memory of her husband. Like the earlier purchase by Constance Eyre-Matcham, a woman's eye had again been needed to save the jewel from loss.

Nelson's famous jewel was unveiled by Lady Barclay in person in the Painted Hall of the Royal Hospital Greenwich – since 1865 home to the Royal Naval College – on 2 July 1930, in front of a packed audience of dignitaries wilting in the summer heat. They watched as Lady Barclay walked the length of the hall to the raised dais, where there now sat a small glazed cabinet draped with a white naval ensign. She was escorted by Admiral William Boyle, president of the college, a short man with fiery red hair and a monocle. In his speech, 'Ginger' Boyle, who had served in the Middle East during the recent war, informed his audience that the jewel was the 'most remarkable decoration conferred upon the greatest English admiral'. He continued:

> Some people in this country were depressed at the international outlook; but there was no need for despondency as long as Nelson was duly honoured and venerated. His spirit would keep us in the path of duty; and his example would continue to be our shield and our strength. But the cultivation of that spirit was immensely facilitated by such relics as those in the Painted Hall; because they made Nelson, for those who looked at them, a living being of flesh and blood and not merely a name in a history book. And yet, wonderful as were the relics in the Painted Hall, they were eclipsed by the Chelengk, the most wonderful of all Nelson relics.[20]

To loud applause, Lady Barclay then pulled back the ensign to reveal the jewel sparkling in its display case. After some closing remarks of Admiral Sir George Hope, former President of the Royal Naval College, the crowd spilled out of the hall into the surrounding courts and colonnades in search of tea.

When Hope spoke, he knew the jewel would not reside in the Painted Hall for long. Its acquisition was a glittering highlight in the accumulation of nautical artefacts for a proposed new institution at Greenwich, grandly titled, by Rudyard Kipling no less, the 'National Maritime Museum'. The museum had been made possible by the removal of the Royal Hospital school to East Anglia, which freed up the Queen's House and neighbouring buildings in the town. Despite the promised loan of the existing collections held at the hospital, such as Nelson's Trafalgar coat and countless important marine paintings, the ambitious aim of the new museum compelled its trustees to spend heavily in the art market. This spending spree was largely financed by Sir James Caird, who, having made a fortune in property and shipping, gave over £300,000 (maybe £17 million today) for acquisitions. These were curated by Geoffrey Callender, appointed first director of the museum, with many items coming from Jack Spink and book dealer Frank Maggs.[21] Fortunately for posterity, as the purchase of the sultan's jewel demonstrated, Callender and Caird were operating in a depressed market, with countless naval treasures appearing for sale from families affected by the financial crash. Despite the perils of their approach, Callender and Caird acquired a huge haul of artworks at bargain prices, including marine paintings sold off by Hitler as 'non-German' from the national collections in Berlin.[22] However, their urgency to acquire a world-class collection at breakneck speed contrasted with the tortuous redevelopment of the museum buildings. It was not until 1934 that the museum was recognised by an act of parliament, and another two years before the jewel could cross Romney Road to its new home. It was placed in Gallery 10 on the ground floor, overlooking Greenwich Park, a room dedicated by Callender to Nelson relics.

Plans for a royal opening were disrupted by the death of King George V, then the abdication of Edward VIII. Finally, on 27 April 1937, the new King George VI, not yet crowned, made the journey to Greenwich by royal barge from Westminster, accompanied by Queen Elizabeth. Queen Mary, an avid collector of Nelson memorabilia, also drove from London for the ceremony, together with her granddaughter Princess Elizabeth, who had just turned 11. When the royal party was fully assembled, the museum was officially opened by the king, with the young princess looking bored during the interminable speeches. They were then taken on a tour of the new galleries, spending most time looking at the relics in the Nelson rooms, where the sultan's jewel sat glittering in its case. So now the jewel touched still living people, extending the line of reigning monarchs who had admired the jewel from George III to the present queen. Having tumbled from hand to hand down the ages, it was stilled at last under electric light in its display case.

Two days later, the public were allowed in, with 5,000 people pouring through the turnstiles on the first day. But the new galleries were open for barely three years before they closed on the outbreak of war. Once again sounds of conflict circled Nelson's jewel, with bombs falling across Greenwich during the Blitz and direct hits on the museum in several places. The larger exhibits were evacuated to safety in locations at Oxford, Cambridge and Somerset. A bomb-proof shelter in the basement of the Queen's House housed medals and some Nelson ceramics. The most precious objects, including the jewel, were entrusted to Jack Spink, who took them away for safekeeping at Dunster Lodge, his country house in Somerset overlooking the sea.[23] Emptied of their exhibits, Callender's galleries were then requisitioned for war work and occupied by the Admiralty's secret service 'M' branch and the Women's Royal Naval Service. Towards the end of the war, Greenwich was assailed by a fresh and more deadly onslaught of flying bombs, which blew out the museum windows and killed two members of staff in the town.

Still occupied by the Admiralty, the museum partially reopened in October 1945. Inevitably, the war wrought change: resources were stretched, and death and retirement left many curatorial positions empty. When Callender dropped dead in his office in 1946, he was replaced as director by the much younger Frank Carr. Likewise, a vacancy on the board of trustees was filled in July 1948 by 27-year-old Prince Philip, Duke of Edinburgh, now husband of the princess who had attended the museum's opening ten years earlier. One problem the trustees did not have to face whilst Sir James Caird still lived was the acquisition of new exhibits. He continued to spend prodigious amounts on rare books, maps, paintings and objects for the collections. Then an opportunity arose for him to purchase a trove of Nelsonian treasures from a quite unexpected source.

Back in 1922, responding to a question in the House of Commons, Chancellor of the Exchequer Stanley Baldwin had revealed that the government was still paying pensions of £2,000 a year to the descendants of Admiral Lord Rodney, victor of the Battle of the Saintes in 1782, and £5,000 a year to the current Earl Nelson. In the wake of a devastating war which had left millions dead and more needing help, largesse on such a scale to the memory of long-dead heroes jarred badly. Isaac Foot, a Liberal MP, thundered:

> It is impossible to go to poor people in this country who are receiving less than 10*s*. per week, and tell them that, while at the same time we are paying out to one gentleman, who is not a descendant of Lord Nelson at all, but is a descendant of his brother, not 10*s*., but £100 per week. I believe that that is indefensible, and that, as soon as Parliament comes to consider it, some arrangement will be insisted upon; and it might be wise if the Financial Secretary could get into communication with those who have been so favoured in the community, and assure them that, unless some reasonable arrangement can soon be made, these pensions may be brought abruptly to an end.[24]

Sensing the shifting mood, in 1925 the Rodney family wisely cashed in their pension for £42,000, leaving Earl Nelson the sole remaining beneficiary of a so-called perpetual state pension. With the country's finances fast deteriorating, the payment became still harder to defend, especially when Winston Churchill, Baldwin's successor at the Treasury, was forced to admit that, 'The present holder of the title is the grandson of the nephew of the first Earl.'[25] Under pressure, the earl reluctantly offered to pay back £500 a year. This gained him time, but failed to silence his critics. Within weeks of the Labour Party's election landslide in 1945, the Trafalgar Estates Bill was introduced to parliament by Chancellor of the Exchequer Hugh Dalton, with the aim of terminating the pension without compensation. The debate was vigorous and, by modern standards, extremely well-informed on both sides, with lengthy and detailed speeches on Nelson's career and his hopes for Emma Hamilton as he lay dying. The decisive contribution came from Isaac Foot's young MP son Michael, an historian and future Labour leader. He closely argued that the original grant to the first earl was 'an act of hypocrisy, for, either through ignorance or hypocrisy, Parliament in 1806 put through an Act which did not carry out the desires and wishes of Lord Nelson's will'. In Foot's opinion, the admiral had wanted to secure Emma, not his brother, a pension from government. Wilson Harris, independent Member of Parliament for Cambridge University, agreed. He said:

> Manifestly, in spite of any moralistic prejudice which the unmarried Mr. Pitt may have entertained, it is clear that Lady Hamilton, and not the Rev. William Nelson, Doctor of Divinity – in spite of the fact that he was a member of my own university – should have been the beneficiary after Lord Nelson's death.

Moreover, Nelson had been amply rewarded in his lifetime with titles, money and many 'gifts of great value by the Tsar of Russia and the Sultan of Turkey'. To then award a pension:

> to his brother, an obscure parson in an eastern county, and to allow it to descend irregularly from uncle to nephew, from father to son, and then to a brother again, in perpetuity, is surely in accordance neither with reason nor common sense.

This was the nub of the argument, with James Callaghan MP, another Labour firebrand and future prime minister, declaring 'that payments of this sort are becoming repugnant to ordinary men and women in the country'. Sympathy for the Nelson family dwindled still further when it was revealed that, back in 1889, the third Earl Nelson had been offered, and refused, £135,000 (maybe £13 million in today's terms) to commute the pension. Since that time, the family had received a further £285,000 in payments, although it was pointed out that had the settlement been accepted in 1889 and wisely invested, their income would have been far higher – and free of further scrutiny. Admiral Sir Ernest Taylor, a Conservative MP, put up a rearguard defence of the pension on patriotic grounds, but it was a hopeless cause.[26]

By the terms of the Trafalgar Estate Act, given royal assent in July 1947, the pension would end with the deaths of the current fourth Earl Nelson and his octogenarian brother and heir. As compensation, an entail in the original grant preventing the family from selling Trafalgar House was removed, allowing its sale on the open market. When the 87-year-old fifth earl duly succeeded, he wasted no time disposing of this millstone now hanging around the family neck, putting the entire estate up for sale. Hopes expressed during the debate in the House of Commons that the house might be saved by the Admiralty as a memorial to Nelson were dashed when a survey revealed its dilapidated state. Instead, on 2 June 1948, the mansion house, together with 3,500 acres of park and arable land, fourteen farms, fifty-five cottages, the chapel and 500 acres of woodland, was split into seventy-five lots and auctioned at the British Legion Hall in Salisbury. Before the sale, Sir James Caird stepped in to buy for £25,000 (less than £1 million today) all the family relics in the house so painstakingly reassembled by the third Earl Nelson following the dispute with the Bridports in the 1840s. It was quite a haul, comprising cabin furniture from *Victory,* porcelain, manuscripts, portraits and silver. Highlights included the large gilded silver vase given to the first earl after Trafalgar by the Patriotic Fund and the silver cup presented to Nelson by the Turkey Company in 1798. The Trafalgar House Collection was installed in the Nelson gallery near the sultan's jewel, where it was seen again by Queen Mary and Princess Elizabeth in April 1948. The remaining contents of the house were sold off after the death of the fifth earl in January 1951, when his son and heir appealed to Prime Minister Sir Winston Churchill for his family to be exempt from crippling death duties. Churchill was sympathetic – after all, his own ancestors the Marlboroughs had once enjoyed similar benefits – but he could do nothing. Disgusted, the new earl called it the 'greatest breach of faith ever perpetrated by any British government'.[27]

19

THE THIEF

George Chatham had been a tough, stocky little kid who knew the personal cost of crime. His father had owned a busy coffee stall in Hammersmith before losing it to a crooked friend when he went off to fight in the First World War. Born in April 1912, just days before the sinking of the *Titanic*, Chatham learned his skills the hard way on the streets of west London, first as a footballer – playing for England as a schoolboy – then as a thief. Petty shoplifting in Kensington High Street quickly escalated to stealing from jewellers and pawnbrokers. He blamed harassment by the local police for accelerating his descent into crime and his life-long loathing of authority. His first serious brush with the law came in 1932 after breaking and entering a shop in Battersea, South London, when he tried to steal a getaway car and was seen viciously kicking a policeman. Imprisonment introduced Chatham to more hardened criminals, and on his release he joined the 'Jelly Gang', a South London outfit which specialised in blowing safes with gelignite. Among the other gang members was Eddie Chapman, a safe-breaker who, famed as 'Agent Zigzag', became a celebrated double agent during the Second World War. In 1938, Chatham was convicted for possession of a detonator and sent to Dartmoor Prison, where his dislike of the cold earned him the nickname 'Taters' (from cockney slang 'potatoes in the mould': cold). Two years later, hearing that his Norwegian wife, an au pair who met on a bus, and their baby daughter had returned to Scandinavia and faced occupation by the Germans, he jumped the wall and started trudging across the moor. He was recaptured and put on bread and water in the punishment block for two weeks, sealing his hatred of the police. 'When I came out, I really went for it,' he recalled. 'I thought I'd make them pay for every day I did.' The death of his daughter in Norway propelled him still deeper into a life of crime and wilful self-indulgence. He liked to portray himself as a 'rebel', but his only cause was to destroy other people's property and fill his own pockets with his ill-gotten gains.[1]

Acting alone or with an accomplice, Chatham now targeted the mansions of the rich in Mayfair. In echoes of the Nelsons' burglary at Portman Square in the 1830s, Chatham would scour the gossip columns for his victims, then creep into their houses when they were at home with their burglar alarms turned off and their guard down. 'They were usually very, very rich people, millionaires,' he would declare by way of justification. 'Some of them regarded it as a nice thing to talk about at dinner parties.' It was said he 'made hay while the sun wasn't shining' as he crept over the rooftops in the pea-souper fogs which then engulfed London.[2] Cat-burgling was a dangerous profession, but it brought a rich reward in jewels easy to dispose of to fund Chatham's gambling, women and his flamboyant lifestyle. 'Money to Taters wasn't money,' remarked Eddie Chapman. 'It was something to gamble with.'[3]

Over a burgling career spanning some sixty years, thirty-five of them spent in prison, Chatham's victims ranged from the Maharajah of Jaipur – from whom he stole £80,000 – to Lady Rothermere, wife of a newspaper magnate, whose furs he took; the Duchess of Argyll, Coco Chanel and the Countess of Dartmouth, daughter of author Barbara Cartland, whose ceiling he fell through. 'His crime sheet read like *Debrett's*,' said Chapman.[4] Despite the admiration of the criminal fraternity, however, Chatham was no Raffles or Robin Hood. Short and combative, he had a reputation for violence, coshing two policemen on one bungled job.[5] His cat-burgling accomplices included Patsy 'Golden Hands' Murphy, an associate of London mobster Billy Hill, 'Human Fly' Peter Scott and a young Bruce Reynolds, who would mastermind the Great Train Robbery. Bruce Reynolds, recalling Taters, said:

> He was an inspiration for young men like me, chiefly for his style. I used to see him in his V12 Lagonda, and he had an air of sophistication that enabled him to move around. But mainly I admired him because he was a one-man crime wave. He didn't need anyone. There wasn't anything that fazed him.[6]

It was a short step from burgling jewels and furs from Mayfair mansions to stealing treasures from national museums. In 1948, two glittering diamond-encrusted swords in an exhibition of relics belonging to the Duke of Wellington at the Victoria & Albert Museum in South Kensington caught Chatham's covetous eye. One of the swords was the magnificent gem-set one given to the duke by the residents of Bombay. As he put it:

> I was sort of besotted by them. And not only that, it was, shall we say, a test. I had no respect for the police whatsoever, and if I could outwit them in any way, I would do my best to do it. I knew there would be a hell of a rumpus, and as long as I was successful I was very very satisfied.[7]

Priding himself on his research and reconnaissance before every job, Chatham visited the museum several times, soon noticing scaffolding outside the building erected by builder George Foreman to repair windows. On the foggy evening of Saturday, 17 April 1948, he used the scaffold to gain entry, lying low until the wardens had gone on their tea break, then running down to the ground floor, where the duke's swords were displayed in a glass cabinet. 'I smashed it, took the swords and was away,' he recalled later.[8] Twelve gold boxes and a sword belonging to Napoleon were left untouched. A warden heard the glass shatter and, glimpsing the shadowy figure, pressed the alarm bell at 11.11 p.m. 'I ran forward,' he said later, 'but could not go quickly in the dark because of the cases.'[9] As all the gates remained locked shut, the museum was searched from top to bottom – even suits of armour were checked for occupants – before Chatham's roof-top escape route was discovered. 'I was lucky, mind you,' he admitted. 'I was up a ladder in the quadrangle and one of the minders comes out. He walked right past me, right past the ladder. Never looked up.'[10] The burglary made front-page news. Interviewed in 2016, the builder George Foreman remembered arriving for work on Monday, 19 April and finding the museum swarming with police and his scaffolding roped off. 'What a fuss there was,' Chatham told Peter Scott in the 1980s. 'The nation nearly went into mourning!'[11] Unconcerned, he had popped the stones from the swords and lost them gambling.

Despite the public outcry, it took until 1951 before the theft of the duke's swords from the V&A was raised in parliament. By then, almost 200,000 visitors a year were visiting the National Maritime Museum on the other side of London, most to see the Nelson relics in Gallery 10 at the rear of the building overlooking Greenwich Park. Today, the room has a mezzanine floor with a gallery above and the museum shop below. Then, high windows sent shafts of daylight onto the exhibits in the large whitewashed room. A pre-war photograph shows a showcase displaying Nelson's uniforms beside a wall dominated by Turner's 'Battle of Trafalgar'. At one end of the gallery was a large vitrine crowded with personal relics such as Nelson's gun and flask from Ali Pasha, together with items of porcelain, silver and glassware. On the upper shelf, behind the plate glass in its own smaller cabinet (the same used in the Painted Hall), was the sultan's jewel propped up in its fitted box.

Sunday, 10 June that year was a lovely early summer's day, and after touring the galleries, people flocked to the tea marquee on the lawn outside. Nothing was untoward until 1.57 a.m. the next day, when an alarm suddenly clattered loudly in the local police station. The same instant, the switchboard operator at the museum went to his control box and saw the red light flashing for Gallery 10. He ran to fetch the duty fireman, and they waited anxiously for the police to arrive before going together to the gallery. The iron gates were still locked so, hoping for a false alarm, the men entered and walked the length of the gallery with torchlights, not noticing anything amiss 'until the warder switched on the light, when they saw the glass on the floor and the window open'.[12] The plate glass of the showcase containing the Nelson relics had been smashed and a crowbar left below it in the shards of broken glass. The warders immediately blew their whistles, whilst the police urgently summoned patrol cars to encircle the museum. A sniffer dog searched Greenwich Park for the intruder, picking up a fresh scent which ran west from the museum towards Crooms Hill before it was lost at the park railings. By then, Reginald Lowen, woken at home by an urgent phone call at 2.20 a.m., had arrived on the scene. As Executive Officer of the museum, he had the unhappy task of confirming to the police that only the jewel, the most precious object in the display, was missing. Nothing else had been touched; even the jewel's fitted case had been left behind. Searching outside, two ladders were quickly discovered in an annex adjoining the gallery, a red wooden one and a set of Commando-style collapsible metal steps. It was obvious the thieves had used the short wooden ladder to reach and then jemmy open a high window into the gallery, before dropping the collapsible steps into the room to gain entry. A watch was immediately placed at the ports and airports, as there was speculation that the jewel had been stolen to order 'by a gang specialising in stealing articles of historic interest for sale to private collectors on the Continent and America'. In fact, capture of the jewel by a collector would have been the least worst outcome.

The museum prepared a press statement stressing, in desperation, that:

> Although the value of the Chelengk as a National Relic is of the greatest sentimental importance, the break-up value of the stones is very small, as they were shallow cut diamonds individually unimportant.

Within hours, a reward of £250 was offered for information leading to the recovery of the jewel. Frank Carr, the Director of the museum, then tried to telephone 'everybody having a particular interest in the Chelengk' before they heard about the theft on the BBC news. They included the king, the prime minister, the chairman of the National Art Collections Fund and the trustees of the museum. A message was sent to the Duke of Edinburgh, who had turned 30 the day before, by coded signal from the Admiralty.[13] However, no one thought to speak with Lady Barclay, the original donor of the jewel, who since her remarriage was now Lady Vansittart. Upset, a week later she wrote to Sir Alec Martin, chairman of Christie's, who had negotiated her original gift, to complain. 'I have not heard from the Museum,' she stormed. 'I feel grieved and rather angry, and your letter of sympathy and understanding has been my consolation – the only one!'[14] Prompted by a furious Sir Alec, an embarrassed Frank Carr responded quickly, limply blaming an administrative error for the confusion and sending his heartfelt apologies and sympathy to Lady Vansittart.

On 26 June, First Lord of the Admiralty Lord Pakenham was grilled about the theft in parliament. His claim that the security arrangements at the museum had been fully adequate was met badly by the other peers. 'The relic has disappeared,' thundered the Marquis of Salisbury, 'and I should have thought that was conclusive evidence that they are not watertight.' There was criticism that the jewel had not been placed in a safe overnight, and it was then that comparisons were made with the recent theft of the Duke of Wellington's swords from the V&A Museum. 'Not one, I fancy, for which I am responsible,' retorted the First Lord, riled by the impression the National Maritime Museum had been in any way negligent. Viscount Samuel then suggested that, like the duke's sword, the jewel might have been stolen to order 'by someone who is specialising in the stealing of relics'. Pakenham agreed, relieved that the debate had shifted from somehow blaming him for the theft. 'I feel that this is a most helpful point,' he replied gratefully, before offering to look at increasing the reward, otherwise 'this connoisseur might well be provoked into further depredations'.[15]

The loss of the sultan's jewel provoked fresh debate about its true value. It was put to the press that it was insured for £20,000 (the sum reportedly refused by Earl Nelson a century earlier). So the claim made by a newspaper from an 'underworld' informer that the largest diamond in the centre star, said to be worth £2,500, had in fact been glass paste caused consternation at the museum. Frank Carr urgently asked his Executive Officer Reginald Lowen for clarification. Lowen retorted that, 'Spink's valued the diamonds before we acquired the Chelengk & I should think they would know whether the stones were paste or not.'[16] It is possible a criminal associate, or the thief himself, had given the information about the fake stone to the press in return for payment or out of disappointment and disgust. Together with inconsistency over its value, the suspicion is that Charlotte Bridport had replaced some diamonds with paste when she altered the jewel, as she was known to have done when she removed the diamonds from the King of Naples' sword hilt. The 'large diamond brooch' specified in her will and sold by Christie's in 1895 as the 'fastening to the "Cloak of Honour"' may have held some missing stones from the Chelengk.

No one was ever arrested for the theft of the sultan's jewel, but in 1994 George Chatham confessed to the crime, which already bore all his hallmarks. The speed and skill of execution and the targeting of a national treasure mirrored his earlier theft of the swords at the V&A Museum, for which crime he was outed by Peter Scott in a 1995 memoir. Living in Kew and, unusually, at liberty at the time of the burglary at the National Maritime Museum, Chatham also had the opportunity and the destructive urges necessary to carry out the daring and spiteful theft. Interviewed for television, he would say only that he had sold the jewel for a 'few thousand' before it was broken up. Whatever the sum, the money was quickly gambled away and the jewel forgotten about when Chatham scooped £15,000 as a driver in the infamous Eastcastle Street robbery the following year. The self-aggrandising confession of a criminal can never be trusted, but Dick Ellis, former head of the Art & Antiques Squad at New Scotland Yard, agrees that the evidence is overwhelming that Chatham was indeed responsible for the theft of the sultan's jewel.[17] He may have had an accomplice, as the police believed at the time, but the clever use of a lightweight collapsible ladder suggests he acted alone. Pulling it up behind him to slow down a pursuit was a classic Chatham feint. As Peter Scott said, 'The times I've seen newspapers describe Taters as a "gang" when in fact it was just George with a bit of wire and a knowledge of how to bend glass doors.'[18]

Dick Ellis well remembers Chatham as he continued cat-burgling into his 70s, only retiring when he fell from a building and broke his ankle. His final, pathetic conviction was for shoplifting a porcelain cup from Harvey Nichols. He died, alone and penniless, of motor neurone disease in 1997. He had nothing to show for stealing millions of pounds in jewels and destroying so many treasures, except the worthless respect of the criminal underworld. 'I don't have any regrets,' he said. 'Everything I did, I did with my eyes open.'

For 150 years, the jewel had passed from hand to hand: from the Sultan of Turkey to Nelson; Nelson to his brother the earl; the earl to his daughter; and so down and down it had fallen through time to a showcase at Greenwich to be admired by the world. It had been loved and cherished, fought over and neglected. For the price of a 'few thousand', it had now reached the hands of a criminal fence who cared nothing for its history but was keenly anxious to avoid trouble. So when Chatham had left for the nearest casino, the jeweller nervously put it on his bench, fixed his loupe to his eye, brought down his lamp, picked up his sharpest pliers and with barely another thought, bent to his task.

20

THE LOST JEWEL AND ITS REBIRTH

The jewel stolen by Chatham was not the jewel presented to Nelson by the Sultan of Turkey. Not exactly. As it passed down from hand to hand, several significant changes were made to his aigrette (as Nelson always called it), stripping it of some of its exoticism and strangeness, but none of its power to amaze.

As soon as news of Nelson's victory reached Constantinople, Selim gave instructions that a 'bejewelled *çelenk* be sent out to the aforementioned admiral in order to honour him'. He then annotated the order himself, adding a fur robe of honour, or *hilat* (a traditional diplomatic gift), and repeated his desire to present Nelson with a 'superior *çelenk*'.[1] The note shows the sultan's desire to define his gift as a gallantry award, as *çelenks* were widely distributed among his troops and janissaries for loyalty and acts of bravery on the battlefield, sometimes to whole regiments. Similar decorations for valour, called chelenkas, had been known in the Balkans – the source of the Ottoman dynasty – as early as the twelfth century. Worn on the turban, the *çelenk* was viewed in Turkey as a purely military decoration with three, five or seven 'fingers' or 'feathers' depending on the award, but with none of the other regulations or titles governing similar decorations in the West. Nevertheless, Spencer Smith declared that the *çelenk* or 'badge', as he called it, 'can hardly, according to the ideas annexed to such insignia here, be considered as less than equal to the first order of Chivalry in Christendom'.[2]

Turkic definitions of *çelenk* ranged from 'a bird feather which one attaches to one's cap as a sign of bravery' – suggesting that the award was once as simple as that (and origin of the term: 'Feather in the cap') – to 'an aigrette with chiselled decorations made of metal or jewels'.[3] These more durable *çelenks* were mass-produced in silver – more rarely in gold – and, in Selim's 'superior' form, set with gems. Surviving requisition orders show the sultan ordering his treasury to produce thousands of silver *çelenks* during the wars with Russia then France, and such an ornament has recently been identified in a portrait of the Greek officer Lambros Katsonis. However, a *çelenk* could also be as rudimentary as those hastily clipped out of metal sheets by Jezzar Pasha and issued on the battlefield at the siege of Acre.

The five-finger 'superior' and 'bejewelled' *çelenk* shown to Spencer Smith in Constantinople conformed to type but was clearly of an exceptional nature, confirming rumours that the jewel had been literally plucked from the sultan's own turban, or at least the imperial treasury. Searching for a means of conveying the exotic nature of the jewel he saw to an English audience, Smith described it in three different ways in his letter to the foreign secretary: 'a superb aigrette … called a Chelengk, or Plume of Triumph.' In so doing, he phonetically anglicised *çelenk*, which is pronounced 'chèlenk', with a soft 'ch' and long 'e'.[4] This pronunciation is evident in press descriptions of the 'Shelengk' or 'Schellengkow' and Emma Hamilton's later recollection, through drink-addled memory, of 'the Shahlerih [*sic*] or Plume of Triumph!'[5] Smith had then scrawled a sketch of the *çelenk* in the margin of his page, which closely mirrors the newly discovered Turkish watercolour showing the same jewel that came into the possession of Josiah Nisbet.

However, as the testimony of Thomas Richards now proves, the *çelenk* seen and sketched by Smith in Constantinople in September 1798 was not the jewel received by Nelson in Naples that December. Richards dined with Nelson and the Hamiltons within hours of its presentation and he described:

> a kind of feather, it represents a hand with thirteen fingers, which are of diamonds and allusive to the thirteen ships taken and destroyed at Alexandria, the size that of child's hand about six years old when opened; the center diamond and the four round it may be worth £1,000 each, and there are about 300 others well set.[6]

Richards' letter, and no doubt other accounts of the jewel actually given to Nelson, was too late to prevent inaccuracies in the design of Nelson's new coat of arms in London, which copied Smith's sketch and showed the *çelenk* highlighted in blue. This expensive error caused William Nelson to later complain, 'that the Nelson arms crests and supporters on the various pieces of plate given by public bodies to his late brother the immortal hero have been *in*correct.'[7]

In fact, the jewel received by Nelson was more closely a *sorguç*, a luxurious bejewelled turban pin. Ottoman court culture drew a clear distinction between *sorguçs*, which were principally decorative and could be worn by men and women, and *çelenks*, which were a purely military reward. Despite Smith's excited claim that a *çelenk* had 'never before [been conferred] upon a disbeliever',[8] it seems the Turkish government had balked at allowing the sultan to breach the rules by awarding such a prestigious Ottoman award to a non-Muslim foreigner. Indeed, Selim had had to be gently reminded of this restriction by his grand vizier once before when he offered a *çelenk* to the King of Prussia back in 1791.[9]

Most cultures have a long tradition of wearing luxurious head ornaments to display status: from crowns and coronets to hat jewels, hair pins and tiaras. In the eighteenth-century Islamic world, specifically Turkey, such jewels were worn on the turbans of high-ranking officials, of whom none was greater than the sultan. The rise of the Ottoman dynasty from the thirteenth century had seen the wearing of crowns by the Turkish ruler replaced by the more Islamic custom of attaching feathered plumes to the turban using a bejewelled pin and socket. Exotic feathers taken from cranes, peacocks, hawks, ostriches or birds of paradise were displayed as high-status symbols. The Turks called this jewel a *sorguç*, or crest, although the English followed the French term '*aigrette*' after the egret, a small variety of heron whose brilliant white plumage often adorned such ornaments.

The aigrette came to embody the sultan's image, and his power. Beside the sultan's throne in the audience chamber of the Seraglio, where dignitaries were received, was a 'niche in which upon blocks are placed the turbans he does not wear, which have plumes formed of some of the most valuable diamonds that are known'.[10] A guild of aigrette makers operated under royal patronage in Constantinople's Grand Bazaar, their creations cared for by the sultan's personal aigrette-keeper. He reported to the Master of the Turbans, one of the most important members of the privy chamber, who had custody of all the sultan's jewels and precious objects. Over time, the aigrette evolved into three well-recognised shapes: the flower-shaped 'rose'; the plain 'ball'; and the 'hand-shaped' aigrette.

From simple beginnings, Ottoman aigrettes became larger and more lavishly and richly ornamented with enamels, diamonds and gemstones. Their symbolic origin was smothered beneath the desire to impress and to project the sultan's vast wealth. Unlike the widespread distribution of *hilats*, bejewelled aigrettes were rarely presented. They were the single most precious gift a sultan could bestow on a foreign dignitary. Selim III sometimes dispatched them with his ambassadors as extravagant presents to foreign courts. It appears, however, that the jewels given to non-Muslims were not fitted with sockets for the highly prized bird plumes, which was a preserve of the Ottomans. Nelson was never depicted wearing plumes in his aigrette, and the only reliable depiction of the jewel awarded to Sir Sidney Smith also shows it without feathers. Queen Charlotte chose to pin the jewel presented to her in London by Ambassador Yusuf Agah 'next to her heart' like a brooch or stomacher. Her daughter the Princess Royal was given a similar jewel, and both women 'looked upon them as talismans of the soul; and showed them with great exultation to the duchesses and ladies, said: "We have now been declared dignified sultanas by the Sublime Porte"'.[11] When the princess died in 1828 as Queen of Wurtemburg, she bequeathed 'the heron aigrette, presented to Her Majesty by the Grand Seignior, Selim III' to the crown jewels of her adopted country, although it cannot now be traced.[12]

The queen and princess were thrilled by their gifts, as dressing *a la Turque* was then the height of fashion throughout Europe. *Turquerie* was the dominant fantasist style of the eighteenth century, infusing the decorative arts and even the music of Mozart, whose 1782 opera *The Abduction from the Seraglio* was set in the palace of 'Pasha Selim'. The craze was fuelled by the best-selling accounts of intrepid travellers to the Orient like Lady Mary Wortley Montagu, wife of the ambassador to Constantinople, and widely circulated portraits of aristocratic grand tourists in Turkish costume. Long before the Ottoman ambassador presented his gifts to the British royal family, Queen Charlotte had been portrayed wearing a jewelled aigrette in her hair beside her two eldest infant sons, George and Frederick, the latter in playful Turkish costume and turban. There was even a folly designed as a mosque in the royal gardens at Kew. As far back as 1743, old King George II, then 60, had appeared at a fete in Hanover, red-faced and sweating 'in Turkish dress; his Turban was ornamented with a magnificent *agraffe* of diamonds'.[13] Emma Hamilton wore Turkish costume for portraits by Elizabeth Vigée-le-Brun in Naples and George Romney in London, years before she met Nelson. When the Princess of Wales sought Sidney Smith's advice for a Turkish room at her Blackheath residence, she was simply following this enduring trend. Apart from the rich and exotic nature of the clothing, the luxuriousness of the artworks and the colourful design, there was a thrilling and liberating sexual charge to the Ottoman world, which was seized upon by free-thinking lovers in the chillier climes of Northern Europe.

It was also not unusual for the Ottomans to design an aigrette to suit a foreign recipient. Just a few months after Nelson's jewel was finished and dispatched, Selim approved the design for several diamond aigrettes to be sent to George III in England, each decorated with the imperial tughra, or cipher. In agreeing the form of the jewel, careful consideration was given to its suitability (for example, visual representation of Allah, the Arabic word for God, was vetoed) and cost, factors that were also in play in the manufacture of Nelson's aigrette.[14] In this way, the thirteen-plume aigrette satisfied Selim's stated aim of presenting Nelson with a 'superior çelenk' whilst avoiding culturally difficult comparison with the usual Ottoman award for gallantry. Nelson referred to his jewel as 'the diamond Aigrette presented to me by the Grand Seignior', not as his 'chelengk', and, according to Alec Hood writing in 1913, the Nelson family always called it an aigrette too.[15] Nevertheless, in his lifetime Nelson was keen to project the aigrette as a military honour, despite it lacking the status of a *çelenk* in Ottoman eyes.

By Selim's day, aigrettes were outsize, even outlandish, and incorporated novelties such as mounting elements of the jewel on tiny springs to move *en tremblent* in wear. As contact with the West grew, a fashionable and more feminine European style filtered into the jewels with the introduction of floral designs, bows and knots. Nelson's aigrette displayed all these innovations, with the fingers mounted *en tremblent* above a bouquet of white enamelled flowers and a large bow or 'lover's knot', tightly tied to show loyalty. This suggests the jewel was *à la mode* and recently made in 1798. The jewel's deluxe and voguish feel was completed by its most striking and memorable feature: hidden behind the diamond star at its heart was a clockwork mechanism which drove the star in circles when wound. An officer who saw the aigrette in Sicily admired the star as it turned with 'a slow and equable motion'.[16] As it spun, the star could throw candlelight around a room like a glitterball, producing, in the words of the enthralled *Lady's Monthly Magazine*, a 'most brilliant effect'.[17] The watercolour of the undelivered *çelenk* shows its star on a blue background, whereas the College of Arms drawing of the aigrette sent to Nelson portrays its star on a red background to more closely resemble the Ottoman naval ensign.

There was great fascination in Ottoman Turkey for Western engineering, mechanics and optics, with a watchmaking quarter in Constantinople populated by Swiss and English émigré workers.

Clockmakers in London competed to feed the Turks' insatiable appetite for these European novelties and to satisfy their fondness for 'show'. 'One could scarcely believe that such prodigious quantities of clockwork could be consumed in Turkey,' recorded one observer, who estimated that the English trade in watches with the Turks was worth an improbable £250,000 a year by 1797, a vast sum equivalent to £200 million today.[18] Famed makers like James Cox exported precious clocks, many with 'curious' features and automaton, *objets d'arts* and complex 'pieces of mechanism' to Constantinople, whilst Markwick Markham & Perigal of London fitted the movement in a luxurious watch with diamond set chatelaine sent to Admiral Lord Keith by the Valida Sultan.[19] Cox eventually overreached himself and went bankrupt, unlike watch and clockwork maker George Prior, who enjoyed substantial trade with Turkey for some fifty years from the 1760s. So successful was Prior's business that the best pocket watches even became known as *Piryol*s in Turkish. Records for just five years from 1784 show Prior selling some 4,500 watches to Turkey, more than any other maker, with further shipments of clocks, clockwork mechanisms and special orders for presentation. Prior believed 'that the streets of the Turkish cities must be paved with English watches'.[20] Given his mass-production and high reputation, if any single maker could be attributed to the clock work mechanism which motored Nelson's jewel, it would be Prior. The sultan had an especial love of these precious toys, and they were a popular present from visiting diplomats like Lord Elgin.

According to Spencer Smith, the çelenk he saw in Constantinople was 'a blaze of brilliants', meaning set with plump, fully faceted diamonds cut in the European style. However, the aigrette sent to Nelson, as eagle-eyed Lady Minto gleefully spotted when she dismissed the Chelengk as 'very ugly and not valuable', was set with 'rose diamonds'.[21] Likewise, the receipt given to Earl Nelson by Rundell, Bridge & Rundell identified 'a Rose Dia^{d} aigrette' and photographs of the aigrette before its theft in 1951 confirm that it was decorated with diamonds 'rose-cut' in this simpler way, with fewer facets and dulled brilliance.[22] It was a method of cutting diamonds, particularly poorer quality examples, which was widespread in the east but disparaged in England. 'I have seldom seen diamonds in Turkey that are *clear* and without *flaws*,' remarked a tourist in 1797, blaming the 'clumsiness' of the Turkish jewellers for breaking many of them.[23] Such stones were mined in large quantities in India before travelling the silk road to Constantinople, despite the assertion by the cataloguer of the Royal United Service Institution that the aigrette was set with more highly prized 'Brazilian diamonds'.[24]

After appraising Nelson's aigrette in Naples, Thomas Richards had calculated there were no less than 300 diamonds in the jewel, with the five largest stones worth at least £1,000 each.[25] They all likely originated in the fabled diamond mines of the Golconda sultanate in southern India, source of such famous stones as the 105-carat *Koh-i-Noor*, now in the British Crown Jewels; the 45-carat Hope blue diamond, today in the Smithsonian Institution, Washington DC; and the 47-carat Pigot diamond, for which Nelson and Emma had competed in the 1801 lottery. These stones were then painstakingly mounted one by one in the aigrette in the Ottoman style, sitting in cups with high collars of gold and silver. To Western eyes, the method looked crude and the stones uneven and poorly matched. In contrast, as Sir William Hamilton noted with approval, when the diamond star for the Order of the Crescent was made under Spencer Smith's personal supervision in Constantinople, it was designed in 'European fashion', which meant with brilliant-cut stones, neatly set close together.[26]

The first portrait of Nelson wearing his aigrette was completed in 1799 by Leonardo Guzzardi within just months of its presentation in Naples. However, it appears the artist did not have access to the jewel, as he painted a strange hybrid apparently constructed from Spencer Smith's drawing of the undelivered five-plume *çelenk*, now widely circulated as a print, and eye-witness accounts, like that of Richards, that the jewel was set with hundreds of small stones and five large ones. This suggests that Nelson did not habitually wear his glamorous new decoration on his hat, perhaps unsure whether he should, or could. Guzzardi's uncertainty was shared by other artists such as Lemuel Abbott, perpetuating the confusion in the public's mind over the exact nature of the sultan's jewel. The only portrait of Nelson with a true representation of the aigrette was completed by William Beechey after the admiral's return to London in November 1800. This clearly depicted the thirteen-plume jewel which Thomas Richards would have recognised.

After Nelson's death, his aigrette shifted in meaning. William Nelson valued it as a precious family heirloom, but not as decoration comparable in prestige to his late brother's British orders and medals. He even allowed his daughter Charlotte to wear it to Court as 'a diamond stomacher composed of part of the aigrette given to her uncle, the late Lord Nelson by the Grand Seignior'.[27] This suggests that the bow on the lower part of the aigrette could be detached and worn separately. Despite its fading potency, Thomas King, an officer at the College of Arms, was permitted to sketch it alongside with Nelson's other decorations for a planned history of Great Yarmouth. His newly discovered watercolour, completed before January 1846, is the best record of the jewel as it appeared during Nelson's lifetime. It provides hitherto unknown and fascinating detail, such as the use of white enamelling on a cluster of flowers around the central red star and a single ruby radiating from the jewel. Rare rubies from Burma were highly prized as talismans to ward off danger and were frequently carried by soldiers into battle, sometimes concealed under the skin. These subtleties, familiar to Ottoman jewels, were lost even in Beechey's highly observant portrait of the admiral. A hint of this hidden complexity came only in the comments of the same officer in Sicily, who had noted the clockwork mechanism when he described the jewel as 'a most superb ornament, which dazzles the eyes by the variety of colours'.[28] Assumed life-size, King's drawing of the Chelengk shows it was an impressive 7 inches long and 3 inches at its widest point: dimensions which match Thomas Richards' rough estimate that the jewel he saw was the size of a 'child's hand about six years old'.

All the personal accounts of the jewel date before Nelson's return to London in November 1800, suggesting he displayed it rarely back in England, finding it difficult to wear and wary perhaps of its ambivalent status. As the aigrette then retreated into the family jewel case, only to be seen at elite private gatherings, opportunities for further description diminished still further, and after King's drawing sixty years would pass before its next known reproduction. Sadly, the photograph published in the catalogue for the Trafalgar Centenary exhibition at the Royal United Service Institution in 1905 shows a reduced jewel, a wreck of its former splendour. Almost all the fragile enamel flowerheads have been stripped off and four of the five largest diamonds and the clockwork mechanism removed, with the star and bow then awkwardly remounted directly below the plumes. Alec Hood assured Constance Eyre-Matcham after she bought the jewel at Christie's that it 'remains in the identical condition to which it was given to Lord Nelson';[29] whilst in 1930, Warren Dawson, the librarian at Lloyd's of London, which had considered buying the aigrette for its collection, declared, 'All the original stones are in place, and the jewel has not been interfered with in any way, except only to remove the watch-work mechanism that formerly rotated the central rose.'[30]

Yet this was obviously not true, as the third Viscount Bridport conceded when he admitted in 1951 'that the chelengk may have been altered by order of my great-grandmother'.[31] Charlotte Bridport may have changed the jewel to make it more wearable, as its fragility would make it prone to damage. The larger diamonds were probably recycled into other jewels, such as a large diamond brooch mentioned in her will. As was reported after the aigrette was stolen in 1951, she may also have swapped some of the remaining diamonds for glass. She did similar when she made a necklace using stones prised from the hilt of the King of Sicily's sword and replacing them with paste. The last person alive who had intimately known Nelson and Emma, Charlotte was perhaps less respectful to their memory than later generations. She also meddled with a pocket watch worn by her uncle at Trafalgar, which she took from its original case and set in an ugly clock for the mantelpiece. The diamonds remaining in the sultan's jewel before it was finally destroyed by Chatham must now reside in countless other pieces scattered across the world.

Despite the obvious disparity with portraits of Nelson wearing his aigrette, Warren Dawson's 1930 judgment that 'the jewel has not been interfered with in any way' since its original gift to the admiral in 1798 has held sway until now. A replica aigrette in glass paste, made by the National Maritime Museum after the jewel's theft, followed this view, as did all subsequent copies, including an example in diamonds gifted to the present Duchess of Cornwall. Only Hollywood bucked this trend. For the 1941 biopic *That Hamilton Woman* (titled *Lady Hamilton* in Britain), celebrated costume jeweller Eugene Joseff returned to original sources before making an aigrette to be worn by Laurence Olivier playing Nelson. Joseff, who had previously supplied jewels for *Gone with the Wind*, was a stickler for accuracy, visiting museums and studying archives before creating his reproductions. Ironically, his replica, which cannot now be traced, more closely resembled the original jewel than the doctored version then still on display at Greenwich. The film, said to be Winston Churchill's favourite, projected Nelson's story to a global audience and gave his jewel lasting fame. It may have fed the young novelist Patrick O'Brian's fascination for the age of fighting sail which emerged in his *Master and Commander* novels. In *Treason's Harbour*, the ninth book in the series, Jack Aubrey, a Nelson acolyte, proudly demonstrates the diamond *çelenk* awarded him by the Sultan of Turkey for defeating rebel Ottoman warlord Mustapha Bey:

> the splendid bauble – two close-packed lines of small diamonds, each topped by a respectable stone and each four or five inches long – had a round, diamond-studded base: this he twisted anti-clockwise for several turns, and as he put on his hat again the chelengk sprang into motion, the round turning with gentle Captain Aubrey sat in a small private coruscation, a confidential prismatic display, astonishingly brilliant in the sun.

Sadly, none of the magnificent diamond aigrettes awarded by Selim III to British officers appear to survive today. Sidney Smith split up his own jewel during his lifetime for the benefit of his sailors, and in 1988 Admiral Viscount Keith's aigrette, like Nelson's before it, was stolen.

The loss of the aigrettes has been compensated by the discovery of Thomas King's illustration of the thirteen-plume aigrette sent by Selim to Nelson, found by chance at the College of Arms whilst I was researching this book, and the Turkish watercolour of the *çelenk* described by Spencer Smith in Constantinople. This came to light following publication of the first edition of *Nelson's Lost Jewel*, having been identified in a private collection in Canada. It was probably 'the drawing of the Aigrette sent by the Sultan to Lord Nelson after the Victory of the Nile', which Fanny Nelson proudly displayed when she dined with Lord and Lady Inchiquin in December 1798.[32] Fanny later gifted the watercolour to her son, Josiah Nisbet, who annotated it: 'a drawing of the Chelingh which was given to his Gallant Father Lord Nelson of the Nile by the Grand Seignior 1798.' Then he, too, gave the watercolour away to a 'Mr Stanley', possibly Joseph Stanley, an old family friend on the Island of Nevis where Josiah was born. On burnished paper, found oil-stained but now conserved, this striking image confirms that there were two jewels, resolving two centuries of confusion over the exact nature of the object received by Nelson.

If the Turkish watercolour of the undelivered *çelenk* solved the identity of Nelson's jewel, the drawing of Nelson's aigrette found at the College of Arms offered the tantalising possibility of re-creating it. With my own professional background in period jewellery it was an opportunity not to be missed. After securing financial assistance from Symbolic & Chase, London dealers who specialise in rare and historic antique jewels, and with the support of the National Museum of the Royal Navy at Portsmouth, master goldsmith Philip Denyer was commissioned to replicate the aigrette using authentic materials and techniques. Before he could even begin, over 300 rose diamonds – and one rare cabochon ruby – had to be sourced and salvaged from damaged or incomplete eighteenth-century jewels. From foil-backed diamond settings and *en tremblant* springs, to figuring out how to fit a period clockwork movement among the delicate enamel flowerheads, every detail had to be worked out from the drawing at the College of Arms, Thomas Richards' eye-witness account and Philip's 40-year experience of handling antique jewels. In the end, with a team of seven craftspeople, it took more than 550 painstaking hours – many filmed by the museum for posterity – to recreate the lost aigrette. And when it was unveiled in the Great Cabin of Nelson's flagship *Victory* on Trafalgar Day, 21 October 2017, it drew the same gasps of astonishment as the original jewel surely generated more than two centuries ago.

The new aigrette was the subject of a symposium at Goldsmiths' Hall in London in March 2018 and then, in May that year, it was exhibited at the Turkish British *Tatli Dil* where it was admired by the Duke of York and by Recep Tayyip Erdoğan, the President of Turkey. In his speech at the forum, the president reviewed the 'nearly 500 years' of history between Turkey and Britain, citing Napoleon's 1798 invasion of Egypt as a landmark event in their shared history. Pointing towards Nelson's jewel, Erdoğan highlighted the aigrette – or Ottoman *Nishan* (medal) as he called it – as representing the deep ties between the two countries, sentiments which Selim in a very different age would have shared and understood. But it was the dazzling glamour of the jewel which caught the imagination of British-based Turkish designer Zeynep Kartal, who unveiled her aigrette-inspired 'Lost Jewel' collection during London Fashion Week later in the year, with models wearing sparkling representations of the jewel on their gowns. When the show travelled to Istanbul in November, it was accompanied by the new jewel which, with historic synchronicity, was displayed at the British Consulate General in Pera. This palatial building, formerly the embassy, stands on land gifted by Selim III to Britain in 1801 for its support against the French in Egypt. With rising interest in Turkey's Ottoman past, it was a fitting location to exhibit a jewel which reaches across the centuries touching hearts and dazzling eyes.

NOTES

Source Abbreviations

ALF	Aikaterini Laskaridis Foundation, Piraeus, Greece.
ASP	Archivio di Stato di Palermo, Sicily.
BL Add	British Library Additional Manuscripts
NMM	National Maritime Museum
NA	National Archives

Prelude

1 Of the two other guns, one is in the collection of the Royal Armouries at the Tower of London, the other was deposited at the now-defunct Rotunda Museum, Woolwich.

Chapter 1 The Battle

1 Gore, 25.
2 Nelson to Sir William Hamilton, 20 July 1798, Nicolas, III, 42.
3 Sir William Hamilton to Nelson, 1 August 1798. BL Add MS 34907, f.99.
4 Thomas Peyton to Nelson, 3 July 1798. BL Add MS 34907, f.62.
5 Sir James Saumarez to Nelson, 23 July 1798. BL Add MS 34907, f.83.
6 Nicol, 185.
7 Nicolas, III, 55.
8 Medical journal of *Vanguard*. Quoted Hill, 104.
9 Nicol, 187.
10 La Jonquière, Clement de, *L'Expedition D'Egypte, 1798-1801*, 5 vols (Paris, 1900); quoted Warner, O., *Nelson's Battles* (1965), p.82.
11 Ibid.
12 Coleridge, S.T., *The Friend* (London, 1818), Vol.3, p.310. Cited Coleman, 160.
13 Pettigrew, 1, 133.

14 Garlick, Farington diary entry for 3 November 1798, III, 1080.
15 Nelson to Emma Hamilton, 13 August 1798. Royal Naval Museum, Portsmouth, 48/64. Quoted Knight, 298.
16 Letter of Nile captains to Nelson, 3 August 1798. BL Add MS34907, f.142. D'Huart, 30. Sugden, 898 n4.
17 Kennedy, 135, 145.
18 Lee, 118.
19 Captain Benjamin Hallowell to Nelson, 23 May 1799. Nicolas, III, 89.
20 Lee, 119.
21 Earl St Vincent to Nelson, 27 September 1798. Quoted Sugden (2014), 114.
22 Nelson to Francis Jackson, 27 August 1798. Nicolas, III, 110.
23 Nelson to Earl St Vincent, 1 September 1798. Nicolas, III, 113.
24 J. Rushout to Nelson, 18 October 1798. Nelson Papers, Monmouth.
25 Spencer Smith to Nelson, 22 August 1798. BL Add MS 34907, f.187.
26 Samuel Hood to Nelson, 27 September 1798. BL Add MS 34907, f.313.
27 Instructions to the Commodore and to each captain of two corvettes destined and dispatched by the Sublime Porte, to attend the English Squadron in the Levant Seas. BL Add MS 34907, f.212.
28 Spencer Smith to Nelson, 12 September 1798. BL Add MS 34907, f.267.
29 *The Times*, 28 September 1797.
30 Spencer Smith to Lord Grenville, 8 September 1798. NA FO 78/20, f.21
31 Hood to Nelson, 25 October 1798. BL Add MS 34908, f.28.
32 Hood to Nelson, 26 November 1798. BL Add MS 34908, f.177.
33 Lee, 127.
34 Hood to Nelson, 26 November 1798. BL Add MS 34907, f.184.
35 Samuel Hood to Spencer Smith, 26 October 1798. NA FO 78/20, f.307.
36 Ship's muster for Alcmene. NA ADM 36/12613.
37 Hood to Nelson, 26 November 1798. BL Add MS 34907, f.184.

Chapter 2 The Sultan

1 George Canning, undersecretary of state for Foreign Affairs, to the Levant Company, 26 September 1798. NA SP105/126, f.296.
2 Edward Nosworthy to his wife, *Minotour*, Naples, 2 October 1798. Watts & Hawkins, 155.
3 John Spencer Smith to Lord Grenville, 3 September 1798. NA FO 78/20, f.3.
4 Sidney Smith to Lord Auckland. BL ADD MS 34449, f.109.
5 Sidney Smith to Lord Grenville, 13 January 1795. Dropmore MSS, IV, 2.
6 Lord Byron to Annabella Millbanke, 29 November 1813. Quoted MacCarthy, 121.
7 Nisbet, 56.
8 'An Account of the English Ambassador's Audience with the Sultan', *The Weekly Entertainer*, 19 September 1808, 744.
9 *The Times*, 31 January 1795.
10 Richard Lee to Lord Elgin, 12 April 1799. NA FO 78/22, f.7.
11 Historic standard of living comparison, see www.measuringworth.com.

12 *True Briton*, Friday, 7 February 1800.
13 Quoted Strathern, 174.
14 Spencer Smith to Nelson, 29 July 1798. BL Add MS 34907, f.87.
15 James, II, Appendix 14, 559.
16 Imperial Decree, 1 September 1798. NA PRO 78/20, f.12.
17 Quoted Eldem, 18.
18 *The Times*, 10 November 1798.
19 Spencer Smith to Lord Grenville, 3 September 1798. NA FO 78/20, f.4.
20 Decree of Selim III. Quoted Eldem, 22.
21 Spencer Smith to Lord Grenville, 8 September 1798. NA FO 78/20, f.21.
22 Casualty figures: Pettigrew, 1, 129.
23 Nicol, 174–75.
24 Spencer Smith to Lord Grenville, 8 September 1798. NA FO 78/20, f.21.
25 Quoted Eldem, 22.
26 Spencer Smith to Lord Grenville, 8 September 1798. NA FO 78/20, f.22.

Chapter 3 The Ambassador's Wife

1 Knight, C., I, 110.
2 Nelson to Fanny (about 25 September 1798). Nicolas, III, 130.
3 Sir William Hamilton to Lord Grenville. NA FO 70/11, f.219.
4 Emma to Nelson, 8 September 1798. BL Add MS 34989, f.4.
5 Thomas Capel to Nelson, 4 September 1798. BL Add MS 34908, f.227.
6 Emma to Nelson, 8 September 1798. BL Add MS 34989, f.7.
7 Hoste, I, 107.
8 Sir William Hamilton to Nelson, 10 September 1798. BL Add MS 34907, f.249.
9 Emma to Nelson, 26 October 1798. BL Add MS 34989, f.18.
10 Emma to Nelson, 27 October 1798. BL Add MS 34989, f.16. Naish, 420.
11 Sir William Hamilton to Nelson, 26 October 1798. BL Add MS 34908, f.38.
12 *Morning Herald* (London, England), Saturday, 26 January.
13 Sir William Hamilton to Nelson, 8 September 1798. Nicolas, III, 72.
14 Sir William Hamilton to Nelson, 22 November 1798, BL Add MS 34908, f.168.
15 Emma to Nelson, 26 October 1798. BL Add MS 34989, f.16. Naish, 420.
16 Emma to Nelson, 27 October 1798. BL Add MS 34989, f.23.
17 Emma to Fanny, 2 December 1798. BL Add MS 34989, f.8. Naish, 462.
18 *Alcmene* log. NA ADM 51/4408.
19 Memorial of Emma Hamilton, March 1813. Morrison, II, 362–63.

Chapter 4 The Hero

1 *Memoirs of Lady Hamilton*, 204.
2 Nelson to Fanny (about 25 September 1798). Nicolas, III, 130.
3 Ibid.

4 Acton, 305.
5 *The United Service magazine with which are incorporated the Army and navy magazine and Naval and military journal,* 1836, pt.1, 202.
6 Nelson to Earl St Vincent, 30 September 1798. Nicolas, III, 138. Nelson to Earl Spencer, 29 September 1798. Nicolas, III, 137.
7 Nelson to Sir William Hamilton, 27 October 1798. Nicolas, III, 161.
8 Nelson to Fanny, 1-6 October 1798. Nicolas, III, 139.
9 Nelson to John Spencer Smith, 26 October 1798. BL Add MS 34908, f.35. Nicolas, III, 159.
10 Nelson to Earl Spencer, 7 December 1798. Nicolas, III, 187.
11 Lawrence H. Officer and Samuel H. Williamson, 'Five Ways to Compute the Relative Value of a UK Pound Amount, 1270 to Present', *Measuring Worth*, 2016 .
12 Extract from journal of Cornelia Knight. Nicolas, III, Appendix 475.
13 Nancy H. Ramage, 'A List of Sir William Hamilton's Property', *The Burlington Magazine* Vol.131, No.1039 (Oct. 1989), pp.704-06. From the list it appears packing was suspended for the day of the presentation.
14 Fraser, 80-81.
15 Sir William Hamilton, *Catalogue of my pictures.* BL Add MS 41200, f.125.
16 Kaimakan to Nelson, [12] September 1798. BL Add MS 34907, f.260.
17 *Naval Chronicle*, I, 340.
18 'List of presents', *Naval Chronicle*, III (April 1800), 187-88.
19 Trench, 108.
20 Nelson codicil to his will, 25 May 1799. Morrison, II, 47. Fraser, 231. Nelson to John Spencer Smith, 12 March 1799. Nicolas, III, 291. Nelson to Emma, 5 February 1801. BL Eg. MS 1614 f.18.
21 Nelson to Spencer Smith, 12 March 1799. Nicolas, III, 291.
22 Nelson to the Grand Vizir, 16 December 1798. Nicolas, III, 203.
23 Spencer Smith to Nelson, 12 September 1798. BL Add MS 34907, f.267.
24 Extract of a letter from the son of a merchant of Birmingham, dated Naples, 17 December. *Northampton Mercury*, 30 March 1799.
25 Spencer Smith memorandum, dated 3 October 1798, 'sent me by Lord Nelson, Frances Nelson and Bronte', Nelson Museum Monmouth. Naish, 405.
26 Nelson to Sultan Selim III, 16 December 1798. Nicolas, III, 202.
27 *Memoirs*, 108.
28 PRO: Greenwich Hospital Records.
29 *The United Service magazine with which are incorporated the Army and navy magazine and Naval and military journal,* 1836, pt.1, 201-08.
30 Captain's Log for *Alcmene*, 21 December 1798. NA ADM 51/4408.
31 Captain's Log for *Alcmene*, 23 December 1798. NA ADM 51/4408.
32 Gordon, I, 196ff.

Chapter 5 The Admiral's Wife

1 Admiral Sir Richard Hughes to Nelson, 9 October 1798. BL Add MS 34907, f.406.
2 Fanny to Nelson, 23 July 1798. Naish, 441.
3 Fanny to Nelson, 15 May 1798. Naish, 430.
4 Harrison, II, 270.
5 Fanny to Nelson, 11 September 1798. Naish, 447.
6 Mrs Mary Lockhart to Fanny, 8 October 1798. Naish, 457.
7 Fanny to Lord Hood, 18 October 1798. Naish, 458.
8 Nelson to Fanny, 16 September 1798. Naish, 401.
9 Fanny to Alexander Davison, 15 June 1801. NMM DAV/2/48.
10 *Morning Post and Gazetteer*, 23 November 1798.
11 Nelson to Fanny, 25 September 1798. Naish, 401.
12 Emma to Fanny, 2 December 1798. BL Add MS 34989 f.8. Naish, 462.
13 *The London Gazette*, 20 October 1798, 993.
14 Memorandum with sketch. Lord Grenville's office, 3 November 1798. Naish, 405.
15 Garlick, Farington diary entry for 11 December 1798, III, 1,100.
16 *The Lady's Monthly Museum*, January 1799, 59.
17 Nelson to Fanny, 11 September 1799. Naish, 489.
18 James de Saumarez to Alexander Davison, 14 January 1799. NMM DAV/3/3.
19 Alexander Davison to Nelson, 7 December 1798. Nicolas, III, 138. It appears Davison may have absent-mindedly confused Nelson's flagship *Vanguard* with HMS *Standard*, another ship of the line.
20 Nelson to Fanny, 10 April 1799. Naish, 482.
21 *London Herald and Evening Post*, 13 February to 16 February 1799. *Observer*, 17 February 1799.
22 Nelson to Fanny, 11 December 1798. Nicolas, III, 194. Naish, 478.
23 *Morning Chronicle*, 28 January 1799.
24 Fanny to Alexander Davison, 11 April 1799; 2 March 1801. NMM DAV/2/7 & 31.
25 *The Times*, 14 November 1799.
26 *Observer*, 24 March 1799.
27 Fanny to Nelson, 8 September 1799; 27 October 1799. Naish, 532, 537.
28 *London Packet or New Lloyd's Evening Post,* 17 May to 20 May 1799.
29 Nelson to Fanny, 2 January 1799. Naish, 480.
30 Nelson to Fanny, 7 November 1799. Naish, 491.

Chapter 6 The Rival

1 *Lloyd's Evening Post,* 28 September to 1 October 1798.
2 *St James's Chronicle or the British Evening Post* (London, England), 27 October to 30 October 1798.
3 Garlick, Farington diary entry for 15 October 1798, III, 1,071.
4 Description of Smith, Earl Spencer to William Windham, 12 August 1794. Windham Papers, I, 221-22.

5 Shankland, 47.
6 Earl Spencer to Smith, 21 October 1798. Barrow, I, 235.
7 Earl St Vincent to Nelson [undated, January 1799]. Howard, I, 147.
8 Smith to Nelson, 11 December 1798. Barrow, I, 249.
9 William Sidney Smith to Lord Grenville, 10 January 1799. BL Add MS 58980, f.39.
10 William Sidney Smith to Lord Grenville, 16 January 1799. BL Add MS 58980, f.41.
11 *St James's Chronicle or the British Evening Post* (London, England), 7 March– to 9 March 1799.
12 Clarke & McArthur, II, 281n.
13 'J.K.' to Spencer Smith, 14 June 1799. *Naval Chronicle*, XXXIV, 355.
14 Spilsbury, 8.
15 Smith to Nelson, 30 May 1799. Barrow, I, 307.
16 Smith to Nelson, 2 June 1799. Barrow, I, 253.
17 Smith to Lord Grenville, 18 October 1799. BL Add MS 58980, f.63.
18 *London Packet or New Lloyd's Evening Post*, 22 July to 24 July 1799; *Lloyd's Evening Post*, 28 October 1799.
19 Howard, I, 203.
20 Imperial Rescript dated 17 June 1799: *Morning Chronicle* (London, England), Friday, 9 August 1799.
21 Barrow, I, 320.
22 *Oracle and Daily Advertiser* (London, England), Tuesday, 10 September 1799.
23 Louis-Marie Larevellière-Lépaux, *Mémoires* (3 vols, Paris, 1873), II, 348. Quoted Strathern, 409.
24 Nelson to Lord Elgin, 31 March 1800. Nicolas, IV, 215.
25 Lord Byron to his mother, the Hon. Mrs Byron, 15 September 1809. *Letters and Journals of Lord Byron* (1840). Byron gifted Constance a yellow diamond ring and immortalised her as Florence in *Childe Harold*.

Chapter 7 The First Knight

1 Nelson to Fanny, 2 January 1799. Naish, 480.
2 Nelson to Earl St Vincent, 30 & 31 December 1798. Nicolas, III, 213, 215.
3 Earl St Vincent to Emma, 30 April 1799. Pettigrew, II, 197–98.
4 Nelson to Fanny, 10 April 1799. Naish, 482.
5 Gordon, I, 201.
6 Gordon, I, 203.
7 Nelson to the Marquis of Niza, 9 January 1799. Nicolas, III, 231.
8 Nelson to Josiah Nisbet, 7 January 1799. Nicolas, III, 229.
9 Gordon, I, 199.
10 Master's log for *Bonne Citoyenne*, 10 August 1798 to 9 August 1799. NA ADM 52/2777.
11 Nelson to Earl St Vincent, 8 March 1799. Nicolas, III, 285.
12 Earl St Vincent to Nelson, 28 April 1799. Barrow, I, 238.
13 Pettigrew, I, 181.
14 Lord Keith to his sister Mary Elphinstone, 10 April 1799. NMM KEI/46.

15 Gordon, I, 209.
16 Paul to Nelson, 8 October 1798. BL Add MS 34907, f.393.
17 Gordon, I, 228–29.
18 Sermoneta, 162ff.
19 Nelson to the Tsar of Russia, undated draft (March 1799). NMM CRK/14/31. White, 217.
20 Nelson codicil to his will, 25 May 1799. Morrison, II, 47.
21 Knight, II, 287.
22 'Horatio Nelson' by John Young, after Leonardo Guzzardi, mezzotint, published 1800. National Portrait Gallery, London. NPG D5334.
23 The portrait of King Ferdinand IV is in the Sala dei Borboni di Napoli di Spagna e Francia at Caserta. Other known portraits by Guzzardi include Monsignor Isidoro del Castillo e Mastrilli painted before 1774; see Ragusa, Ignazio: *Saggio Storico vita Isidoro del Castillo Mastrilli* (Palermo, 1778), where engraved portrait after Guzzardi is illustrated as the frontispiece; portrait of Salvatore di Maria Blasi completed by 1802: see Equizzi, Rosanna: *Palermo San Martino delle Scale. La Collezione Archeologica. Storia della Collezione e Catalogo della Ceramica* (2007), discussed p.71; illustrated p.72. Guzzardi also painted his fellow Sicilian artist Domenico Provenzani (1736–1794): see Equizzi, p.71 (painting assumed lost).
24 *Naval Chronicle*, XX (1808), 111. Quoted Walker, 88.
25 Nelson to Spencer Smith, 25 July 1799. Nicolas, III, 422.
26 Nelson to Smith, 20 August 1799. Nicolas, III, 455.
27 Nelson to Spencer Smith, 31 August 1799. Nicolas, III, 471.
28 Emma to Charles Greville, 19 July 1799. Sichel, 308.
29 Nelson to Abraham Gibbs, 11 August 1803. Nicolas, V, 160.
30 Sermoneta, 200.
31 Parsons, 5.
32 Nelson to Fanny, 4 August 1799. Naish, 487.
33 Damas, 278.
34 Parsons, 17. Sermoneta, 181.
35 Nelson to Earl Spencer, 6 September 1799. Nicolas, IV, 6.
36 Nelson to Maurice Nelson, 7 September 1799. Nelson Papers, Monmouth, E605.
37 King Ferdinand IV of Naples to Nelson, 13 August 1799. Translation copy, ALF L15, ex Lot 70 The Alexander Davison Collection, Sotheby's, 21 October 2002.
38 Southey, 66.
39 Nelson to Rev. Edmund Nelson, 15 August 1799. Nicolas, III, 441.
40 Sugden, 524.
41 Thomas Masterman Hardy to John Manfield, 7 November 1801. Broadley, 77.

Chapter 8 The Mistress

1 Lawrence H. Officer and Samuel H. Williamson, 'Five Ways to Compute the Relative Value of a UK Pound Amount, 1270 to Present', *Measuring Worth*, 2016.

2 *Description of a Piece of Plate presented by Alexander Davison Esq. to Admiral Lord Nelson.* Lot 15: Sotheby's The Alexander Davison Collection, 21 October 2002. The ornament is now lost.
3 Nelson to John McArthur, 15 October 1799. Nicolas, IV, 53.
4 Nelson to Sir Isaac Heard, 1 November 1799. Nicolas, IV, 81.
5 Translation of a dispatch from Bekir Pasha, deputy of the grand vizir at Constantinople, to Nelson, 8 September 1799. Clarke and McArthur, appendix 6, vol.2, 481–82.
6 Translation of a design for a medallion to Lord Nelson and other British Officers. Undated [1799]. BL Add MS 34917, f.392.
7 Smith to Nelson, 8/9 September 1799. Nicolas, IV, 81–82n.
8 *Lloyd's Evening Post* (London, England), 28 October to 30 October 1799.
9 Sir William Hamilton to Lord Grenville, 8 November 1799. NA FO 70/12, f.316.
10 Nelson to the Grand Vizir, 4 November 1799. Nicolas, IV, 87.
11 Nelson to Earl Spencer, 6 November 1799. Nicolas, IV, 90.
12 Addington to Nelson, 19 February 1802. Morrison, II, 185–86.
13 Southey, II, 68.
14 Nelson to the Inhabitants of Zante, 21 December 1799. Nicolas, IV, 151.
15 Nelson to Evan Nepean, 28 November 1799. Nicolas, IV, 115.
16 Nelson to Earl Spencer, 18 December 1799. Nicolas, IV, 146.
17 Nelson to the Grand Vizir, 22 December 1799. Nicolas, IV, 156.
18 Nelson to Spencer Smith, 22 December 1799. Nicolas, IV, 157.
19 Ali Pasha to Nelson, 16 January 1800. BL Add MS 34916, f.240. These gifts were later misattributed to the Sultan of Turkey.
20 Lord Byron to his mother, 12 November 1809. 548. *Letters and Journals of Lord Byron* (1840), 548
21 François Charles Hugues Laurent Pouqueville, *Histoire de la régénération de la Grèce* (1824), Vol. I, p.140.
22 Nelson to Spiridon Foresti, 22 October 1803. Nicolas, V, 269.
23 Nelson to Henry Addington, 24 August 1803. Nicolas, V, 173.
24 Ali Pasha to Nelson, 30 August 1801. Dawson, 173.
25 Nelson to Davison, 23 August 1799. Nicolas, III, 460.
26 Grant, 17.
27 Grant, 25–26.
28 Damas, 278.
29 Parsons, 53.
30 Admiral Lord Keith to his wife, 22 June 1800.
31 Harrison, II, 149.
32 Sir William Hamilton to Charles Greville, 21 September 1790, Morrison, I, 185.
33 Sir William Hamilton to Charles Greville. Quoted Scarisbrick, 20.
34 Grant, 24.
35 Fraser, 267.
36 Trench, 109.
37 Lady Minto to Lady Malmersbury, 6 July 1800. Minto, 138.
38 Nelson to Evan Nepean, 14 December 1799. Nicolas, IV, 141.

39 Tsar Paul to Nelson, 24 December 1799, translation. NMM BRP/5. Emma has annotated the letter 'Translation of the Emperors letter to Lord N'.
40 Emma to Charles Greville, 25 February 1800. Gamlin, I, 115.
41 *Morning Herald* (London, England), Wednesday, 19 November 1800.
42 Fraser, 267.
43 Emma to Charles Greville, 25 February 1800. Robinson, 225.
44 Nelson to Emma, 30 January 1800. Private Collection. Quoted Williams, 232.
45 Earl Spencer to Nelson, 9 May 1800. Nicolas, IV, 242n.
46 Sugden, 307.
47 Sir John Acton to Nelson, 8 June 1800. Nicolas, IV, 250n.
48 Downer, 9ff.
49 Nelson to the Caimaken Pasha, 7 April 1800. Nicolas, IV, 223.

Chapter 9 The Grand Turk

1 *The Times* (London, England) 21 September 1798, 2; 2 October 1798, 2; 3 October 1798, 2. *The Times Digital Archive*.
2 Nelson to the Lord Mayor of London, 8 August 1798. Nicolas, III, 95.
3 City cash account for 1798. Prentice, 161.
4 *The Times*, 18 October 1798.
5 *General Evening Post* (London, England), 1 November to 3 November 1798.
6 *Lloyd's Evening Post* (London, England), 24 October to 26 October 1798.
7 *The European Magazine*, January 1808, 54.
8 *The Lady's Monthly Museum*, January 1799, 59.
9 *Morning Herald* (London, England), Saturday, 19 January 1799.
10 Wyndham, H. (ed.), *Correspondence of Sarah Spencer, Lady Lyttelton 1787-1870* (1912), p.14. Quoted Gattrell, 206.
11 Advertisement of W. Kirtland, No.1 Lower Ormond Quay, Dublin, *Hibernian Journal*, 15 January 1806.
12 *British Gazette and Sunday Monitor*, 23 December 1798.
13 'RANELAGH. Under the Patronage of his Royal Highness the Prince of WALES', *The Times* (London, England), 23 January 1800.
14 Jane Austen to Cassandra Austen, 8 January 1799. Deirdre Le Faye (ed.), *Jane Austen's letters* (Oxford, 1995), p.33.
15 Vote of Thanks of the Levant Company, 2 November 1798. BL Add MS 34908, f.108.
16 The original grant has not survived. For correspondence see Dawson, 2.
17 Bill for plate purchased for Nelson by Lloyd's from Rundell & Bridge, 24 November 1800. Private Collection. Formerly lot 25, The Alexander Davison Collection, Sotheby's London, 21 October 2002.
18 *Naval Chronicle*, III (1800), 187–88.
19 Fanny to Nelson, 4 March 1800. Naish, 552.
20 Nelson to Earl Spencer, 6 November 1799. Nicolas, IV, 91.
21 Nelson to Earl Spencer, 6 November 1799. Nicolas, IV, 90. *Naval Chronicle*, III (1800), 191.

22 Minto (1874), III, 146.
23 Quoted Deutsch, 92. Thomas Blumel, 'Nelson's Overland Journey', *ND*, 7 (2000), 166.
24 Westminster, 105–06.
25 Westminster, 111–12.
26 Minto (1874), III, 147.
27 Kennedy, 145.
28 D'Huart, 30.
29 Nelson to Emma, 13 June 1801. Pettigrew, II, 101.
30 Nelson to Isaac Heard, 1 November 1799. Nicolas, IV, 81.
31 Sir Isaac Heard to the Duke of Portland, 20 December 1799. College of Arms, Nayler GCB LMN, f. 125.
32 Nelson to Isaac Heard, 20 September 1800. Letter book, Nelson papers, Monmouth, III, E79.
33 *Morning Chronicle*, 13 November 1800.
34 Rose, I, 219.
35 Stuart, 88.
36 *Memoirs of Lord Collingwood*, Vol. 1, 110. Quoted Nicholas, IV, 278.
37 Earl St Vincent to Evan Nepean, 17 January 1801. NMM AGC/J/6/2.
38 Quoted Naish, 561.
39 *Morning Herald*, 13 November 1800.
40 Harrison, II, 270.
41 *Memoirs*, 145–46.
42 *Morning Herald* (London, England), Wednesday, 19 November 1800.
43 *Memoirs*, 148.
44 Fanny to Alexander Davison, 26 June 1801. NMM DAV 2/50.
45 *The Cabinet of Modern Art, and Literary Souvenir* (1836), 102. Quoted Walker, 124. The portrait, hat and sword are still in the collection of the City of Norwich. The hat still shows a ragged hole where the Chelengk had once been pinned.
46 Nicolas, VII, 347–48n.
47 John McArthur to Nelson, 1 December 1800. NMM. Quoted Walker, 49–50.
48 Brian Connell, *Portrait of a Whig Peer* (London, 1957), 440. Quoted Walker, 128.
49 *Naval Chronicle*, Volume 1 (1799), 340.
50 Nelson to Alexander Davison, 8 February 1801. BL Add MS 34988, f. 380.
51 Prince of Wales loan, July 1809. Royal Archives GEO/31557.
52 Nelson to Lady Nelson, 3 February 1801. Naish, 619.
53 Fanny to Alexander Davison, 24 February 1801. NMM DAV 2/30.
54 Nelson, 'Codicil to my last will and testament', 25 May 1799. Morrison, II, 47.
55 Nelson to Emma, 5 February 1801. Pettigrew, II, 648. Nelson to Emma (undated February 1801). Pettigrew, I, 428. Nelson to Emma, 6 March 1801. Pettigrew, I, 436.
56 Nelson to Emma, (undated, February 1801). Pettigrew, I, 428.
57 Nelson to unknown correspondent, 13 December 1800, private collection. Pettigrew, I, 390.
58 Codicil dated 16 March 1801. Morrison, II, 131.
59 Nelson to Fanny, 9 January 1801. BL ADD MS 34902, f. 181.

Chapter 10 The Doctor

1 Rev. William Nelson to unknown, 'Monday 5 o'clock afternoon', 1 October 1798. BL Add MS 34907, f.334.
2 Lady Spencer to Nelson, 2 October 1798 (tr. by Earl Nelson, 24 May 1808). BL Add MS 34907, f.339.
3 Matcham, 161.
4 Oman, 4.
5 The Rev. William Nelson to Nelson, 7 June 1798. BL Add MS 34988, f.247 / 17 October 1798. NMM BRP/1/2.
6 Pay certificate, dated 31 December 1785. NMM BRP6. Quoted Coleman, 77.
7 Fanny to Nelson, 7 June 1799. BL Add MS 34988, f.309. Naish, 529.
8 Nelson to Fanny, 16 September 1798. Naish, 400.
9 *The Times*, 28 September 1797.
10 William Nelson to Nelson, 30 November 1797. Monmouth IV, quoted Coleman, 145.
11 Catherine Matcham to Nelson, 6 October 1798. BL Add 34988, quoted Coleman, 167.
12 William to Nelson, 26 May 1804, NMM, CRK/9/33, quoted Knight, 658.
13 Colonel John Drinkwater, *A Narrative of the Battle of Cape St Vincent* (1840), quoted Hibbert, 110.
14 Nelson to William Nelson, 6 April 1797. Nicolas, III, 370.
15 Nelson to Fanny, 29 June 1797. Naish, 327.
16 Nelson to William Nelson, 18 January 1798. Nicolas, III, 235.
17 Maurice Nelson to Fanny, 6 October 1798. Naish, 453.
18 Nelson to Fanny, 2 January 1799. Naish, 479.
19 Fanny to Nelson, 26 December 1799. Naish, 544.
20 A panel from the coach decorated with Nelson's coat of arms is in the collection of NMM Greenwich, ID: BHC1078.
21 Armorial panel in the collection of the Nelson Museum, Monmouth.
22 The Rev. William Nelson to Lady Nelson, 1 April 1799. Naish, 467. Nelson Papers, Monmouth, III, E663.
23 Fanny to Nelson, 18 June 1799. Naish, 529.
24 Nelson to Emma, 16 February 1801. Pettigrew, I, 426.
25 Fanny to Nelson, 10 December 1799, quoted Sugden (2014), 359.
26 Emma to Sarah Nelson, February 1801, Naish, 577.
27 William to Emma, 19 February 1801. Pettigew, I, 429.
28 William to Emma, 6 September 1801, Letters 1814, quoted Coleman, 275.
29 Fanny to Alexander Davison, 26 April 1801, NMM, DAV/2/37 & (undated, May 1801?) NMM, DAV/2/40.
30 Sir William Hamilton to Nelson, 16 April 1801, Naish, 585.
31 Alexander Davison to Nelson, 29 June 1803, private collection. Lot 70, Sotheby's, 21 October 2002.
32 Alexander Davison to Maurice Nelson, 22 April 1801, private collection. Lot 70, Sotheby's, 21 October 2002.
33 Nelson to Emma, 7 August 1801. Pettigrew, II, 144.

34 William to Emma, 6 August 1801, private collection. Pettigrew, II, 124, where remark about Fanny is edited out.
35 William to Emma, 20 August 1801. Pettigrew, II, 167.
36 William to Emma, 6 September 1801. *Letters*, I, 207.
37 William to Emma, 13 August 1801, private collection. Pettigrew, II, 153.
38 William to Nelson, 6 July 1802. Pettigrew, II, 258.
39 Sarah Nelson to William, 2 September 1801. NMM BRP/3. Sugden, 522.
40 Fanny to Sarah Nelson, September 1801. NMM BRP MS 9292 f. Naish, 592.
41 Nelson to Davison, 27 April 1802. Lot 62, The Alexander Davison Collection, Sotheby's London, 21 October 2002.
42 Sir William Hamilton to Nelson, 12 August 1801. *Letters*, II, 218.
43 Nelson to Emma, 14 October 1801. Lot 432, International Auctions, Malaga, Spain, 3 June 2017.
44 Harrison, II, 391. Harrison (writing under Emma Hamilton's supervision) misidentifies the painting as the portrait of Nelson completed by Heinrich Füger in Vienna in 1800. The mistake suggests that the Vienna portrait was also given away by Nelson, possibly because it showed the Order of the Crescent above the Bath Star. Füger's painting was lost until the 1920s. It is now in the collection of the Museum of the Royal Navy, Portsmouth.
45 Sir William Hamilton to Charles Greville, 24 January 1802. Morrison II, 182., quoted Fraser, 295.
46 Harrison, II, 386.
47 Nelson to Emma, 11 August 1801. *Letters*, I, 47.
48 Stuart, 123-24.
49 *The Morning Post*, 19 January 1802.
50 *The Morning Post*, 4 June 1803.
51 Gilbert, Rev. George, *Reminiscences* (ed. Rev. John Shirley, 1938), quoted Gérin, 103.
52 *Memoirs*, 168.
53 Nelson to William, 19 August 1805. Nicolas, VII, 13.
54 Quoted by Abbé Campbell to Emma, 8 December 1805. Monmouth, E216, quoted Knight, 658.
55 Emma to Nelson, 8 October 1805. Morrison, II, 268.

Chapter 11 The Invasion

1 William Sidney Smith to Lord Grenville, 22 February 1799. BL Add MS 58980, f.45.
2 Lloyd, *Keith Papers*, II, 62. Despite his misgivings about Nelson, it appears Sir John Moore acquired a version of the admiral's portrait by Guzzardi at, or following their meeting in Leghorn.
3 Lord Keith to his sister, quoted Lloyd, II, 230.
4 William Sidney Smith to Lord Keith, 14 March 1801. Barrow, I, 345.
5 Parsons, 81.
6 Parsons, 90.

7 'Extract of a letter from a lieutenant on board Lord Keith's Fleet', *British Gazette and Sunday Monitor*, Sunday, 24 May 1801.
8 Admiral Lord Keith's diamond Chelengk was stolen in 1988 but a fine replica is on display at Bowood House, Wilshire.
9 Quoted Shankland, 136.
10 Ibid., 143.
11 Howard, I, 296–99.
12 Smith to General Hely-Hutchinson, 28 August 1801. Barrow, I, 435.
13 21 September 1801, *Nisbet*, 111 ff.
14 Diary of Ahmed Efendi. Translation quoted Eldem, 41.
15 *Nisbet*, 119.
16 NA HO 42/69, f.240–49. In addition to Nelson, the list recipients were the Marquis of Wellesley, Earl of Elgin, Earl of Cavan, Lord Keith, Lord Hutchinson, Sir Eyre Coote, Sir John Warren, Sir John Craddock, Sir David Baird, Sir John Stuart, Admiral Sir Richard Bickerton and 'Mr Drummond' (William Drummond, who succeeded Lord Elgin as ambassador in Constantinople in 1803).
17 'Egypt', *The Times* (London, England), 22 January 1802, 3.
18 *The Times* (London, England), 11 November 1801.
19 Howard, I, 304.
20 *The Morning Post*, 17 May 1802.
21 *Naval Chronicle*, Vol. 7 (January-July 1802), 516.
22 *The Morning Post*, 19 June 1802.
23 Sir William Hamilton to General Edward Smith, 15 December 1800. Barrow, II, 115, quoted Shankland, 170.
24 George Matcham to Nelson (October 1798). BL Add MS 34988, f.276.
25 Earl St Vincent to Emma, 28 October 1798. Nelson Papers, Monmouth, II, E415.
26 Nelson to Emma, 22 February 1801. Morrison, II, 121.
27 *Inquiry*, 84.
28 Ibid., 106.
29 Ibid., Appendixes, 87.
30 Ibid., 77–78.
31 Howard, I, 367–68.
32 Howard, I, 399.

Chapter 12 The Farewell

1 Nelson to Henry Addington, 31 January 1802. Nicolas, V, 3.
2 Nelson to Fanny, 7 November 1799. Naish, 491.
3 Robinson, 249. Memorial of Emma Hamilton, March 1813. Morrison, II, 364.
4 Maltese cross and earrings sold Christie's, London, 10 May 1932, Lot 54. NMM NWD/5. John Salter's bill for ninety-one items of jewellery supplied to Emma Hamilton between June 1802 and March 1803 amounted to £169 11*s* 7*d*. NMM NWD/32.
5 Nelson to Emma, 10 September 1803. *Letters*, I, 150.

6 *The Morning Post and Gazetteer* (London, England), Saturday, 28 February 1801.
7 Nelson to Emma (March 1801). *Letters*, I, 38.
8 Nelson to Emma, 31 August 1801. *Letters*, I, 54.
9 Nelson to Alexander Davison, 8 February 1801. BL Add MS 34988, f.380.
10 Nelson to Alexander Davison, 18 December 1801. Pettigrew, II, 240.
11 Nelson to William Marsh, 29 December 1801. Pettigrew, II, 242.
12 John Salter trade label. Comfort, 63.
13 Trade card of John Salter. Southwick, 215.
14 Pettigrew, II, 171n.
15 Comfort, 49. The sword was sold by Sotheby's on 22 December 1919 and is now in the collection of the Nelson Museum, Monmouth. Nelson's hats, each supplied with a regulation cockade, started at £1 11s 6d (about £120 today) rising to £2 6s 0d (£170) with a shade. William Nelson also ordered 'Round' hats from Locks for himself and 'Livery' hats braided in gold for his servants.
16 John Salter to Nelson, 24 August 1801. NMM CRK/12/11.
17 *List of Nelson's plate to go afloat and at Merton 1801-02*. NMM BRP/14/9292.
18 Mrs Cadogan to Emma, 31 August 1804. NMM CRK /20/63.
19 Silliman, I, 335.
20 Account with William Peddieson, 10 September 1805. Nelson Papers, Monmouth, E400.
21 Minto (1874), III, 243.
22 Nelson to Alexander Davison, 4 October 1803. Nicolas, V, 219.
23 Harrison, II, 465.
24 Emma to Alexander Davison, 6 September 1805. Sotheby's, 155.
25 Lot 184, Sotheby's, London, 5 October 2005. The watch was made by James McCabe, 97 Cornhill, Royal Exchange.
26 Eyre Matcham, 230.
27 *The Morning Post*, 14 September 1805.
28 Smith to Henry Addington (n.d. 1805). Quoted Knight, 498.
29 Jennings, L.J. (ed.), *The Croker Papers: Correspondence and Diaries of the Late Right Honourable John Wilson Croker* (London, 1884), II, 233-34.
30 Harrison, II, 472.
31 Silliman, II, 242.

Chapter 13 The Death

1 Miss Susanna Bolton to Emma, 7 July 1805. Naish, 605.
2 Lord Barham to Fanny, 6 November 1805. Naish, 605.
3 Stuart, 127ff.
4 Sidney Smith to Lord Castlereagh, 8 November 1805. Londonderry, V, 126.
5 Gilbert, Rev. George, *Reminiscences* (ed. by Rev. John Shirley, 1938), quoted Gérin, 106.
6 William Haslewood to his partner Frederick Booth, 'Saturday night eleven o'clock', 9 November 1805. Lot 207A, Bonhams, London, 5 July 2005. The award was published in the *London Gazette*, No. 15859 (5-9 November 1805), 1,376.
7 William Pitt to William Nelson, 9 November 1805. Hood Papers.

8 William Nelson to William Pitt, 9 November 1805. Hood Papers.
9 William Nelson to unnamed duke ('My Lord Duke'), BL Add 34992, f.28, quoted Coleman, 328.
10 Hibbert, 389.
11 Nelson's Will, 10 May 1803. Nicolas, VII, ccxxi.
12 Emma to Alexander Davison, 7 June 1806. BL Add MS 40739 f.106.
13 John Salter Statement of Account. NMM NWD/5.
14 Nelson's Will, 10 May 1803, Nicolas, VII, ccxxviii.
15 Codicil No.II, 6 September 1803. Nicolas, VII, ccxxxv.
16 Captain Thomas Masterman Hardy to Alexander Davison, 7 December 1805. NMM DAV 52/44.
17 Codicil VIII, 21 October 1805. Nicolas, VII, ccxl.
18 Beatty, 42.
19 Captain Thomas Masterman Hardy to Emma, 8 December 1805. Stuart, 128.
20 Beatty, 42.
21 Sarah Nelson to Emma, 5 December 1805. Lot 181, Sotheby's London, 17 May 1905.
22 Sarah Nelson to Emma, 13 February 1806. NMM/AGC/18/14.
23 'Journal of Lionel Goldsmid', *Transactions of the Jewish Historical Society*, XIV, 225–45, quoted Gérin, 111.
24 A receipt from the Earl Nelson to Lady Hamilton, 22 February 1806. Morrison, II, 277.
25 Earl Nelson to William Haslewood, 26 February 1806. NMM HAS/1. Same to same, 9 May 1806. NMM MS80/050.
26 Stuart, 128.
27 Earl Nelson, 'Receipt from Rundle, Bridge & Co for Aigrette, Sword & Gold Box dated 23rd May 1807'. NMM BRP/5.
28 Hartop, 135.
29 Emma to Alexander Davison, 5 September 1806. NMM LKB/7 MS9640. Sold Sotheby's London, 21 October 2002. An ivory-handled Persian Shamshir (scimitar) in the collection of the Nelson Museum, Monmouth, is the best candidate for Ali Pasha's lost sword.
30 Earl Nelson to Fanny, 9 November 1805. Draft. NMM BRP/11/9292.
31 Fanny to Earl Nelson, 23 November 1805. Hood Papers.
32 Fanny to William Marsh, 29 January 1810. NMM 37 MS 1254. Naish, 617.
33 Invoice of E. Franks, Milliner & Dressmaker, St James's Street, London. Nelson Museum, Monmouth.
34 Farington diary, 9 May 1806, VII, 2,754.
35 Codicil No.II. Nicolas, VII, Addenda ccxxxvi.
36 Nelson to James Dodds, 31 August 1801. Nelson Papers, Monmouth, E97.
37 Fanny to Alexander Davison, 3 September 1801. NMM DAV 2/54.
38 The Nelson Collection from a direct descendant of Josiah Nisbet. Christie's London, 3 July 2012.
39 Earl Nelson to Lord Grenville, 5 March 1806, BL Add MS 59380, ff.71–76.
40 House of Commons Debate, 15 July 1806, Vol.7. 1,151
41 Memorial of Emma Hamilton, March 1813. Morrison, II, 365.
42 Farington diary, 7 February 1807. IV.

43 For discussion relating to the commission of the 'official' biography of Nelson with royal patronage see correspondence of Earl Nelson, BL Add MS 34992 ff.95–146.
44 Harrison, II, 277.
45 Harrison, II, 465.
46 Fanny to John McArthur, 28 February 1807. Naish, 615.
47 *Memoirs*, 188. Annotated frontispiece to *Memoirs of Lady Hamilton* (London, 1815) belonging to Florence Horatia Suckling. Author's collection.
48 *The Times*, 25 December 1805. Emma to George Rose, 29 November 1805. Gérin, 109.

Chapter 14 The Earl

1 Earl Nelson to (William Haslewood?), undated. NMM MS80/050.
2 *The Times* (London, England), 6 January 1806. 3.
3 Gatty, A. & M., *Recollections of the Life of the Reverend A.J. Scott* (London, 1842), 197–98.
4 Alexander Scott to Emma, 3 January 1806. Pettigrew, II, 554.
5 Gatty, 203.
6 Ibid., 204.
7 *The Times* (London, England), 9 January 1806. 3.
8 *The Morning Post*, 27 December 1805. Fanny to Davison, 14 December 1805. NMM DAV 2/65.
9 Earl Nelson to William Marsh (?), 25 December 1805. NMM MS80/050.
10 Journal of George Matcham, 6 January 1805. Eyre Matcham, 242.
11 William Nelson to George Nayler, Genealogist of the Order of the Bath. College of Heralds, quoted White, 69.
12 William Nelson, 'List of Person to whom mourning rings were sent' (undated 1806). BL Add MS 34988, f.412.
13 Matcham, 242.
14 'Tradesman Bills', BL Add MS 34992, f.80. Salter statement of Account, NMM MSS/80/050.
15 Account of late Admiral Viscount Nelson. Hood Papers.
16 Earl Nelson to William Haslewood, 26 February 1806. NMM HAS/1.
17 *The Morning Chronicle*, Saturday, 11 January 1806.
18 For papers relating to parliament's grant to Nelson's family, see BL Add MS 79200.
19 Earl Nelson to William Haslewood (undated, August 1806). NMM HAS/1.
20 Lawrence H. Officer and Samuel H. Williamson, 'Five Ways to Compute the Relative Value of a UK Pound Amount, 1270 to Present', *Measuring Worth*, 2016.
21 Earl Nelson to Alexander Davison. BL Add MS 79200, f.4.
22 House of Commons Debate, 13 May 1806. Hansard Vol.7, 141–45.
23 Earl Nelson to unknown (Alexander Davison?), 27 May 1806. NMM MS80/050.
24 Earl Nelson note. BL Add 79200, f.14.
25 Farington diary, 9 May 1806, VII, 2755.
26 *The Gentleman's Magazine, and Historical Chronicle*, Vol.LXXVIII (March 1808), 188.
27 Naish, 597.

28 *The Gentleman's Magazine, and Historical Chronicle*, Vol. LXXVIII (March 1808), 188.
29 Farington diary, 16 June 1808, IX, 3,198.
30 Quoted Gérin, 153..
31 Catherine Matcham to Emma, 31 December 1808. Morrison, II, 322.
32 Earl Nelson to George Nayler, 23 February 1808. College of Arms, Nayler GCB LMN, f.136.
33 'An Account of the English Ambassador's Audience with the Sultan', *The Weekly Entertainer*, 19 September 1808, 745.
34 *The Times* (London, England), 16 September 1808.
35 Farington diary, 20 April 1807, VIII, 3,027.
36 Emma to Alexander Davison, 3 April 1814. NMM LBK/7.
37 Alexander Davison to Earl Nelson, 30 July 1806. NMM BRP/5.
38 *The Bury and Norwich Post*, 22 October 1806.
39 Journals of the House of Commons, LXX, 997.
40 Quoted MacCarthy, 88.
41 Eyre Matcham, 273.
42 Pettigrew, II, 540.
43 Gordon, II, 389-90.
44 Nelson to Emma, 16 October 1801. *Letters*, I, 83. Nelson to Emma, 26 August 1803. *Letters*, I, 143.
45 William to Emma, 29 March & 23 August 1801. *Letters*, I, 200 & 203.
46 Hood Papers.
47 Codicil 4, 19 February 1804. Nicolas, VII, Addenda ccxxxviii.
48 Earl Nelson to Antonio Forcella (1807), quoted Pratt, 110.
49 Emma to Alexander Davison, 8 April 1809. NMM LBK/7.
50 Hood, *Jottings*, I, 44.
51 Emma to Earl Nelson, 29 April 1814. NMM BRP/4/1.
52 Gérin, 251.
53 Matcham, 279.
54 Longman's Annual Biography and Obituary for 1823, 251.
55 Lot 152, *Catalogue of The Entire Property of Alexander Davison Esq.*, 21 April 1817 and fifteen following days.
56 *The Gardener's Magazine*, Vol. 9 (1833), 15.
57 Eyre Matcham, 289.
58 Tom Bolton to George Matcham, 18 November 1818. Gérin, 234.
59 Farington diary, 28 January 1817, XIV, 4,965.

Chapter 15 The Bride

1 *The Belfast News-Letter*, 7 August 1829.
2 Quoted Pratt, 104.
3 Earl Nelson to Lord Bridport, 12 February 1829. Hood Papers.
4 Hood Papers.

5 Earl Nelson to Lord Hood, 29 September 1831. NMM BRP/9.
6 *Testamento della famiglia Nelson*. ASP 284/B.
7 *John Bull*, 4 May 1829.
8 *Morning Post*, 10 May 1833.
9 *Arnold's Magazine of the Fine Arts*, Vol. IV (1834), 200.
10 Hardy, 305.
11 Susannah Bolton to Emma (October 1808), Gamlin, II, 94.
12 Stirling, II, 218.
13 Ibid.
14 Gore, 149. The battle vases can be identified as the pair of vases by Chamberlains Worcester circa 1805, National Maritime Museum, Object ID: AAA4740.
15 *The Morning Chronicle* (London, England), Monday, 16 May 1831.
16 *The Times*, 16 May 1831.
17 *The Times* (London, England), 13 May 1831, 2.
18 *The Morning Chronicle* (London, England), Monday, 16 May 1831.
19 *The Times*, 16 May 1831. Lawrence H. Officer and Samuel H. Williamson, 'Five Ways to Compute the Relative Value of a UK Pound Amount, 1270 to Present', *Measuring Worth*, 2016.
20 *Naval & Military Gazette*, 20 March 1841.
21 Barrow, II, 460.
22 Will of Sir Sidney Smith, Barrow, II, 581.
23 Russell, 201.
24 Rumbold, 20.
25 Ibid., 21.
26 Will of Admiral Sir Sidney Smith, NA PROB 11/1930/18. Barrow, II, 498.
27 *The Morning Post*, 15 November 1833.
28 *The Morning Post*, 22 November 1833.
29 Stirling, II, 267.
30 *Hampshire Advertiser*, Saturday, 4 October 1834. Stirling, II, 267.
31 Thomas Bolton to Miss Bolton, 2 March 1835. NMM GIR/5.
32 Earl Nelson to William Haslewood, 15 August 1806. NMM HAS/1.
33 *The Times*, 4 November 1852. Gamlin, II, 264-66.
34 Personal assets. BL Add MS 34992, f.259.
35 The earl's full-length portrait of his brother was another version by John Hoppner of the painting eventually presented to the Prince of Wales in 1810. The earl's portrait, since cut-down, has also been insecurely attributed to Hoppner. The painting of Sir Robert Walpole 'in his hunting dress', now in the same private collection as the earl's portrait, is by Joseph Richardson (1667-1745) and may be identified as hanging in Walpole's bed chamber at Downing Street in 1736 (John Kerslake, *Early Georgian Portraits*, 1977).
36 Earl Nelson to Admiral Sir Richard Keats, 24 March 1814. Morton & Eden catalogue for the sale of the breast star by direct descent from Admiral Keats on 22 October 2010.
37 George Matcham to Emma Hamilton, May 1808. Gamlin, II, 94.

Chapter 16 The Duchess

1 26 October 1798, Monmouth E.662, quoted Hibbert, 158.
2 Hood, *Jottings*, I, 46.
3 Charlotte Nelson to Nelson, 5 February 1799. NMM BRP/1/1. Naish, 466.
4 Charlotte Nelson to Sarah Nelson (January 1800). NMM BRP/1/1. Naish, 546. William Nelson to Emma, 23 May 1805, 'Most Secret and Confidential'. Gamlin, II, 16.
5 Sarah Nelson to Charlotte, October 1802. NMM BRP/1/1, quoted Williams, 281.
6 Sarah Nelson to Emma, 6 November 1804, quoted Williams, 303.
7 Charlotte to Sarah Nelson, 11 November 1803. NMM BRP/1/1.
8 Emma to Nelson, 8 October 1805. NMM/NWD/9594, quoted Gérin, 103.
9 Emma to Sarah Nelson (undated, 1804), quoted Fraser, 309.
10 Emma to Sarah Nelson, (undated). NMM BRP 9292/4.
11 Sugden, 549.
12 Quoted Pocock (1987) 262; ibid., 270.
13 Quoted Pocock, 262.
14 Emma to Sarah Nelson (December 1801), private collection, quoted Pocock (2002), 183.
15 Quoted Pocock (2002), 188.
16 *The Morning Post and Gazetteer*, 10 November 1802.
17 Monmouth, E206, quoted Williams, 282.
18 Sarah Nelson to Charlotte, 29 October 1805, quoted Pocock (2002), 224.
19 *The Morning Chronicle,* 7 February 1806.
20 Miss Bolton to Emma, 3 June 1807. Morrison, II, 299.
21 Charlotte Nelson to Emma, undated 1806. Gamlin, II, 173.
22 Farington diary entry, 19 January 1808, Vol. V, 8.
23 *The Morning Post*, 6 June 1809.
24 Keate, 284.
25 Quoted Riall, 165.
26 *The Morning Post* (London, England), Friday, 16 June 1820.
27 Mrs Bolton to Emma, 17 January 1811. Morrison, II, 346.
28 Hood, *Jottings*, I, 46.
29 Earl Nelson to Samuel Hood (undated, 1828), quoted Pratt, 144.
30 Thomas Bolton, second Earl Nelson to his solicitor, 16 June 1835. Lot 134, Sotheby's London, 17 May 1905. NMM NWD/32.
31 Hood, *Jottings*, I, 46.
32 Earl Nelson v. Lord Bridport. Beavan, 547ff.
33 Pettigrew, I, xix.
34 Horatio, third Earl Nelson, 'Nelson Relics and Relic Hunters', *The Windsor Magazine*, October 1904, 516.
35 Queen Victoria journal entry for 10 October 1838. www.queenvictoriasjournals.org.
36 Prince Albert to Duke Ernest of Saxe-Coburg-Gotha, 22 June 1841. Martin, I, 113n.
37 Marble bust of Nelson by Sir Francis Chantrey, 1835. Now in the collection of the National Portrait Gallery, London. Walker, 187, 272.
38 Sarah Nelson to Emma, 13 February 1806. NMM/AGC/18/14.

39 Inventory of goods held by Alderman Smith (unsigned, 1844), private collection.
40 Evans, 2.
41 Ibid., 13.
42 Ibid., 16.
43 Lady Hamilton account with John Salter. NMM NWD/5/1 part.
44 List of securities deposited with Mr Trickey. NMM NWD/5/1 part.
45 Horatia Nelson to Joshua Smith, 1 May 1816. NMM TRA/22.
46 *A Catalogue of the Elegant Household Furniture, The Property of a Lady of Distinction* (8 July 1813), NMM.
47 Nelson Papers, Monmouth E178.
48 Horatia Ward to Sir N.H. Nicolas, 15 March 1846. NMM NWD/34.
49 'Horatia Nelson Thompson', Nicolas VII, 388.
50 Journal of George Matcham, 6 November 1805. Eyre Matcham, 237.
51 Quoted Prentice, 98.
52 *Illustrated London News* (London, England), 26 July 1845.
53 Evans, 14.

Chapter 17 The General

1 Byron, *Don Juan*, Canto 1, IV (London, 1820).
2 Hood, *Jottings*, I, 27.
3 *The Morning Post*, Friday, 3 August 1838.
4 Benjamin Disraeli to Sarah Williams, 18 October 1860. Wiebe, 62.
5 *London Gazette*, 21 September 1841.
6 Hood, *Jottings*, I, 30 & 32.
7 Benjamin Disraeli to Sarah Williams, 18 October 1860. Wiebe, 61
8 Queen Victoria's Journal entry for Sunday, 14 November 1869. www.queenvictorias-journals.org.
9 Hood, *Jottings*, I, 29.
10 Will of Charlotte Mary, Duchess of Bronte, dated 13 May 1863. ASP 284/B.
11 Viscount Bridport to James Risk (undated, circa 1955), Hood Papers.
12 *The Morning Post*, 13 July 1867.
13 Queen Victoria's Journal entry for Saturday, 13 July 1867. www.queenvictoriasjournals.org.
14 Queen Victoria's Journal entry for Wednesday, 17 July 1867. www.queenvictoriasjournals.org.
15 Queen Victoria's Journal entry for Sunday, 4 June 1876. www.queenvictoriasjournals.org.
16 George Pulman, *The Book of the Axe* (London, 1875), 386.
17 Nelson to Alexander Davison, 8 February 1801. BL Add MS 34988, f.380.
18 *The Times* (London, England), 26 May 1891, 10.
19 *The Times*, 17–18 January 1895.
20 Francis Capel Cure to Alec Hood, 17 March 1895. Archivio della Ducca di Bronte – Archivio Nelson, Volume 601/A. ASP.

21 Lawrence H. Officer and Samuel H. Williamson, 'Five Ways to Compute the Relative Value of a UK Pound Amount, 1270 to Present', *Measuring Worth*, 2017. *The Commercial Gazette*, 22 May 1895, 3.
22 Cricket St Thomas & Bronte mortgage details: Archivio della Ducca di Bronte – Archivio Nelson, Volume 371/C. ASP.
23 Capel Cure & Ball to Fladgate & Co., Solicitors, 15 May 1895. Archivio della Ducca di Bronte – Archivio Nelson, Volume 601/A. ASP.
24 Francis Capel Cure to General Viscount Bridport, 16 May 1895. Ibid.
25 General Viscount Bridport to Alec Hood, 17 May 1895. Ibid.
26 General Viscount Bridport to Alec Hood, 28 May 1895. Ibid.
27 *The Times*, 13 July 1895.
28 *The Morning Post*, 15 July 1895.
29 Catalogue of Old English silver … GOLD SWORD HILTS MEDALS, ORDERS and other Highly Interesting Objects formerly in the possession of ADMIRAL LORD NELSON … the Property of The Right Hon. Viscount Bridport, Christie's London, 12 July 1895. NMM NWD/32.
30 *The Standard*, 13 July 1895.
31 The hilt was stolen from the Nelson Museum, Monmouth, on 9 November 1953.
32 Catalogue of Old English silver … GOLD SWORD HILTS MEDALS, ORDERS and other Highly Interesting Objects formerly in the possession of ADMIRAL LORD NELSON … the Property of The Right Hon. Viscount Bridport, Christie's London, 12 July 1895. NMM NWD/32.
33 Hood, *Jottings*, I, 29.
34 Statement of Funds in Hand, 28 October 1895. Archivio della Ducca di Bronte – Archivio Nelson, Volume 594/A. Archivio di Stato di Palermo (ASP).

Chapter 18 The People

1 A.O. Bell (ed.), *The Diary of Virginia Woolf* (1980), Vol. 3, 72–73, quoted Littlewood, 45.
2 Lord Charles Beresford & H.W. Wilson, *Nelson and His Times* Part 5 (n.d., 1897–98).
3 *Hampshire Telegraph and Naval Chronicle,* 15 December 1900.
4 Horatio, third Earl Nelson, 'Nelson Relics and Relic Hunters', *The Windsor Magazine*, October 1904, 513–16.
5 *The Times*, 17 September 1904
6 Charles Arrow, *Rogues and Others* (London, 1926), 131–36.
7 Littlewood, 30.
8 Horatio, third Earl Nelson, 'Nelson Relics and Relic Hunters', *The Windsor Magazine*, October 1904, 513.
9 Official Catalogue of the United Service Museum, Whitehall (London, 1914), cat. nos 92 (hat), 93 (foul weather hat), 3,031 (sword), 3,038 (cane).
10 Official Catalogue of the United Service Museum, Whitehall (London, 1914).
11 *Daily Express*, 10 May 1928.

12 Mrs Valentine Jeffreys to Lord Bridport, 11 February 1952. Hood Papers. Sale leaflet for the Chelengk, Society of Nautical Research (undated, 1929).
13 Cat. No. 112: Loan Exhibition of Nelson Relics, Spink & Son, 1928.
14 *The Times* (London), 12 May 1928.
15 The City of London presentation sword is now in the collection of the Museum of London, MOL11952.
16 Sale leaflet for the Chelengk, Society of Nautical Research (undated 1929).
17 Sale leaflet for the Chelengk, Society of Nautical Research (undated 1929).
18 *The Times*, 8 November 1929.
19 ODNB entry for Sarita Barclay's second husband Robert Vansittart, Baron Vansittart.
20 Annual General Meeting of the Society for Nautical Research, 2 July 1930. Report published in *Mariner's Mirror*, vol.16, October 1930, p.387ff.
21 Littlewood, 55.
22 Littlewood, 81.
23 Littlewood, 102.
24 HC Deb, 28 February 1924. Vol.170, c841.
25 HC Deb, 29 June 1926. Vol.197, c988W.
26 HC Deb, 3 December 1946. Vol.431, cc212-79.
27 Obituary of 9th Earl Nelson, Daily Telegraph, 1 April 2009.

Chapter 19 The Thief

1 Weir, Andrew, 'Thieves like Him', *The Independent Magazine*, 12 February 1994, 32-33.
2 Obituary, *The Guardian*, 7 June 1997.
3 Weir, Andrew, 'Thieves like Him', *The Independent Magazine*, 12 February 1994, 32-33.
4 Campbell, 35.
5 Obituary, *The Guardian*, 7 June 1997.
6 Weir, Andrew, 'Thieves like Him', *The Independent Magazine*, 12 February 1994, 32-33.
7 Weir, Andrew, 'Thieves like Him', *The Independent Magazine*, 12 February 1994, 32-33.
8 Campbell, Duncan, *The Guardian*, 14 February 1994.
9 *Daily Mail*, 19 April 1948.
10 Scott, 150.
11 Scott, 150.
12 Statement of Reginald Lowen, 11 June 1951. NMM10 C63.
13 Frank Carr to Sir Alec Martin, Christie's, 22 June 1951.
14 Lady Vansittart to Sir Alec Martin, 17 June 1951. NMM10 C63.
15 Parliamentary Debates, 26 June 1951. Hansard, Vol.172, No.76.
16 NMM10 C63.
17 Conversation with Dick Ellis, February 2016.
18 Scott, 3.

Chapter 20 The Lost Jewel and its Rebirth

1 Decree of Selim III. Quoted Eldem, 22.
2 Spencer Smith to Lord Grenville, 8 September 1798. NA FO 78/20, f.22.
3 Eldem, 24n.
4 James W. Redhouse, *An English and Turkish Dictionary, in two parts, English and Turkish, and Turkish and English* (London, 1856).
5 Memorial of Emma, Lady Hamilton, March 1813. Morrison, II, 363.
6 Extract of a letter from the son of a merchant of Birmingham, dated Naples, 17 December. *Northampton Mercury*, 30 March 1799.
7 Alexander Davison to George Nayler, 20 March 1806. College of Arms, Nelson Peerage Papers.
8 Spencer Smith to Lord Grenville, 8 September 1798. NA FO 78/20, f.21.
9 Irepoğlu, 231.
10 Dalloway, 25.
11 'Account of the Mission of Yusuf Agha, Ambassador from Turkey to the British written by himself translated from the Turkish by the Ritter Joseph Von Hammer', Transactions of the Royal Asiatic Society of Great Britain and Ireland, Vol. III (1833), 9.
12 *Gentleman's Magazine, and Historical Chronicle*, Vol. XCVIII (July–December 1828), 651. Enquiry to Landesmuseum Württemberg, July 2016.
13 Thackeray, W.M., *The Four Georges* (London, 1860), 114.
14 Michael Talbot, *British-Ottoman Relations, 1661-1807* (Woodbridge, 2017), 105.
15 Prentice, 72.
16 *Recreations in Arts and Literature*, 1 May 1799, 96.
17 Prentice, 70.
18 De Beaujour, 241.
19 Admiral Lord Keith's diamond watch and chatelaine are on display at Bowood House, Wiltshire.
20 De Beaujour, 241.
21 Minto (1874), III, 147.
22 Earl Nelson, 'Receipt from Rundle, Bridge & Co for Aigrette, Sword & Gold Box dated 23rd May 1807'. NMM BRP/5.
23 De Beaujour, 248.
24 Official Catalogue of the United Service Museum, Whitehall (London, 1914).
25 Extract of a letter from the son of a merchant of Birmingham, dated Naples, 17 December. *Northampton Mercury*, 30 March 1799.
26 Sir William Hamilton to Lord Grenville, 8 November 1799. NA FO 70/12, f.316.
27 *The Morning Post* (London, England), Friday, 16 June 1820.
28 *Recreations in Arts and Literature*, 1 May 1799, 96.
29 Sir Alexander Nelson Hood to Constance Eyre-Matcham, 3 May 1913, quoted Prentice, 72.
30 Dawson, 496
31 Letter of Viscount Bridport, *Country Life*, Vol. 110 (24 August 1951), 578
32 Garlick, Farington diary entry for 11 December 1798, III, 1,100.

BIBLIOGRAPHY

Barrow, J., *Life and Correspondence of Admiral Sir William Sidney Smith* (2 vols, London, 1848).

Beatty, W., *Authentic Narrative of the Death of Lord Nelson* (second ed., 1808).

Beavan, C., Report of Cases in Chancery: Argued and Determined in the Rolls Court During the time of Lord Langdale Master of the Rolls, (Vol. 8, London, 1847).

Beresford, Lord Charles, and Wilson, H.W., *Nelson and his Times* (1897-98).

Broadley, A.M., and Bartelot, R.G., *The Three Dorset Captains at Trafalgar* (1906).

Browne, G.L., *Nelson* (London, 1890).

Campbell, D., *The Underworld* (London, 1994).

Clarke, J.S., and McArthur, J. (eds), *The Life and Services of Horatio, Viscount Nelson, Duke of Bronte, Vice-Admiral of the White, K.B.* (3 vols, London, 1840).

Cliff, K., *Mr Lock: Hatter to Lord Nelson and his Norfolk Neighbours* (Norwich, 2000)

Coleman, T., *Nelson: The Man and the Legend* (London, 2001).

Comfort, S., *Lord Nelson's Swords* (London, 2014).

The Costume of Turkey illustrated by a series of Engravings; with Descriptions in English and French, printed for William Miller (London, 1802).

Cross, A., 'An Offence Against the Nation: An Account of the Theft of Lord Nelson's Relics from the Painted Hall, Greenwich, December 1900', *TC*, 13 (2003), pp.92-110.

Dalloway, J., *Constantinople, Ancient and Modern* (London, 1797).

Damas, Roger de, *Memoirs of the Comte Roger de Damas* (1913).

Dawson, W.R., *The Nelson Collection at Lloyd's* (London, 1932).

De Beaujour, L.A.F., *A View of the Commerce of Greece, formed after an Annual Average, from 1787 to 1797* (London, 1800).

D'Huart, S., *Journal de Marie-Amélie, reine de Français* (Paris, 1981).

Eldem, E., *Pride and Privilege: A History of Ottoman Orders, Medals and Decorations* (Istanbul, 2004).

Elgood, R., *The Arms of Greece and her Balkan Neighbours in the Ottoman Period* (London, 2009)

Evans, T., *A Statement of the Means by which the Nelson Coat … Was Obtained* (London, 1846).

Gamlin, H., *Emma, Lady Hamilton* (Liverpool, 1891).

Gamlin, H., *Nelson's Friendships* (2 vols, London, 1899).

Garlick, K., Macintyre, A., Cave, K., and Newby, E. (eds), *The diary of Joseph Farington* (17 vols, 1978–98).

Gatrell, V., *City of Laughter: Sex and Satire in Eighteenth Century London* (London, 2007).

Gatty, A. and M., *Recollections of the Life of the Reverend A.J. Scott, D.D., Lord Nelson's Chaplain* (London, 1842).

Gérin, W., *Horatia Nelson* (Oxford, 1970).

Gordon, Pryce Lockhart, *Personal Memoirs* (2 vols, London, 1830).

Gore, P., *Nelson's Band of Brothers* (Barnsley, 2015).

Grant, N.H. (ed.), *The Letters of Mary Nisbet of Dirleton, Countess of Elgin* (1926).

Hardy, S., Frances, *Lady Nelson: The Life and Times of an Admirable Wife* (Staplehurst, 2005).

Harrison, J., *The Life of the Rt. Hon. Horatio Lord Viscount Nelson* (2 vols, London, 1806).

Hartop, C., *Royal Goldsmiths: The Art of Rundell & Bridge* (Cambridge, 2005).

Hibbert, C., *Nelson: A Personal History* (London, 1994).

Hills, Dr A-M.E., *Nelson: A Medical Casebook* (Stroud, 2006).

Hoste, H. (ed.), *Memoirs and Letters of Captain Sir William Hoste* (2 vols, London, 1833).

Howard, The Hon. E.C.G., *Memoirs of Sir Sidney Smith* (2 vols, London, 1839).

James, W., *Naval History of Great Britain* (6 vols, London, 1822–24).

Keate, E.M., *Nelson's Wife* (London, 1939).

Kennedy, L., *Nelson and his Captains* (London, 1975).

Knight, C., *Autobiography of Miss Cornelia Knight* (2 vols, London, 1861).

Knight, R., *The Pursuit of Victory: The Life and Achievements of Horatio Nelson* (London, 2005).

Lee, J.T., *Memoirs of the Life and Services of Sir J. Theophilus Lee, of the Elms, Hampshire* (London, 1836).

Letters of Lord Nelson to Lady Hamilton (2 vols, London, 1814).

Littlewood, K., & Butler, B., *Of ships and stars: maritime heritage and the founding of the National Maritime Museum, Greenwich* (London, 1998).

Lloyd, C.C. (ed.), *The Keith Papers* (3 vols, 1927–55).

Londonderry, Marquess of (ed.), *Correspondence and Dispatches of Viscount Castlereagh* (5 vols, London, 1851).

MacCarthy, F., *Byron: Life and Legend* (London, 2002).

Matcham, M. Eyre, *The Nelsons of Burnham Thorpe* (London, 1911).

Memoirs of Lady Hamilton with Illustrative Anecdotes (London, 1815).

Minto, Countess of(ed.), *The Life and Letters of Sir Gilbert Elliott, First Earl of Minto from 1751 to 1806* (3 vols, London, 1874).

Moore, T., *Life of Lord Byron with His Letters and Journals* (6 vols, London).

Morrison, A., *The Hamilton and Nelson Papers* (2 vols, 1894).

Naish, G.B.P. (ed.), *Nelson's Letters to his Wife and Other Documents* (London, 1958).

The Naval Chronicle.

The Nelson Dispatch (Nelson Society).

Nicol, J., *The Life and Adventures of John Nicol, Mariner*, ed. Gordon Grant (Edinburgh, 1822, reprinted London, 1937).

The Letters of Mary Nisbet, Countess of Elgin (1936).

Oman, C., *Nelson* (London, 1946, reprinted 1996).

The Oxford Dictionary of National Biography (ODNB).

Parsons, G.S., *Nelsonian Reminiscences* (London, 1843).

Perceval, Spencer, *The Genuine Book: An Inquiry or The Delicate Investigation into the conduct of Her Royal Highness The Princess of Wales* (London, 1813).

Pettigrew, T.J., *Memoirs of the Life of Vice-Admiral Lord Viscount Nelson* (2 vols, London, 1849).

Pocock, T., *A Thirst for Glory: The Life of Admiral Sir Sidney Smith* (London, 1996).

Pocock, T., *Horatio Nelson* (London, 1987).

Pocock, T., *Nelson's Women* (London, 2002).

Pointon, M., *Brilliant Effects: A Cultural History of Gem Stones and Jewellery* (London, 2009).

Pratt, M., *Nelson's Duchy* (Staplehurst, 2005).

Prentice, R., *The Authentic Nelson* (London, 2005).

Riall, L., *Under the Volcano: Revolution in a Sicilian Town* (Oxford, 2013).

Robinson, S.K., *In Defence of Emma* (Croydon, 2016).

Rumbold, Sir Horace, *Recollections of a diplomatist* (London, 1902).

Russell, Lord, *Knight of the Sword: The Life and Letters of Admiral Sir Sidney William Smith* (London, 1964).

St Clair, W., *Lord Elgin and the marbles: The Controversial history of the Parthenon sculptures* (Oxford, 1998).

Scarisbrick, D., 'Emma Hamilton and her Jewellery', in the handbook to the International Silver and Jewellery Fair and Seminar (London, February 1985).

Scott, P., *Gentleman Thief* (London, 1995).

Sermonata, Vittoria, Duchess of, *The Locks of Norbury* (London, 1940).

Shankland, P., *Beware of Heroes: Admiral Sir Sidney Smith's War against Napoleon* (London, 1975).

Shaw, S.J., *Between Old and New: The Ottoman Empire under Sultan Selim III 1789-1807* (Cambridge, Mass., 1971).

Silliman, B., *A Journey of Travels in England, Holland and Scotland … in the years 1805 and 1806* (3 vols, Boston, 1812).

Sotheby's, *Nelson: The Alexander Davison Collection, London 21 October 2002* (2002).

Southey, R., *The Life of Nelson* (2 vols, London, 1813).

Southwick, L., *London silver-hilted swords: their makers, suppliers and allied traders, with directory* (Leeds, 2001).

Spilsbury, F.B., *Picturesque scenery in the Holy Land and Syria: delineated during the campaigns of 1799 and 1800* (London, 1803).

Stirling, A.M.W., *Pages & Portraits from the Past: being the private papers of Admiral Sir William Hotham* (2 vols, London, 1919).

Strathern, P., *Napoleon in Egypt* (London, 2008).

Stuart, D.M., *Dearest Bess* (London, 1955).

Sugden, J., *Nelson: The Sword of Albion* (London, 2012).

Tarihi, B., *Ottoman Medals and Orders Documented History* (Istanbul, 2001).

Trafalgar Chronicle: Yearbook of the 1805 Club.

Vernon-Harcourt, L. (ed.), *The Diaries and Correspondence of the Rt. Hon. George Rose* (2 vols, London, 1860).

Walker, R., *The Nelson Portraits* (Portsmouth, 1998).

Watt, H. & Hawkins, A., *Letters of Seamen in the Wars with France, 1793-1815* (Woodbridge, 2016)

Westminster, Dean of (ed. by Trench, R. Chevenix), *The Remains of the late Mrs Richard Trench* (London, 1862).

White, C., *Nelson: The New Letters* (Woodbridge, 2007).

White, D., 'Heralds and their Clients: The Arms of Nelson', *Trafalgar Chronicle*, 8 (1998), pp.56–73.

White, I., *English Clocks for the Eastern Market* (Ticehurst, 2012).

Wiebe, M.G., Millar, M.S., & Robson, A.P. (eds), *Benjamin Disraeli Letters. Volume VIII: 1860–1864* (Toronto, 2009).

Williams, H., *Turquerie: An Eighteenth-Century European Fantasy* (London, 2014).

Williams, K,. *England's Mistress: The Infamous Life of Emma Hamilton* (London, 2006).

Yarrington, A., *The Commemoration of the Hero* (London, 1988).

ACKNOWLEDGEMENTS

A book of this sort accumulates many debts from friends, family and people I cannot thank in person but who gave me their time and expertise out of kindness and their interest in Nelson's lost jewel. In Turkey, Gül İrepoğlu, the leading authority on Imperial Ottoman jewellery, offered warm encouragement and, when I visited Istanbul with the new jewel, wonderful hospitality over dinner with her family. In Sicily, Nino Liuzzo of the Associazione Bronte Insieme Onlus provided CDs of the massive Duchy of Bronte archives, and then essential help in navigating them. In Greece, Konstantinos Mazarakis revealed the treasures of the Nelson Collection at the Aikaterini Laskaridis Foundation in Piraeus. It was with Konstantinos at the National Historical Museum in Athens that I discovered the portrait of Lambros Katsonis wearing a çelenk. At the College of Arms, Somerset Herald David White showed me Nelson's and Sir William Sidney Smith's original grants of arms, then hit the jackpot when he stumbled across Thomas King's drawing of the sultan's aigrette which has transformed our understanding of the jewel. The staff at the National Maritime Museum, Greenwich, and National Museum of the Royal Navy in Portsmouth have been wonderfully helpful as usual. In particular, I would like to thank Quintin Colville, Pieter van der Merwe and Geraldine Charles at NMM, and Professor Dominic Tweedle and Matthew Sheldon at NMRN which hosted an exhibition of the new jewel for six months in 2018.

Special mention is also due to Ann Rainsbury and Sue Miles for an unforgettable day exploring the trove of Nelson treasures at the Monmouth Museum under their expert guidance.

For a book which deals with several generations of their family, I am incredibly grateful to Peregrine Nelson Hood and his father Alex Bridport for all their support and enthusiasm. Access to the Bridport family papers yielded many gems, including the poignant and important letter revealing Fanny Nelson's feelings after Trafalgar. Peregrine was also brilliantly effective at locating the hitherto untraced portraits of Earl Nelson and his children Charlotte and Horace, which led to a magical day in Jersey with James and Sinead Lynch and the truly remarkable Lady Cook.

It was always a hope of this project that a replica jewel in diamonds and precious stones could be made to recreate the excitement of the original jewel. Martin Travis and Sophie Jackson of Symbolic & Chase rose to this challenge,which was envisaged by Hannah Fagerstrom-Day's drawings then realised by master goldsmith Philip Denyer under the expert guidance of jewellery historian and broadcaster Joanna Hardy. Joanna also provided wonderful insight into the symbolism of the jewel for the film of its making by Rob White of Maritime Films who was assisted by photographer David Botwinik (film available to view on YouTube). Grateful thanks, too, to Roger Stephenson of Lock & Co. for entertaining stories of his famous former customer and for arranging a replica hat to Nelson's original specifications (size '7 1/8 Full') for displaying a new jewel.

Understanding Nelson's world is a team effort, and I have received advice and inspiration from many professionals, scholars and collectors who like me are captivated by it. I value them all as my good friends. They include Michael Naxton, Andrew Guy, Tim Spicer, Sim Comfort, Charles Miller, Anthony Cross at the Warwick Leadlay Gallery, and Emma Rutherford and Philip Mould at the Philip Mould Gallery, which also hosted an exhibition of the new jewel. Sabitri Ghosh shared many sparkling finds whilst researching the controversies surrounding Nelson's death and its aftermath for her own forthcoming book.

This book would not have been possible without the vision of Mark Beynon, my editor at The History Press, who commissioned it and has been a wise and supportive companion from the start. His colleagues have all helped to produce this stunning tribute to Nelson's beautiful jewel.

Above all, I wish to thank my wife Sam, who read the whole manuscript twice making some brilliant observations; and my children Tabitha, William and Mary, who have yet again endured a woefully preoccupied father. My love for her and them is in every word. The book, however, is dedicated to my brother Jeremy, from whom so many years of love and laughter were taken.

INDEX